New

Second Edition

DIRECTIONS

Reading, Writing, and Critical Thinking

PETER S. GARDNER

CAMBRIDGE UNIVERSITY PRESS
Cambridge, New York, Melbourne, Madrid, Cape Town,
Singapore, São Paulo, Delhi, Mexico City

Cambridge University Press
32 Avenue of the Americas, New York, NY 10013–2473, USA

www.cambridge.org
Information on this title: www.cambridge.org/9780521541725

First published 2005
18th printing 2013

Printed in the United States of America

A catalog record for this publication is available from the British Library.

ISBN 978-0-521-54172-5 paperback

Art direction and book design: Adventure House, NYC
Layout Services: Page Designs International

To my parents, whose love of learning
has inspired my own

TABLE OF CONTENTS

The Essentials of Writing   *102*

3 Mass Media and Technology   *134*
A Writer's Technique: *Figures of Speech*

INTRODUCTION

Audience

New Directions: Reading, Writing, and Critical Thinking is written for students who are studying, or preparing for study, at an English-speaking college or university. It may be used by advanced ESL or EFL students in courses that stress the connection between reading and writing, by native English speakers in developmental writing and expository writing classes at the college level, or by anyone wishing to improve his or her reading, writing, and critical thinking skills for personal or professional purposes.

Overview

New Directions is a thematically based, interactive reader designed to help students meet the demands of reading and writing assignments in college and university classes. To this end, the text offers a number of challenging reading and writing activities that encourage the higher-order thinking skills of analysis, synthesis, interpretation, evaluation, and application necessary for academic success. Through integrated reading, writing, speaking, and listening activities, students learn to generate hypotheses, argue, analyze critically, interpret a writer's meaning inferentially as well as literally, discriminate between opinion and fact, detect fallacies in reasoning, reach conclusions and judgments based on supportable criteria, and propose new ideas. The book also stresses the development of students' academic vocabulary.

Writing Skills

New Directions takes students through the major stages of the writing process (assessing the writing situation, exploring and planning, drafting, revising, editing and proofreading). The book teaches strategies that will help learners compose expository and argumentative essays and use sources effectively in researched writing. It provides many opportunities for formal and informal writing, including journal entries, freewriting, summaries, reports, and personal narratives. A number of activities, often overlooked in other textbooks, focus on how writers employ tone, take into account purpose and audience, and use figurative language.

The Readings

New Directions contains 35 readings of varying length and difficulty, though all are appropriate for the college level. The selections are interdisciplinary and include excerpts from college texts and nonfiction books, newspaper and magazine articles, personal essays, letters, short stories, folktales, fables, and poems. Provocative and challenging, the readings are diverse in subject matter, aim, voice, style, and rhetorical technique and represent a balance of descriptive, narrative, expository, and argumentative writing. All of the readings are original and unadapted, though some have been abridged. They are written by authors from a wide range of cultural backgrounds. Accompanying many of the readings are sidebars that contain short high-interest texts or content-related graphs, charts, and tables. The diverse selections and graphic material engage students in important social issues and promote a stimulating context for developing reading, writing, and critical thinking skills.

Structure of the Book

New Directions is divided into five thematically based chapters. An informational section on writing skills, titled "The Essentials of Writing," is placed between Chapters 2 and 3.

The Thematic Chapters

The five chapter themes in the book were selected because of their relevance and interest to students. The themes and activities in *New Directions* are not sequenced, allowing the chapters to be taught in any order. Besides the thematic content, each of the five chapters also focuses on an important writing technique. The five chapters and the five writing techniques are:

Chapter 1: Intercultural Communication
              Main Ideas and Supporting Details
Chapter 2: Education
              Purpose and Audience
Chapter 3: Mass Media and Technology
              Figures of Speech
Chapter 4: Gender Roles
              Summarizing and Paraphrasing
Chapter 5: Work
              Tone

The Essentials of Writing

This writing section appears between Chapters 2 and 3. It is printed in a second color so that it may be easily located at any time in the course. It contains no tasks, only essential information about writing and plentiful examples. Students are encouraged to go to the information whenever they have a writing assignment. The writing section is in three parts.

Part One: The Structure of an Essay
                    The Introduction, Body Paragraphs, The Conclusion
Part Two: The Writing Process
                    Assessing the Writing Situation, Exploring and Planning, Drafting, Revising, Editing and Proofreading
Part Three: Writing with Sources
                    Types of Sources, Locating Sources, Evaluating Sources, Taking Notes from Sources, Documenting Sources

The Organization of a Chapter

Each chapter has an opening activity that raises students' awareness of the chapter theme; a series of core readings, with pre- and post-reading activities; an activity that requires students to synthesize information and make connections among the core readings; several additional readings, with a pre- and post-reading activity for each; and a final activity with essay topics based on the theme of the chapter.

Unit Opener

Each chapter begins with a brief introduction describing the major theme of the chapter, followed by a list of questions and quotations relating to the readings. To raise awareness of, and interest in, the chapter topic, students discuss the questions and quotations in a small group and share personal opinions and experiences.

Core Readings

Each chapter has three core readings containing a balance of academic and personal writing. The core readings have a full range of pre- and post-reading activities. (For details of the reading activities, see Activities Accompanying the Core Readings on the next page.)

Making Connections

This section may be used as the basis of a writing or discussion activity. The questions help students to synthesize the information presented in the core readings – to combine facts, ideas, and beliefs to form their own opinions and judgments about issues. Students compare and contrast the authors' ideas and writing techniques, imagine how the authors might respond to each other, and apply concepts discussed in one reading to another.

Additional Readings

Each chapter contains five additional readings (two prose pieces, a story, a poem, a joke) and a cartoon. These readings have only a few accompanying tasks. Instructors may choose to study these readings in class or simply assign them as extra reading to be done out of class. The additional material allows students to explore issues in greater depth, to apply the writing technique learned earlier in the chapter, and to practice their intensive and extensive reading skills.

Essay Topics

This concluding section of each chapter presents five essay topics that require students to use various rhetorical strategies, such as compare and contrast, cause and effect, and division and classification, and higher-order thinking skills, especially synthesis, interpretation, and application. The assignments include expository, argumentative, and narrative writing. For each assignment, students support their ideas with references to the chapter readings, library and Internet sources, and personal experience.

Activities Accompanying the Core Readings

The core readings have a full set of pre- and post-reading activities, which are described below. The additional readings have only one pre-reading activity, a note-taking activity, and a post-reading activity.

Journal Writing

Students write journal entries about topics relating to the readings, focusing on personal opinions and experiences. They are often asked to respond to a brief quotation, agree or disagree with a statement, or make a prediction about an issue raised in the reading. In their journal writing, students also practice the pre-writing techniques that are discussed in the writing section (brainstorming, freewriting, clustering, the journalist's questions).

Previewing the Topic

In a small group, students discuss an issue or perform a task relating to the topic of the reading and then share their opinions and experiences with the rest of the class. Similar to journal writing, this activity encourages students to examine personal and cultural beliefs, helping them better understand, analyze, and take issue with perspectives reflected in the reading.

Agreeing and Disagreeing

Students indicate the extent to which they agree with statements relating to the topic of the selection and then compare their responses with those of several classmates. This activity encourages students to express their opinions clearly and to reach conclusions and judgments based on supportable criteria.

Taking Notes While You Read

While reading the selection, students are asked to underline, highlight, and annotate ideas in the piece, often indicating points of agreement and disagreement and relationships to their own culture and experience. Taking notes actively engages students with the texts, provides practice with an important academic skill, and helps with the reading, writing, and critical thinking activities that follow.

Reading Journal

After reading a selection, students write an entry in their reading journal. These entries include discussions of specific topics relating to the reading, interpretations, points of agreement and disagreement with the author, likes and dislikes, and personal experiences.

Main Ideas

This section helps students understand the main ideas in the reading, while referring to the notes they took when reading the selection. The final question asks students to summarize the main idea of the reading in one or two sentences.

Reflecting on Content

Students think critically about major issues raised in the reading, relating them to their own knowledge and experience. In contrast to the more literal focus of the previous section, these questions help students develop the skills of analysis, synthesis, evaluation, interpretation, inference, and application needed to fully appreciate a writer's ideas.

A Writer's Technique

Students learn about the major writing technique introduced in the chapter, focusing on the ways in which the author of the reading uses the strategy. Students think critically about such aspects of writing as main ideas, supporting details, purpose, audience, and tone.

Vocabulary

This is the first of two vocabulary exercises. The vocabulary focus of each exercise varies from chapter to chapter and from reading to reading. Some exercises turn students' attention to multi-word items, such as phrasal verbs, idioms, and collocations; others examine the denotations and connotations of words; and still others work on determining meaning through the analysis of word parts (prefixes, roots, suffixes), and the study of context clues, including synonyms and antonyms.

Vocabulary In Context

Students determine the meaning of vocabulary items from their context in the reading and then think of an example or situation that illustrates each word or idiom. Through this content-based approach, students actively develop their vocabulary by using words and idioms in personalized contexts.

Discussion

These collaborative activities encourage students to search for connections between the ideas in the selections and their own lives, to take issue with the opinions expressed by the authors and their classmates, and to interact with sources of knowledge outside the classroom. The activities focus on cross-cultural similarities and differences. They include group discussions, debates, presentations, and community-related projects, such as interviews, surveys, and trips to stores and museums. The last discussion activity for each core reading involves a Web or library task, such as conducting research, filling out a questionnaire, or listening to a broadcast on National Public Radio.

Writing Follow-up

These short writing tasks are paired with the discussion activities and include summaries, reports, letters, and case studies. Students also practice the writing technique introduced in the chapter. These varied activities, some of which are collaborative, encourage different rhetorical strategies and modes of writing (description, narration, exposition, argumentation) and focus students' attention on content, purpose, audience, tone, and other important aspects of composition.

Changes in the Second Edition

This new edition of *New Directions* represents a substantial revision of the first edition, while retaining the integrated approach to reading, writing, and critical thinking. Major changes in the second edition include the following:

- A new chapter on the mass media and technology
- An increased development of writing skills, with new sections to accompany the core readings – *A Writer's Technique* and *Writing Follow-up*
- A major new section in the middle of the book – "The Essentials of Writing" – that can be used as a handy reference tool for all writing assignments
- Many new and updated readings
- Sidebars within the readings, presenting varied points of view and additional information
- A note-taking task that students engage in while reading
- A humor section for each chapter, with a thematically related joke and cartoon
- Internet and library activities to develop students' language and research skills
- One Web-based activity per chapter in which students practice listening comprehension skills
- More charts, graphs, and tables for practice in understanding numerical presentation of information

ACKNOWLEDGEMENTS

The second edition of *New Directions* would not have been possible without the help and support of many people. I would like to thank my colleagues Sally Blazar, Walter Harp, Sheila Katz, Joe Coroniti, Doug Kohn, and Leslie Greffenius for their friendship and encouragement during the long birth of this project. My thanks also go to Berklee College of Music for providing me with the sabbatical time necessary to undertake an extensive revision; Charles Combs, Chair of the General Education Department and Lawrence McClellan, Dean of the Professional Education Division, for their continued support; Chee-Ping Ho, Professional Education Division Technology Coordinator, for his assistance with technical matters; and my many students, whose insightful responses to the readings and activities helped shape the final form of the book.

I am grateful to the following reviewers for their thoughtful criticism: Lida Baker, American Language Center, University of California, Los Angeles; Jon Beesing, American Language Institute, New York University; Wayne Conrad, El Centro College, Dallas, Texas; Carolyn M. Heard, American Language Institute, New York University; Barbara Hockman, The City College of San Francisco; April Muchmore-Vokoun, English Language Institute, University of Florida; and Cynthia Zeki, Roosevelt University, Chicago.

For the editing and production of the book, I would like to thank Susan Joseph, freelance copyeditor, for her sharp eye and pedagogical suggestions and Don Williams for his creative typesetting. I am particularly indebted to the editors and staff at Cambridge University Press: Ann Garrett and Helen Lee, project editors, for their guidance; Mary Sandre, Editorial Controller, and Pam Harris, Assistant Editor, for their help with the permissions process; and, especially, Joe McVeigh, development editor, for his judgment, comradeship, and keen use of Occam's razor; and Bernard Seal, commissioning editor, for his counsel, wit, and unfailing ability to detect infelicities.

I am ever grateful to my parents – to my mother, for her enthusiasm, compassion, and good cheer and to my father, whose artistic passion and insight into human nature inform every aspect of my teaching. I am also thankful to my daughters, Claire and Renee, for sustaining me with their energy, laughter, and curiosity and for helping me hear the mermaids sing. Finally, my special thanks to Clotilde Raemy-Gardner, my wife, for her honesty, forbearance, and moral support. Without her help, this book would not have been completed.

Intercultural Communication

A WRITER'S TECHNIQUE
Main Ideas and Supporting Details

In this chapter, you will explore cultural differences in values, beliefs, and behaviors and the intercultural problems that sometimes result from these differences. You will consider how people from diverse cultures regard time, express themselves verbally and nonverbally, and interact successfully.

Questions Raised in Chapter One

Working with a partner or in a small group, discuss two or three of the following questions.

1 Are there more similarities or more differences among people around the world in the way they think, behave, and communicate?

2 What are the most important social and cultural values influencing your own beliefs and behavior?

3 What are the major obstacles to intercultural communication? How can they be reduced?

4 If you live in another culture for an extended period of time, should you embrace the proverb "When in Rome, do as the Romans do"?

5 Do you think that when you live in a new culture your values, opinions, or behavior change in any way?

Brief Quotations

The following quotations deal with intercultural issues considered in this chapter. Working with a partner or in a small group, choose two or three quotations and discuss them.

1 *There never were, in the world, two opinions alike, no more than two hairs, or two grains; the most universal quality is diversity.* (Montaigne, French essayist)

2 *There is no longer division between what is foreign and what is domestic – the world economy, the world environment, the world AIDS crisis, the world arms race – they affect us all.* (William Jefferson Clinton, U.S. president)

3 *All people are the same. It is only their habits that are different.* (Confucius, Chinese philosopher)

4 *Prejudices, it is well known, are most difficult to eradicate from the heart whose soil has never been loosened or fertilized by education; they grow there, firm as weeds among stones.* (Charlotte Brontë, English writer)

5 *I consider myself a Hindu, Christian, Moslem, Jew, Buddhist, and Confucian.* (Mohandas Gandhi, Indian nationalist and spiritual leader)

6 *No object is mysterious. The mystery is in your eye.* (Elizabeth Bowen, U.S. author)

CORE READING 1
American Values and Assumptions

Journal Writing

In your journal, write for ten to fifteen minutes about one or two cultural differences you've noticed while living in a foreign country or in a place that is culturally different from where you grew up. Then share your thoughts with several classmates.

Previewing the Topic

Read the first paragraph of "American Values and Assumptions," in which the author discusses the concept of values. Then write a list of three or four major values in your culture. Discuss your list in a small group and then write a list of all the cultural values on the board.

Agreeing and Disagreeing

To what extent do you agree with the following statements? Fill in each blank with SA (strongly agree), A (agree), U (undecided), D (disagree), or SD (strongly disagree). Then share your responses with several classmates.

_____ 1 It's usually better to do things by yourself than to accept help from other people.

_____ 2 Not everyone's opinions are equally valid and worthy of consideration.

_____ 3 People do not have control over their own destinies.

_____ 4 Nature should be controlled and used in the service of human beings.

_____ 5 When young people are eighteen years old, they should be encouraged to move away from home.

_____ 6 Competition is a strong value in my culture.

_____ 7 If someone does something that bothers you, you should express your feelings openly and directly to the person.

_____ 8 When living in a foreign country, you should try to assimilate by embracing the nation's customs and practices.

_____ 9 People in my culture are quite informal in their personal and professional relationships.

_____ 10 It's better to focus on the future than to think too much about your culture's past – its customs, traditions, and heritage.

As you read the selection, underline or highlight the passages that identify major U.S. values. Then, in the margin next to a marked passage, indicate how prominent the value is in your culture by writing "very strong," "strong," "not very strong," or "weak."

 # American Values and Assumptions
Gary Althen

Gary Althen was a foreign student adviser at the University of Iowa for many years. He has written several books based on his experiences living in Peru and Malaysia and on his extensive work with students, immigrants, and other visitors to the United States. This reading is taken from a chapter in American Ways: A Guide for Foreigners in the United States, *second edition (2003).*

People who grow up in a particular culture share certain values and assumptions. 1
That does not mean they all share exactly the same values to exactly the same extent. It does mean that most of them, most of the time, agree with each other's ideas about what is right and wrong, desirable and undesirable, and so on. They also agree, mostly, with each other's assumptions about human nature, social relationships, and so on. . . .

Notice that the values and assumptions discussed below overlap with and support 2
each other. In general, they agree with each other. They fit together. A culture can be viewed as a collection of values and assumptions that go together to shape the way a group of people perceives and relates to the world around them.

INDIVIDUALISM

The most important thing to understand about Americans is probably their 3
devotion to individualism. They are trained from very early in their lives to consider themselves as separate individuals who are responsible for their own situations in life and their own destinies. They're not trained to see themselves as members of a close-knit interdependent family, religious group, tribe, nation, or any other collectivity.

You can see it in the way Americans treat their children. One day I was at a local 4
shopping mall, waiting in line to buy an Orange Julius. (An Orange Julius is a cool drink made in a blender with orange juice, ice, and some other ingredients.) Behind me in the line was a woman with two children, a boy who was about three years old and a girl who was about five. The boy had his hand in the pocket of his blue jeans, and I could hear that he had some coins in there.

The boy asked his mother, "Can I get an Orange Julius?" 5

"No," she said to him. "You don't have enough money left for an Orange Julius. 6
Remember you bought that cookie a while ago. You do have enough money for a hot dog. So you could get a hot dog now if you want to. Or, you could save your money, and sometime later when you have enough money, we could come back here and you could get an Orange Julius."

When I tell this story to people from other countries, they usually react with 7 disbelief. The idea that a child so young would even have his own money to spend, let alone be expected to decide how to spend it, seems beyond their comprehension. Here is a young child whose own mother is forcing him to make a decision that affects not just his situation at the moment – whether or not to get a hot dog – but that will affect him at some unspecified time in the future, when he will have more money.

But when Americans hear the story, they usually understand it perfectly well. This 8 mother is helping her son learn to make his own decisions and to be accountable for his own money. Some American parents might not expect a three-year-old to make a decision about how to spend money, but they certainly understand what the mother is doing. She is getting her son ready for a world in which he will be responsible for his choices and their consequences. Even his own mother won't be helping him later in life, and he needs to be ready for that.

This particular mother may or may not have owned a copy of Dr. Benjamin 9 Spock's famous book, *Dr. Spock's Baby and Child Care*, to which millions of American parents have long turned for information and advice on raising their children. The most recent version of the book makes this observation:

> In the United States . . . very few children are raised to believe that their personal destiny is to serve their family, their country, their God [as is the practice in some other countries]. Generally children [in the United States] are given the feeling that they can set their own aims and occupation in life, according to their inclinations. We're raising them to be rugged individualists. . . . (1998; p. 7)

While it has become more acceptable in light of changing economic circumstances 10 (especially higher housing costs) for young adults to live in their parents' house, the ideal of independence after high school graduation remains. If it is economically feasible for them to do so, young adult Americans are expected to live apart from their parents, either on their own or in college, or risk being viewed as immature, "tied to their mother's apron strings," or otherwise unable to lead a normal, independent life. . . .

Americans are trained to conceive of themselves as separate individuals, and 11 they assume everyone else in the world is too. When they encounter a person from abroad who seems to them excessively concerned with the opinions of parents, with following traditions, or with fulfilling obligations to others, they assume that the person feels trapped or is weak, indecisive, or "overly dependent." They assume all people must resent being in situations where they are not "free to make up their own minds." They assume, furthermore, that after living for a time in the United States, people will come to feel "liberated" from constraints arising outside themselves and will be grateful for the opportunity to "do their own thing" and "have it their own way." As indeed, many are. . . .

The individual that Americans idealize prefers an atmosphere of freedom, where 12 neither the government nor any other external force or agency dictates what the individual does. For Americans, the idea of individual freedom has strong, positive connotations.

By contrast, people from many other cultures regard some of the behavior 13
Americans legitimize by the label "individual freedom" to be self-centered and
lacking in consideration for others. . . .

Foreign visitors who understand the degree to which Americans are imbued 14
with the notion that the free, self-reliant individual is the ideal kind of human being
will be able to understand many aspects of American behavior and thinking that
otherwise might not make sense. A very few of the many possible examples:

- Americans see as heroes those individuals who "stand out from the crowd"
  by doing something first, longest, most often, or otherwise "best." Examples
  are aviators Charles Lindbergh[1] and Amelia Earhart,[2] golfer Tiger Woods,
  and basketball player Michael Jordan. Perhaps the best example from the
  world of fiction is the American cowboy as portrayed by such motion-
  picture actors as John Wayne and Clint Eastwood.

- Americans admire people who have overcome adverse circumstances (for
  example, poverty or a physical handicap) and "succeeded" in life. Black
  educator Booker T. Washington[3] is one example; the blind and deaf author
  and lecturer Helen Keller[4] is another.

- Many Americans do not display the degree of respect for their parents that
  people in more traditional or family-oriented societies commonly do. From
  their point of view, being born to particular parents was a sort of historical
  or biological accident. The parents fulfilled their responsibilities to the
  children while the children were young, and now that the children have
  reached "the age of independence," the close child-parent tie is loosened,
  occasionally even broken.

- It is not unusual for Americans who are beyond the age of about twenty-
  two (and sometimes younger) and who are still living with their parents
  to pay their parents for room and board. Elderly parents living with their
  grown children may do likewise. Paying for room and board is a way of
  showing independence, self-reliance, and responsibility for oneself.

- Certain phrases one commonly hears among Americans capture their
  devotion to individualism: "You'll have to decide that for yourself." "If you
  don't look out for yourself, no one else will." "Look out for number one."
  "Be your own best friend."

COMPETITION

Individualistic Americans naturally see themselves as being in competition with 15
others. Competitiveness pervades the society. It is obvious in the attention given
to athletic events and star athletes, who are praised for being "real competitors."

---

[1] *Charles Lindbergh* (1902–1974): American pilot who, in 1927, made the first solo, nonstop transatlantic flight.

[2] *Amelia Earhart* (1897–1937): First woman to fly across the Atlantic Ocean (in 1928) and to fly across it alone (in 1932).

[3] *Booker T. Washington* (1856–1915): Son of a slave who went from working in coal mines to founding a university for African-American students and becoming one of the leading educators of his day.

[4] *Helen Keller* (1880–1968): Graduate of Radcliffe College who went on to write and lecture extensively about social causes.

It is also obvious in schools and extracurricular activities for children, where games and contests are assumed to be desirable and beneficial. Competitiveness is less obvious when it is in the minds of people who are consistently comparing themselves with others: who is faster, smarter, richer, better looking; whose children are the most successful; whose husband is the best provider or the best cook or the best lover; which salesperson sold the most during the past quarter; who earned his first million dollars at the earliest age; and so on. People who are competing with others are essentially alone, trying to maintain their superiority and, implicitly, their separateness from others.

PRIVACY

Also closely associated with the value they place on individualism is the importance Americans assign to privacy. Americans assume that people "need some time to themselves" or "some time alone" to think about things or recover their spent psychological energy. Americans have great difficulty understanding people who always want to be with another person, who dislike being alone. Americans tend to regard such people as weak or dependent. . . . 16

Americans' attitudes about privacy can be difficult for foreigners to understand. Americans' houses, yards, and even their offices can seem open and inviting, yet, in the Americans' minds, there are boundaries that other people are simply not supposed to cross. When the boundaries are crossed, the Americans' bodies will visibly stiffen and their manner will become cool and aloof. 17

EQUALITY

Americans are also distinctive in the degree to which they believe in the ideal, as stated in their Declaration of Independence,[5] that "all men are created equal." Although they sometimes violate the ideal in their daily lives, particularly in matters of interracial relationships and sometimes relationships among people from different social classes, Americans have a deep faith that in some fundamental way all people (at least all American people) are of equal value, that no one is born superior to anyone else. "One person, one vote," they say, conveying the idea that any person's opinion is as valid and worthy of attention as any other person's opinion. 18

Americans are generally quite uncomfortable when someone treats them with obvious deference. They dislike being the subjects of open displays of respect – being bowed to, being deferred to, being treated as though they could do no wrong or make no unreasonable requests. . . . 19

Foreigners who are accustomed to more obvious displays of respect (such as bowing, averting eyes from the face of the higher status person, or using honorific titles[6]) often overlook the ways in which Americans show respect for people of higher status. They think, incorrectly, that Americans are generally unaware of status differences and disrespectful of other people. What is distinctive about the American outlook on the matter of equality are the underlying assumptions that (1) no matter what a person's initial station in life, he or she has the opportunity to 20

---

[5] *Declaration of Independence:* Document announcing the creation of the United States and its separation from Great Britain (1776).

[6] *honorific titles:* Titles of honor or respect.

achieve high standing and (2) everyone, no matter how unfortunate, deserves some basic level of respectful treatment.

INFORMALITY

Their notions of equality lead Americans to be quite informal in their general 21
behavior and in their relationships with other people. Store clerks and table servers, for example, may introduce themselves by their first (given) names and treat customers in a casual, friendly manner. American clerks, like other Americans, have been trained to believe that they are as valuable as any other people, even if they happen to be engaged at a given time in an occupation that others might consider lowly. This informal behavior can outrage foreign visitors who hold high stations in countries where it is not assumed that "all men are created equal." . . .

People from societies where general behavior is more formal than it is in America 22
are struck by the informality of American speech, dress, and body language. Idiomatic speech and slang are liberally used on most occasions, with formal speech reserved for public events and fairly formal situations. People of almost any station in life can be seen in public wearing jeans, sandals, or other informal attire. People slouch down in chairs or lean on walls or furniture when they talk, rather than maintaining an erect bearing.

A brochure advertising a highly-regarded liberal-arts college contains a 23
photograph showing the college's president, dressed in shorts and an old T-shirt, jogging past one of the classroom buildings on his campus. Americans are likely to find the photograph appealing: "Here is a college president who's just like anyone else. He doesn't think he's too good for us."

Likewise, U.S. President George W. Bush frequently allowed himself to be 24
photographed in his jogging attire while out for one of his frequent runs.

The superficial friendliness for which Americans are so well known is related to 25
their informal, egalitarian approach to other people. "Hi!" they will say to just about anyone, or "Howya doin'?" (that is, "How are you doing?" or "How are you?"). This behavior reflects not so much a special interest in the person addressed as a concern (not conscious) for showing that one is a "regular guy," part of a group of normal, pleasant people – like the jogging college president and the jogging president of his superpower country. . . .

THE FUTURE, CHANGE, AND PROGRESS

Americans are generally less concerned about history and traditions than are people 26
from older societies. "History doesn't matter," many of them will say. "It's the future that counts." They look ahead. They have the idea that what happens in the future is within their control, or at least subject to their influence. The mature, sensible person, they think, sets goals for the future and works systematically toward them. Americans believe that people, as individuals or working cooperatively together, can change most aspects of the physical and social environment if they decide to do so, then make appropriate plans and get to work. Changes will presumably produce improvements. New things are better than old things.

Closely associated with their assumption that they can bring about desirable 27
changes in the future is the Americans' assumption that their physical and social environments are subject to human domination or control. Early Americans cleared

forests, drained swamps, and altered the course of rivers in order to "build" the country. Contemporary Americans have gone to the moon in part just to prove they could do so! "If you want to be an American," says cross-cultural trainer L. Robert Kohls, "you have to believe you can fix it." . . .

This fundamental American belief in progress and a better future contrasts 28 sharply with the *fatalistic* (Americans are likely to use that term with a negative or critical connotation) attitude that characterizes people from many other cultures, notably Latin American, Asian, and Arab, where there is a pronounced reverence for the past. In those cultures the future is often considered to be in the hands of fate, God, or at least the few powerful people or families that dominate the society. The idea that they could somehow shape their own futures seems naive, arrogant, or even sacrilegious.

Americans are generally impatient with people they see as passively accepting 29 conditions that are less than desirable. "Why don't they do something about it?" Americans will ask. Americans don't realize that a large portion of the world's population sees the world around them not as something they can change, but rather as something to which they must submit, or at least something with which they must seek to live in harmony. . . .

TIME

For Americans, time is a resource that, like water or coal, can be used well or poorly. 30 "Time is money," they say. "You only get so much time in this life; you'd best use it wisely." As Americans are trained to see things, the future will not be better than the past or the present unless people use their time for constructive, future-oriented activities. Thus, Americans admire a "well-organized" person, one who has a written list of things to do and a schedule for doing them. The ideal person is punctual (that is, arrives at the scheduled time for a meeting or event) and is considerate of other people's time (that is, does not "waste people's time" with conversation or other activity that has no visible, beneficial outcome). . . .

The American attitude toward time is not necessarily shared by others, especially 31 non-Europeans. They are more likely to conceive of time as something that is simply there, around them, not something they can "use." One of the more difficult things many foreign businessmen and students must adjust to in the United States is the notion that time must be saved whenever possible and used wisely every day.

In their efforts to use their time wisely, Americans are sometimes seen by foreign 32 visitors as automatons, unhuman creatures who are so tied to their clocks, their schedules, and their daily planners that they cannot participate in or enjoy the human interactions that are the truly important things in life. "They are like little machines running around," one foreign visitor said.

The premium Americans place on *efficiency* is closely related to their concepts of 33 the future, change, and time. To do something efficiently is to do it in the way that is quickest and requires the smallest expenditure of resources. This may be why e-mail has become such a popular means of communication in American society. Students commonly correspond with their professors by e-mail rather than waiting to talk with them during their office hours. Likewise, businesspeople frequently check their e-mail before and after work, on the weekend, and even while on vacation.

American businesses sometimes hire "efficiency experts" to review their operations and to suggest ways in which they could accomplish more with the resources they are investing. Popular magazines offer suggestions for more efficient ways to shop, cook, clean house, do errands, raise children, tend the yard, and on and on. The Internet provides immediate access to all kinds of information and products. Americans have come to expect instant responses to phone calls, e-mails, faxes, and other forms of communication. Many quickly become impatient if the responses aren't immediately forthcoming, even when there is no apparent urgency. . . .

ACHIEVEMENT, ACTION, WORK, AND MATERIALISM

34 "He's a hard worker," one American might say in praise of another. Or, "She gets the job done." These expressions convey the typical American's admiration for a person who approaches a task conscientiously and persistently, seeing it through to a successful conclusion. More than that, these expressions convey an admiration for *achievers*, people whose lives are centered around efforts to accomplish some physical, measurable task. . . .

35 Visitors from abroad commonly remark, "Americans work harder than I expected them to." (Perhaps these visitors have been excessively influenced by American movies and television programs, which are less likely to show people working than to show them driving around in fast cars or pursuing members of the opposite sex.) While the so-called "Protestant work ethic"[7] may have lost some of its hold on Americans, there is still a strong belief that the ideal person is a "hard worker." A hard worker is one who "gets right to work" on a task, works efficiently, and completes the task in a way that meets reasonably high standards of quality. . . .

36 More generally, Americans like *action*. They do indeed believe it is important to devote significant energy to their jobs or to other daily responsibilities. Beyond that, they tend to believe they should be *doing* something most of the time. They are usually not content, as people from many countries are, to sit for hours and talk with other people. They get restless and impatient. They believe they should be doing something, or at least making plans and arrangements for doing something later.

37 People without the Americans' action orientation often see Americans as frenzied, always "on the go," never satisfied, compulsively active, and often impatient. They may, beyond that, evaluate Americans negatively for being unable to relax and enjoy life's pleasures. Even recreation, for Americans, is often a matter of acquiring lavish equipment, making elaborate plans, then going somewhere to *do* something. . . .

38 Americans tend to define and evaluate people by the jobs they have. ("Who is she?" "She's the vice president in charge of personal loans at the bank.") Family backgrounds, educational attainments, and other characteristics are considered less important in identifying people than the jobs they have. . . .

39 Americans tend to spend money rather freely on material goods. Items that were once considered luxuries, such as personal computers, telephone answering machines, microwave ovens, and electric garage-door openers are now considered "necessities" by many Americans. Credit cards, which are widely available even to teenagers, encourage spending, and of course the scale and scope of the advertising

---

7 *Protestant work ethic*: Belief that with hard work and self-discipline, a person will eventually succeed.

industry is well known. Americans are often criticized for being so "materialistic," so concerned with acquiring possessions. For Americans, though, this materialism is natural and proper. They have been taught that it is a good thing to achieve, to work hard, acquire more material badges of their success, and in the process assure a better future for themselves and their immediate families. And, like people elsewhere, they do what they are taught.

DIRECTNESS AND ASSERTIVENESS

Americans, as we've said before, generally consider themselves to be frank, open, and direct in their dealings with other people. "Let's lay our cards on the table,"[8] they say. Or, "Let's stop playing games and get to the point." These and many other common expressions convey the Americans' idea that people should explicitly state what they think and what they want from other people. 40

Americans usually assume that conflicts or disagreements are best settled by means of forthright discussions among the people involved. If I dislike something you are doing, I should tell you about it directly so you will know, clearly and from me personally, how I feel about it. Bringing in other people to mediate a dispute is considered somewhat cowardly, the act of a person without enough courage to speak directly to someone else. Mediation is, however, slowly gaining in popularity in recent years. 41

The word *assertive* is the adjective Americans commonly use to describe the person who plainly and directly expresses feelings and requests. People who are inadequately assertive can take "assertiveness-training classes." What Americans consider assertive is, however, often judged as aggressive by some non-Americans and sometimes by Americans – if the person referred to is a woman. . . . 42

Americans are not taught, as people in many Asian countries are, that they should mask their emotional responses. Their words, the tone of their voices, or their facial expressions will usually reveal when they are feeling angry, unhappy, confused, or happy and content. They do not think it improper to display these feelings, at least within limits. Many Asians feel embarrassed around Americans who are exhibiting a strong emotional response to something. On the other hand, Latin Americans and Arabs are generally inclined to display their emotions more openly than Americans do, and to view Americans as unemotional and "cold." 43

Americans, however, are often less direct and open than they realize. There are, in fact, many restrictions on their willingness to discuss things openly. It is difficult to categorize those restrictions, and the restrictions are often not "logical" in the sense of being consistent with each other. Generally, though, Americans are reluctant to speak openly when: 44

- the topic is in an area they consider excessively personal, such as unpleasant body or mouth odors, sexual functioning, or personal inadequacies;
- they want to say "no" to a request that has been made of them but do not want to offend or "hurt the feelings of" the person who made the request;
- they are not well enough acquainted with the other person to be confident

---

[8] *to lay one's cards on the table:* To state one's opinion honestly.

that direct discussion will be accepted in the constructive way that is intended; and, paradoxically,

- they know the other person very well (it might be a spouse or close friend) and they do not wish to risk giving offense and creating negative feelings by talking about some delicate problem. . . .

All of this is to say that Americans, even though they see themselves as properly assertive and even though they often behave in open and direct ways, have limits on their openness. It is not unusual for them to try to avoid direct confrontations with other people when they are not confident that the interaction can be carried out in a constructive way that will result in an acceptable compromise. . . . **45**

Despite these limitations, Americans are generally more direct and open than people from almost all other countries with the exception of Israel and Australia. They will not try to mask their emotions, as Scandinavians or Japanese tend to do. They are much less concerned with "face" (that is, avoiding embarrassment to themselves or others) than most Asians are. To them, being honest is usually more important than preserving harmony in interpersonal relationships. **46**

Americans use the words *pushy* or *aggressive* to describe a person who is excessively assertive in expressing opinions or making requests. The line between acceptable assertiveness and unacceptable aggressiveness is difficult to draw. Iranians and people from other countries where forceful arguing and negotiating are common forms of interaction risk being seen as aggressive or pushy when they treat Americans in the way they treat people at home. **47**

Reading Journal

In your journal, write about one of the following topics.

1 Explain what a visitor to your country should know in order to avoid intercultural misunderstandings.
2 Describe an experience you had in a foreign country or culture that helped you understand it better.
3 Choose a topic of your own related to the reading.

Main Ideas

One of the most important skills you can develop as a good reader is the ability to recognize the **main idea** in a piece of writing. Although writers often include many ideas, there is usually a central point, or message, they wish to convey. When you read something, you should ask yourself the following questions:

- What main idea is the writer trying to communicate?
- How does the main idea relate to other ideas in the reading?
- How does the writer develop his or her main point? What does the writer want me to remember about this subject?

Answer the following questions, referring to the notes you took when reading the selection. Then share your answers with a partner.

1 According to the reading, what is the most important thing to understand about U.S. culture? Explain.

2 In the reading, Althen provides many examples of cross-cultural differences in values and assumptions. Which consequences of these differences does he focus on? Give two examples.

3 What is the main point Althen makes in the reading? Summarize his central idea in one or two sentences. Use your own words. Begin with the sentence *In the chapter "American Values and Assumptions," Gary Althen maintains that . . .*

Reflecting on Content

Answer the following questions with a partner. When possible, support your answers with observations based on your own experiences.

1 In paragraph 2, Althen says that the values and assumptions discussed in the reading "overlap with and support each other. In general, they agree with each other. They fit together." Give two examples of cultural values mentioned in the reading that you think overlap with and support each other.

2 Are the U.S. values that Althen discusses similar to or different from those in the culture with which you are most familiar? Explain. Focus on one or two of the values mentioned in the reading.

3 Can you tell how Althen feels about the issues he discusses? How objective do you consider his writing to be? Be as specific as possible.

A Writer's Technique: *Supporting Details*

Good writers provide sufficient details such as examples, facts, quotations, and definitions to support their ideas. Writers use this information, known as **supporting detail**, to explain, clarify, or illustrate their main points. Without such specific material, a writer's ideas remain abstract and unconvincing. Experienced writers try, whenever possible, to show rather than simply tell their readers what their ideas mean.

Look at these statements from "American Values and Assumptions." Locate them in the reading and then write a sentence that describes the main idea the statement supports or illustrates. Then share your answers with a partner.

Example: *A brochure . . . contains a photograph showing the college's president, dressed in shorts and an old T-shirt, jogging past one of the classroom buildings on his campus. (par. 23)*

Main Idea: *People from the United States value informality and equality in their everyday lives.*

1 If it is economically feasible for them to do so, young adult Americans are expected to live apart from their parents, either on their own or in college, or risk being viewed as immature. (par. 10)

2 Americans' houses, yards, and even their offices can seem open and inviting, yet, in the Americans' minds, there are boundaries that other people are simply not supposed to cross. (par. 17)

3 Early Americans cleared forests, drained swamps, and altered the course of rivers in order to "build" the country. (par. 27)

4 Thus, Americans admire a "well-organized" person, one who has a written list of things to do and a schedule for doing them. (par. 30)

5 Even recreation, for Americans, is often a matter of acquiring lavish equipment, making elaborate plans, then going somewhere to *do* something. (par. 37)

Vocabulary: *Negative Prefixes*

Studying the parts of words is a good way to develop your vocabulary. Often in English a word is formed by adding a group of letters to the beginning or the end of the **word root** – the basic part of the word. Groups of letters attached to the beginning of a word root are called **prefixes**. Those attached to the end of a word root are called **suffixes**. In general, prefixes change the meaning of a word and suffixes change its part of speech (noun, verb, adjective, and adverb).

Look at the following examples of roots, prefixes, and suffixes.

Root	Prefix	Suffix
operate (*verb*)	**co**operate (*verb*)	cooperation (*noun*)
conscious (*adjective*)	**un**conscious (*adjective*)	unconscious**ly** (*adverb*)

In English, many prefixes indicate something negative – that is, the prefixes mean "not," "the opposite of," or "lacking in."

1 Following are twelve words from the reading, each with its negative prefix removed. Fill in the blank with the proper negative prefix from the list below. In some cases, there might be more than one possible response. Then find the words in the reading and check your answers.

un-, in-, im-, il-, ir-, a-, ab-, non-, dis-, mis-

a. ____desirable (par. 1)

b. ____belief (par. 7)

c. ____specified (par. 7)

d. ____mature (par. 10)

e. ____decisive (par. 11)

f. ____respectful (par. 20)

g. ____formal (par. 25)

h. ____patient (par. 29)

i. ____Europeans (par. 31)

j. ____human (par. 32)

k. ____adequately (par. 42)

l. ____emotional (par. 43)

2 The following words appear in the reading without negative prefixes. Make each word negative by filling in the blank with the proper prefix or prefixes from the list on page 15.

a. ____normal (par. 10)   f. ____typical (par. 34)

b. ____associated (par. 16)   g. ____proper (par. 39)

c. ____appealing (par. 23)   h. ____inclined (par. 43)

d. ____reverence (par. 28)   i. ____logical (par. 44)

e. ____considerate (par. 30)   j. ____behave (par. 45)

Vocabulary in Context

Locate the following italicized vocabulary items in the reading and see if you can determine their meaning from the context. Then think of an example or situation to illustrate each item, using your personal experience if possible. Do not just define the italicized words and expressions. When you are done, share your answers with a partner.

1 a time in a new culture when you felt liberated from certain *constraints* (par. 11)

2 an idea that has strong, positive *connotations* in your culture (par. 12)

3 someone you think *stands out from the crowd*, and why (par. 14)

4 whether *self-reliance* is valued in your culture (par. 14)

5 a reason someone might behave in an *aloof* manner (par. 17)

6 something you *place a premium on*, and why (par. 33)

7 a time when you *saw something through* to a successful conclusion (par. 34)

8 a situation in which someone might say, "Let's *lay our cards on the table*" (par. 40)

9 the degree to which speaking in a direct and *forthright* manner is valued in your culture (par. 41)

10 whether people in your culture are *inclined to* display their emotions in public (par. 43)

Discussion

Choose one of the following activities to do with a partner or in a small group.

1 Review the major categories of U.S. values and assumptions in Althen's chapter. Choose two or three of the categories and discuss whether similar cultural patterns are seen in the culture with which you are most familiar. Think of examples that reflect the existence or the lack of such ways of thinking, behaving, and viewing the world.

2 One way to get a sense of the values and assumptions of a culture is to look at its proverbs and sayings. Following are ten common proverbs in English. Choose five of the proverbs and discuss (1) the meaning of each proverb, (2) a

situation in which it might be used, (3) the values it reflects, and (4) whether an equivalent exists in another language that you know. See the example below.

Proverb: *The early bird catches the worm.*

Meaning: *The person who starts early on something has the best chance of success.*

Situation: *Claire began looking for a summer job in December. She knew that the early bird catches the worm.*

Values: *Diligence, action, punctuality*

Other language: *The German equivalent translates as "The morning hour has gold in its mouth."*

a. Don't cry over spilled milk.

b. God helps those who help themselves.

c. Too many cooks spoil the broth.

d. You can lead a horse to water but you can't make it drink.

e. The squeaky wheel gets the grease.

f. A penny saved is a penny earned.

g. Don't count your chickens before they're hatched.

h. Strike while the iron is hot.

i. A man's home is his castle.

j. A bird in the hand is worth two in the bush.

3 In a library or on the World Wide Web, locate an interview with a person who has lived in a new culture. In class, discuss the person's intercultural experience. Focus on the differences in values and assumptions between the two societies in which the individual has lived, and on any problems resulting from these differences. Compare this person's experiences with your own.

Writing Follow-up

Follow up the discussion activity you chose (item 1, 2, or 3) with the matching writing assignment below.

1 Imagine you are a member of a government agency that helps immigrants adapt to your country. You have been asked to speak to a large group of new arrivals. The topic of your presentation is "How to Better Understand Your New Homeland." Write a short speech welcoming the immigrants to your country and discussing the major values and assumptions they should be aware of in order to adapt more easily and avoid cross-cultural misunderstandings.

2 Write one or two paragraphs describing the values reflected in the proverbs you selected and their cross-cultural equivalents. What conclusions can you draw about cultural variations in beliefs, attitudes, and other patterns?

3 Briefly, compare the intercultural experience of the person interviewed with an experience you've had. Focus on similarities and differences.

CORE READING 2
Where Do We Stand?

Journal Writing

In your journal, **freewrite** for ten minutes on the topic of nonverbal communication. Don't worry about spelling, grammar, punctuation, or organization. Just write for ten minutes, without stopping, about whatever comes to mind when you think of nonverbal communication. (See the discussion of freewriting, a prewriting strategy, on page 114.) Then share your ideas with several classmates.

Previewing the Topic

Specialists in the field of communication look at three factors when trying to determine what people really mean when they are speaking: (1) the literal meaning of the words (the verbal element); (2) the manner of speaking, including tone, volume, pitch, rhythm, and tempo (the vocal element); and (3) the speaker's body movements, especially facial expressions (the nonverbal element, sometimes called body language). Think of a face-to-face conversation you had recently. As the two of you talked, what percentage of the conversation did each element – the verbal, the vocal, and the nonverbal – play in conveying meaning? Write your answers in the blanks. Then share your answer with the rest of the class.

> Verbal = _____%   Vocal = _____%   Nonverbal = _____%

Agreeing and Disagreeing

To what extent do you agree with the following statements? Answer in the context of the culture with which you are most familiar. Fill in each blank with SA (strongly agree), A (agree), U (undecided), D (disagree), or SD (strongly disagree). Then share your responses with several classmates.

_____ 1 People usually greet each other with some form of touching.

_____ 2 It is common for students to avoid eye contact when being reprimanded by a teacher.

_____ 3 Men frequently link arms or hold hands in public.

_____ 4 People tend to gesture a lot with their hands while conversing.

_____ 5 People often smile at each other when passing on the sidewalk.

_____ 6 Silence is a strong cultural value.

_____ 7 People often show physical affection in public.

_____ 8 When people converse, they usually stand very close to each other.

As you read the article, underline or highlight the passages describing the nonverbal behavior of various cultures. Then, in the margin next to each marked passage, indicate whether the behavior is commonly seen in your culture.

Where Do We Stand?
Lisa Davis

In the following article, Lisa Davis, a freelance writer in the United States, focuses on cultural differences in the use of personal space – one type of nonverbal communication – and on problems arising from these differences. "Where Do We Stand?" was originally published in the magazine In Health *in 1990.*

Call it the dance of the jet set,[1] the diplomat's tango: A man from the Middle East, say, falls into conversation with an American, becomes animated, takes a step forward. The American makes a slight postural adjustment, shifts his feet, edges backward. A little more talk and the Arab advances; a little more talk and the American retreats. "By the end of the cocktail party," says Middle East expert Peter Bechtold, of the State Department's Foreign Service Institute, "you have an American in each corner of the room, because that's as far as they can back up." 1

What do you do when an amiable chat leaves one person feeling vaguely bullied, the other unaccountably chilled? Things would be simpler if these jet-setters were speaking different languages – they'd just get themselves a translator. But the problem's a little tougher, because they're using different languages of space. 2

---

[1] *jet set:* Wealthy people who travel around the world from one fashionable place to another.

Everyone who's ever felt cramped in a crowd knows that the skin is not the body's only boundary. We each wear a zone of privacy like a hoop skirt,[2] inviting others in or keeping them out with body language – by how closely we approach, the angle at which we face them, the speed with which we break a gaze. It's a subtle code, but one we use and interpret easily, indeed automatically, having absorbed the vocabulary from infancy.

At least, we *assume* we're reading it right. But from culture to culture, from group to group within a single country, even between the sexes, the language of space has distinctive accents, confusing umlauts.[3] That leaves a lot of room for misinterpretation, and the stakes have gotten higher as business has become increasingly international and populations multicultural. So a new breed of consultants has appeared in the last few years, interpreting for globe-trotters of all nationalities the meaning and use of personal space.

For instance, says international business consultant Sondra Snowdon, Saudi Arabians like to conduct business discussions from within spitting distance – literally. They bathe in each other's breath as part of building the relationship. "Americans back up," says Snowdon, "but they're harming their chances of winning the contracts." In seminars, Snowdon discusses the close quarters common in Middle Eastern conversations, and has her students practice talking with each other at very chummy distances.

Still, her clients had better be careful where they take their shrunken "space bubble," because cultures are idiosyncratic in their spatial needs. Japanese subways bring people about as close together as humanly possible, for instance, yet even a handshake can be offensively physical in a Japanese office. And, says researcher and writer Mildred Reed Hall, Americans can even make their business counterparts in Japan uncomfortable with the kind of direct eye contact that's normal here. "Not only do most Japanese businessmen not look at you, they keep their eyes down," Hall says. "*We* look at people for hours, and they feel like they're under a searchlight."

The study of personal space got under way in the early 1950s, when anthropologist Edward Hall described a sort of cultural continuum of personal space. (Hall has frequently collaborated with his wife, Mildred.) According to Hall, on the "high-contact" side of the continuum – in Mediterranean and South American societies, for instance – social conversations include much eye contact, touching, and smiling, typically while standing at a distance of about a foot. On the other end of the scale, say in Northern European cultures, a lingering gaze may feel invasive, manipulative, or disrespectful; a social chat takes place at a remove of about two and a half feet.

In the middle-of-the-road United States, people usually stand about 18 inches apart for this sort of conversation – unless we want to win foreign friends and influence people, in which case, research shows, we'd better adjust our posture. In one study, when British graduate students were trained to adopt Arab patterns of behavior (facing their partners straight on, with lots of eye contact and smiling), Middle Eastern exchange students found them more likable and trustworthy than

---

[2] *hoop skirt:* A long, full skirt supported by a series of connected hoops, or rings (popular in the late 1850s).

[3] *umlaut:* Change in a vowel sound, often indicated by the symbol (¨).

typical British students. In contrast, the *mis*use of space can call whole personalities into suspicion: When researchers seated pairs of women for conversation, those forced to talk at an uncomfortably large distance were more likely to describe their partners as cold and rejecting.

Don't snuggle up too fast, though. Men in that study were more irritated by their partners when they were forced to talk at close range. Spatially speaking, it seems men and women are subtly foreign to each other. No matter whether a society operates at arm's length or cheek-to-jowl,[4] the women look at each other more and stand a bit closer than do the men. 9

It just goes to show that you can't take things for granted even within the borders of a single country. Take that unwilling amalgamation of ethnic minorities, the Soviet Union. According to psychologist Robert Sommer, who along with Hall sparked the study of personal space, spatial needs collide in the republics. "The Estonians are a non-contact people," says Sommer, of the University of California at Davis. "I went to a 'Hands Around the Baltic'[5] event, and nobody touched hands. The Russians, on the other hand, are high-contact. The Estonians say the Russians are pushy, and the Russians say the Estonians are cold." 10

Nor are things easier within the United States. Researchers have found, for instance, that middle-class, Caucasian schoolteachers often jump to mistaken conclusions when dealing with a child from a different background: If a girl from an Asian family averts her eyes out of respect for her teacher's authority, the teacher may well go on alert, convinced that the child is trying to hide some misbehavior. Ethnically diverse workplaces can be similarly booby-trapped. 11

Such glitches[6] are all the more likely because spatial behavior is automatic – it snaps into focus only when someone doesn't play by the rules. Say an American businessman is alone in a roomy elevator when another man enters. The newcomer fails to perform the national ritual of taking a corner and staring into 12

SPATIAL PATTERNS OF NORTH AMERICANS			
	Distance	**Description**	**Voice**
Intimate	Touching to 18 inches	Private situations with people who are emotionally close. If others invade this space, they feel threatened or angry.	Whisper
Personal	18 inches to 4 feet	The lower end is "handshake" distance – the distance most couples stand in public. Friends also use the personal zone.	Soft voice
Social	4 feet to 12 feet	The lower end is the distance between salespeople and customers and between people who work together. This zone is also common in social gatherings.	Full voice
Public	Greater than 12 feet	Situations such as teaching in a classroom or delivering a speech.	Loud voice

SOURCE: Adapted from *The Silent Language* by Edward Hall (New York: Anchor Books, 1959), pp. 184–185.

[4] *cheek-to-jowl*: Cheek-to-cheek (very close).

[5] *Hands Around the Baltic*: Large group of people expressing solidarity by holding hands in a long line.

[6] *glitches*: Minor problems or malfunctions.

space; instead, he stands a few inches away, smiling, which is simple politeness in some cultures. "You start to search for a reasonable explanation," says psychologist Eric Knowles, at the University of Arkansas. "In many cases you come up with one without even being aware of it. You say, 'Is this guy a pickpocket? Is he psychotic?' If no explanation seems to fit, you just think, 'This guy's weird, I better get out of here.'"

In fact, such caution is not always unwarranted, because an abnormal use of 13 space can indicate that something odd is going on. Research has shown that when people with schizophrenia approach another person, they often either get closer than normal or stay unusually distant. And a small study of prisoners seemed to show that those with a history of violence needed up to three times the space taken by nonviolent inmates. These are reminders that the human need for space is based in an animal reality: The closer you allow a stranger, the more vulnerable you become.

But the spatial differences among cultures point to something beyond self- 14 protection. Anthropologist Edward Hall suggests that a culture's use of space is also evidence of a reliance on one sense over another: Middle Easterners get much of their information through their senses of smell and touch, he says, which require a close approach; Americans rely primarily on visual information, backing up in order to see an intelligible picture.

Conversational distances also tend to reflect the standard greeting distance in 15 each culture, says State Department expert Bechtold. Americans shake hands, and then talk at arm's length. Arabs do a Hollywood-style, cheek-to-cheek social kiss, and their conversation is similarly up close and personal. And, at a distance great enough to keep heads from knocking together – about two feet – the Japanese bow and talk to each other. On the other hand, the need for more or less space may reflect something of a cultural temperament. "There's no word for privacy in Arab cultures," says Bechtold. "They think it means loneliness."

Whatever their origin, spatial styles are very real. In fact, even those who set 16 out to transgress find it uncomfortable to intrude on the space of strangers, says psychologist John R. Aiello, at Rutgers University. "I've had students say, 'Boy, that was the hardest thing I ever had to do – to stand six inches away when I was asking those questions.'"

Luckily, given coaching and time, it seems to get easier to acculturate to foreign 17 habits of contact. Says Bechtold, "You often see men holding hands in the Middle East and walking down the street together. It's just that they're concerned and don't want you to cross the street unescorted, but I've had American pilots come in here and say, 'I don't want some s.o.b.[7] holding my hand.' Then I see them there, holding the hand of a Saudi.

"Personal space isn't so hard for people to learn," Bechtold adds. "What is really 18 much harder is the business of dinner being served at midnight."

---

[7] *s.o.b.*: Son of a bitch; vulgar term referring to an offensive or disagreeable person, usually a male.

Reading Journal

In your journal, write about one of the following topics.

1 You've probably noticed differences in people's nonverbal behavior depending on their cultural background or their nationality. Describe one difference.

2 Discuss a misunderstanding you've experienced as a result of cultural differences in nonverbal behavior.

3 Choose a topic of your own related to the reading.

Main Ideas

Answer the following questions, referring to the notes you took when reading the article. Then share your answers with a partner.

1 Which types of nonverbal communication are mentioned in the reading?

2 What is the major cause of the nonverbal conflicts described in the article?

3 What is the main point Davis makes in the article? Summarize her central idea in one or two sentences. Use your own words. Begin with the sentence *In her article "Where Do We Stand?," Lisa Davis maintains that . . .*

Reflecting on Content

Answer the following questions with a partner. When possible, support your answers with observations based on your own experiences.

1 In paragraph 4, Davis refers to "the language of space." In which ways is the use of space like a spoken language? Think of at least two similarities.

2 Why do you think differences in nonverbal communication exist around the world? Are there any contexts in which nonverbal behaviors are the same in almost every society? Explain your answer.

3 How do you think Davis would recommend avoiding intercultural misunderstandings that result from differences in body language?

A Writer's Technique: *Supporting Details*

Review the discussion of supporting details on page 14.

The following four general statements appear in Davis's article. Find one or two details in the reading that support or illustrate each general idea. The supporting details may come from the same paragraph as the general statement or from another paragraph in the article. Describe these details in your own words. Share your answers with a partner.

1 But from culture to culture, from group to group within a single country, even between the sexes, the language of space has distinctive accents, confusing umlauts. (par. 4)

2 Spatially speaking, it seems men and women are subtly foreign to each other. (par. 9)

3 It just goes to show that you can't take things for granted even within the borders of a single country. (par. 10)

4 Such glitches are all the more likely because spatial behavior is automatic – it snaps into focus only when someone doesn't play by the rules. (par. 12)

Vocabulary: *Idioms*

An **idiom** is a phrase or an expression with a special meaning that is different from the individual meanings of the words – for example, *to sleep like a log* means to sleep very soundly; *to rain cats and dogs* means to rain heavily. Because idioms occur frequently in English and because their meaning cannot be determined from the literal definitions of the words, understanding idioms is essential for effective communication.

Many idioms in English are based on parts of the body – for example, *to bang one's head against a wall,* which means to waste time on a hopeless activity, and *to pull someone's leg,* which means to play a joke on someone by saying something that is not true.

Think of five idioms based on parts of the body. Give the meaning of each idiom and use the idiom correctly in a sentence (as in the example below). You may use a dictionary to help you. Then share the idioms with several classmates.

> **Idiom:** *to cross one's fingers (for someone)*
> **Meaning:** *to wish someone good luck*
> **Sentence:** *I'll cross my fingers (for you) when you take the test.*

Vocabulary in Context

Locate the following italicized vocabulary items in the reading and see if you can determine their meaning from the context. Then think of an example or situation to illustrate each item, using your personal experience if possible. Do not just define the italicized words and expressions. When you are done, share your answers with a partner.

1 a person with whom you have an *amiable* relationship (par. 2)

2 a *distinctive* type of food, clothing, or architecture that you've encountered in a new culture (par. 4)

3 an *idiosyncratic* way of dealing with an issue or a problem (par. 6)

4 a way in which a teacher might communicate nonverbally that it was time for a student to stop *lingering* in her office (par. 7)

5 an example of *manipulative* behavior (par. 7)

6 something you think many people in your culture *take for granted,* and why (par. 10)

7 an example of a person *jumping to a conclusion* about a foreign culture (par. 11)

8 one or two ways to *avert* cross-cultural misunderstandings (par. 11)

9 an example of an *unwarranted* statement or behavior (par. 13)

10 one or two reasons someone might feel *vulnerable* living in a new culture (par. 13)

Discussion

Choose one of the following activities to do with a partner or in a small group.

1 Demonstrate some common gestures in your culture and discuss restrictions regarding their appropriate use. Next, show how you would indicate the following comments and behaviors nonverbally:

Comments	**Behaviors**
"I don't know."	greeting someone
"That person is intelligent / crazy / beautiful."	saying goodbye to someone
"That's expensive."	insulting someone
"That was stupid."	flirting with someone
"I feel happy / sad / angry / afraid / surprised / ashamed / disgusted."	getting a waiter's attention
	ending a conversation

2 Below are seven photographs showing universal facial expressions. In the space beneath each picture, write an adjective that describes the emotion the person is experiencing. Then compare your answers with those of your partner or group. Do you think there are any other facial expressions of emotion seen in all cultures?

a. _____   b. _____   c. _____   d. _____

 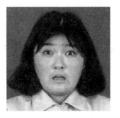 

e. _____   f. _____   g. _____

3 Do a library or Internet search of a particular form of nonverbal communication. Look for information dealing with cross-cultural similarities and differences. In class, discuss the material you found with your partner or group. Then share your findings and conclusions with the rest of the class.

Writing Follow-up

Follow up the discussion activity you chose (item 1, 2, or 3) with the matching writing assignment below.

1 Imagine that two people from different societies have a misunderstanding based on cultural variations in the use of gestures or another form of nonverbal communication. Write two paragraphs discussing the problem. In the first paragraph, describe the misunderstanding; in the second paragraph, explain the reason for it.

2 Describe the process of analyzing the pictures as though you were describing a small scientific experiment. Write up what happened, give the results, and interpret them.

3 In one or two paragraphs, summarize the information you found in your library or Internet search.

CORE READING 3
Time Talks, with an Accent

Journal Writing

In your journal, write for ten to fifteen minutes about a cultural difference you've noticed in perceptions of time, especially the pace of life and attitudes toward punctuality (arriving on time, early, and late). You may focus on different countries or various parts of your own country. Then share your observations with several classmates.

Previewing the Topic

In a small group, discuss cultural differences in concepts of punctuality. Consider the following questions: If you were attending a dinner party at a friend's house, when would you typically arrive? At the scheduled time? Earlier? Later? What would be considered an early or a late arrival? Would the concept of punctuality be the same for someone going to a class, a job, or an interview, or meeting with a friend?

Agreeing and Disagreeing

To what extent do you agree with the following statements? Fill in each blank with SA (strongly agree), A (agree), U (undecided), D (disagree), or SD (strongly disagree). Then share your responses with several classmates.

_____ 1 Punctuality is a strong value in my culture.

_____ 2 One of the hardest things for many people to adjust to in a new culture is the concept of time.

_____ 3 In my culture, it is acceptable for students to arrive late to class.

_____ 4 It doesn't make much sense to worry about the future, since fate largely determines people's lives.

_____ 5 Tradition is highly valued in my culture.

_____ 6 In my culture, one has to wait for a lot of things, such as trains, store purchases, and bank transactions.

_____ 7 Never put off until tomorrow what you can do today.

_____ 8 Getting together with friends and family is one of the important pleasures in life.

_____ 9 In my culture, schedules, plans, and deadlines are easily changed.

_____ 10 Time is a limited resource and shouldn't be wasted.

Taking Notes While You Read

As you read the selection, note in the margin the cultural differences the author discusses in perceptions of time. Also indicate which perceptions are similar to and different from those in your culture.

Time Talks, with an Accent
Robert Levine

Robert Levine is a social psychologist and professor of psychology at California State University, Fresno. He has lived and taught in many countries, including Brazil, Japan, and Sweden. The following reading is an excerpt from Levine's book A Geography of Time *(1997), which explores cross-cultural differences in concepts of time – a subject to which he has devoted his career.*

> Every culture has its own unique set of temporal fingerprints. To know a people is to know the time values they live by.
>
> Jeremy Rifkin, *Time Wars*

Time has intrigued me for as long as I remember. Like most young Americans, I was initially taught that time is simply measured by a clock – in seconds and minutes, hours and days, months and years. But when I looked around at my elders, the numbers never seemed to add up the same way twice. Why was it, I wondered, that

1

some adults appeared to be perpetually running out of daylight hours while others seemed to have all the time in the world? I thought of this second group of people – the ones who would go to the movies in the middle of the workday or take their families on six-month sabbaticals to the South Pacific – as temporal millionaires, and I vowed to become one of them.

When planning my career, I ignored my peers' unwavering concern with the amount of money a job would pay and tuned in instead to the temporal lifestyle it offered. To what extent would I be able to set my own pace? How much control would I have over my time? Could I take a bike ride during the day? Thoreau[1] spoke to me when he observed, "To affect the quality of the day, that is the highest of arts." I chose a profession – that of a university professor – which offers the temporal mobility I sought. And to my good fortune, I encountered a specialty – social psychology – that has allowed me to pursue the very concept of time that fascinated me as a child.

I trace the beginning of my scientific journey to an experience early in my career. . . . I had just begun an appointment as a visiting professor of psychology at the Federal University in Niteroi, Brazil, a midsized city across the bay from Rio de Janeiro. I arrived anxious to observe at first hand just what characteristics of this alien environment would require the greatest readjustment from me. From my past travel experiences, I anticipated difficulties with such issues as the language, my privacy, and standards of cleanliness. But these turned out to be a piece of cake compared to the distress that Brazilians' ideas of time and punctuality were to cause me.

I was aware before arriving, of course, of the stereotype of the *amanhã* attitude of Brazilians (the Portuguese version of *a mañana*[2]), whereby it is said that whenever it is conceivably possible the business of today is put off until tomorrow. I knew I'd need to slow down and to reduce my expectations of accomplishment. But I was a kid from Brooklyn,[3] where one is taught at an early age to move fast or get out of the way. Years ago I had learned to survive life in the foreign culture of Fresno, California, a city where even laid-back Los Angelenos must learn to decelerate. Adjusting to the pace of life in Brazil, I figured, would call for no more than a bit of fine tuning. What I got instead was a dose of culture shock I wouldn't wish on a hijacker.

My lessons began soon after arriving. As I left home for my first day of teaching, I asked someone the time. It was 9:05 A.M., allowing me plenty of time to get to my 10 o'clock lecture. After what I judged to be half an hour, I glanced at a clock I was passing. It said 10:20! In panic, I broke for the classroom, followed by gentle calls of "*Alô, Professor*" and "*Tudo bem, Professor?*"[4] from unhurried students, many of whom, I later realized, were my own. I arrived breathless to find an empty room.

Frantically, I exited the room to ask a passerby the time. "Nine forty-five," came the answer. No, that couldn't be. I asked someone else. "Nine fifty-five." Another

---

[1] *Thoreau, Henry David* (1817–1862): Well-known U.S. writer who spent two years living by himself in the woods and observing nature (an experience he described in his book *Walden*).

[2] *a mañana*: Spanish for "tomorrow."

[3] *Brooklyn*: One of the five major divisions, called boroughs, of New York City.

[4] "*Alô, Professor*" and "*Tudo bem, Professor?*": Portuguese for "Hello, Professor" and "How are you, Professor?"

squinted down at his watch and called out proudly: "Exactly nine forty-three." The clock in a nearby office read 3:15. I had received my first two lessons: Brazilian timepieces are consistently inaccurate; and nobody seemed to mind but me.

My class was scheduled from ten until noon. Many students came late. Several arrived after 10:30. A few showed up closer to eleven. Two came after that. All of the latecomers wore the relaxed smiles I later came to enjoy. Each one greeted me, and although a few apologized briefly, none seemed terribly concerned about being late. They assumed that I understood.   **7**

That Brazilians would arrive late was no surprise, although it was certainly a new personal experience to watch students casually enter a classroom more than one hour late for a two-hour class. The real surprise came at noon that first day, when the class came to a close.   **8**

Back home in California, I never need to look at a clock to know when the class hour is ending. The shuffling of books is accompanied by strained expressions screaming: "I'm hungry / I'm thirsty / I've got to go to the bathroom / I'm going to suffocate if you keep us one more second." (The pain, I find, usually becomes unbearable at two minutes to the hour for undergraduates and at about five minutes to the hour for graduate students.) But when noon arrived for my first Brazilian class, only a few students left right away. Others slowly drifted out during the next fifteen minutes, and some continued asking me questions long after that. When several remaining students kicked off their shoes at 12:30, I went into *my* own hungry / thirsty / bathroom / suffocation plea. (I could not, with any honesty, attribute their lingering to my superb teaching style. I had, in fact, just spent two hours lecturing on statistics in halting Portuguese. Forgive me, *meus pobres estudantes.*[5]) In the hope of understanding my students' behavior, I made an appointment for 11 A.M. the next morning with my new *chefe*, or department head. I arrived at her office on time. Neither she nor her secretary was there. In fact, I had to turn on the lights to read the magazines in the waiting room: a year-old copy of *Time* and a three-year-old copy of *Sports Illustrated.*   **9**

At 11:30 the secretary arrived, said *alô*, asked me if I wanted a *cafézinho* (the traditional Brazilian drink consisting of one-half thick coffee and one-half sugar, which, as best I can tell, gets everyone so wired that they no longer bother to move), and left. At 11:45 my new *chefe* arrived, also offered me a *cafézinho*, and also went off. Ten minutes later she returned, sat down at her desk, and began reading her mail. At 12:20, she finally called me into her office, casually apologized for making me wait, chatted for a few minutes and then excused herself to "run" to another appointment for which she was late. I learned later that this was no lie. It was her habit to make lots of appointments for the same time and to be late for all of them. She apparently liked appointments.   **10**

Later that day I had a meeting scheduled with several students from my class. When I got to my "office" two of them were already there and acting quite at home. They seemed undisturbed that I was a few minutes late and, in fact, were in no hurry to begin. One had kicked his feet up on my desk and was reading his *Sports Illustrated* (which, I noted, was only three months old).   **11**

---

[5] *meus pobres estudantes:* Portuguese for "my poor students."

Some fifteen minutes after the scheduled conclusion I stood up and explained 12
that I had other appointments waiting. The students stayed put and asked pleasantly,
"Who with?" When I listed the names of two of their associates, one fellow excitedly
reported that he knew them both. He rushed to the door and escorted one of
them from the waiting area – the other hadn't arrived yet – into my office. They
all then proceeded to chit-chat and turn the pages of the *Sports Illustrated*. By the
time his associate sauntered in, five minutes before the scheduled conclusion of
our appointment, I was beginning to lose track of who was early and who was late
– which, I was eventually to learn, was exactly the lesson that I should have been
learning. For now, though, I was just plain confused.

My last appointment of the day was with the owner of an apartment I wanted to 13
rent. This time I thought I could spot the little train coming. As soon as I arrived
I asked his secretary how long I would have to wait. She said that her boss was
running late. "How late?," I asked. "A half an hour, *mais ou menos*,"[6] she replied.
Would I like a *cafézinho*? I declined and said I'd be back in twenty minutes. Upon my
return, she said it would be a little while longer. I left again. When I came back ten
minutes later, she told me her boss had gotten tired of waiting for me and had left
for the day. When I began to snap out an angry message to give to her Sr. Landlord,
the secretary explained that I'd left him no choice but to skip out on me. "Don't
you understand, he's the owner and you're not. You're an arrogant man, Dr. Levine."
That was the last time I tried to outmaneuver a Brazilian at the waiting game.

During my year in Brazil, I was repeatedly bewildered, frustrated, fascinated, and 14
obsessed by the customs and ideas of social time that Brazilians sent my way. The
reason that Brazilians' rules of punctuality so confused me, it soon become apparent,
was that they are inseparably intertwined with cultural values. And when we enter
the web of culture, answers come neither simply nor cleanly. Cultural beliefs are
like the air we breathe, so taken for granted that they are rarely discussed or even
articulated. But there is often a volatile reaction when these unwritten rules are violated. Unsuspecting outsiders like myself can walk into a cultural minefield.

No beliefs are more 15
ingrained and subsequently hidden than those about time. Almost thirty years ago anthropologist Edward Hall labeled rules of social time the "silent language." The world over, children simply pick up their society's conceptions of early and late; of waiting and rushing; of the past, the

THE PACE OF LIFE IN SIX COUNTRIES			
	Accuracy of Bank Clocks	Walking Speed	Post Office Speed
Japan	1	1	1
United States	2	3	2
England	4	2	3
Italy	5	4	6
Taiwan	3	5	4
Indonesia	6	6	5

The first indicator of time sense refers to the accuracy of a country's bank clocks, the second to the speed at which pedestrians walk, and the third to the average time it takes a postal clerk to sell a single stamp. Numbers (1 is the top value) indicate the comparative rankings of each country for each indicator of time sense.

Source: "Social Time: The Heartbeat of Culture" by Robert Levine and Ellen Wolff, (*Psychology Today* 19, 1985: pp. 28–35)

---
[6] *mais ou menos*: Portuguese for "more or less."

present, and the future. There is no dictionary to define these rules of time for them, or for strangers who stumble over the maddening incongruities between the time sense they bring with them and the one they face in a new land. . . .

Brazil made it clear to me that time was talking. But understanding what it was saying was no simple matter. After several months of temporal blunders, I designed my first systematic experiments about time in an attempt to understand Brazilians' beliefs and rules about punctuality. This work, at first to my frustration but eventually my appreciation, raised more questions than it answered. What I found so intrigued me that I have spent most of the past two decades continuing to research both the psychology of time and the psychology of places. My research has evolved from studies of punctuality to those about the broader pace of life; further study has raised questions about the consequences the pace of life has for the physical and psychological well-being of people and their communities. This work has taken me through many of the cities of the United States and across much of the rest of the world. It has confirmed my earliest intuitions: that how people construe the time of their lives comprises a world of diversity. There are drastic differences on every level: from culture to culture, city to city, and from neighbor to neighbor. And most of all, I have learned, the time on the clock only begins to tell the story. 16

Reading Journal

In your journal, write about one of the following topics.

1 Explain the significance of the title of the article, "Time Talks, with an Accent."
2 Discuss a difficulty or misunderstanding you've experienced as a result of cultural differences in perceptions of time.
3 Choose a topic of your own related to the reading.

Main Ideas

Answer the following questions, referring to the notes you took when reading the selection. Then share your answers with a partner.

1 How does Levine define the term "social time"? What are its components?
2 According to Levine, why is adjusting to a foreign concept of time so difficult?
3 What is the main point Levine makes in the reading? Summarize his central idea in one or two sentences. Use your own words. Begin with the sentence *In the excerpt "Time Talks, with an Accent," Robert Levine maintains that . . .*

Reflecting on Content

Answer the following questions with a partner. When possible, support your answers with observations based on your own experiences.

1 What does Levine mean when he says that the rules of punctuality are "inseparably intertwined with cultural values" (par. 14)? In which ways does a society's concept of time reflect cultural values?

2 Edward Hall, a noted intercultural scholar, refers to rules of social time as a "silent language" (par. 15). What does he mean by this? How does a culture's concept of time resemble a language? Think of two or three similarities.

3 What feelings does Levine experience while encountering cultural differences in perceptions of time? Have you experienced any of these feelings when confronted with a different orientation to time?

A Writer's Technique: *Supporting Details*

Review the discussion of supporting details on page 14.

One type of evidence that writers frequently use to support their main points, especially in narrative and descriptive essays, is the **anecdote** – a brief story that presents an interesting or amusing incident. Sometimes these anecdotes are based on the author's personal experiences and sometimes on other peoples' experiences with which the author is familiar.

Answer the following questions. Then compare your responses with a partner.

1 In "Time Talks, with an Accent," Levine provides a number of personal anecdotes to illustrate his main idea. The paragraphs listed below contain anecdotes. Reread the paragraphs and explain the single main idea that all the anecdotes illustrate.
   • Paragraph 10
   • Paragraphs 11–12
   • Paragraph 13

2 How effective do you think Levine's anecdotes are in illustrating his thesis? Should he have included any other type of detail to support his points?

Vocabulary: *Guessing Meaning from the Context*

If you are reading a passage and come across an unfamiliar word or expression, don't immediately reach for your dictionary. Often by looking at the context of the vocabulary item – the sentence and paragraph in which the word or expression appears – you can get a good sense of its general meaning. Good readers often use **context clues** to figure out the meaning of an unknown vocabulary item. When you use context clues, you use the words you are familiar with in a passage and your own experiences to make an educated guess about the meaning of an unfamiliar word or expression. Developing the ability to guess meaning from context will help improve your reading comprehension and build your vocabulary.

Look at these sentences from "Time Talks, with an Accent" and do the following.
   • Guess the meaning of each italicized word or expression from the context.
   • Write one or two **synonyms** for each vocabulary item, or write your own definition. A synonym is a word with the same, or nearly the same, meaning. Do this exercise first without using a dictionary.
   • Write a sentence of your own, using the vocabulary item correctly.

> **Example:** *Why was it, I wondered, that some adults appeared to be* **perpetually** *running out of daylight hours while others seemed to have all the time in the world? (par. 1)*
>
> **Synonyms:** *continually, forever*
>
> **Sentence:** *Because of his lack of flexibility, Ari was* **perpetually** *running into problems while living abroad.*

1 When planning my career, I ignored my peers' *unwavering* concern with the amount of money a job would pay and tuned in instead to the temporal lifestyle it offered. (par. 2)

2 From my past travel experiences, I anticipated difficulties with such issues as the language, my privacy, and standards of cleanliness. But these turned out to be *a piece of cake* compared to the distress that Brazilians' ideas of time and punctuality were to cause me. (par. 3)

3 Back home in California, I never need to look at a clock to know when the class hour is ending. The *shuffling* of books is accompanied by strained expressions screaming: "I'm hungry / I'm thirsty / I've got to go to the bathroom / I'm going to suffocate if you keep us one more second." (par. 9)

4 The reason that Brazilians' rules of punctuality so confused me, it soon became apparent, was that they are inseparably *intertwined* with cultural values. And when we enter the web of culture, answers come neither simply nor cleanly. (par. 14)

5 Cultural beliefs are like the air we breathe, so taken for granted that they are rarely discussed or even articulated. But there is often a *volatile* reaction when these unwritten rules are violated. (par. 14)

Vocabulary in Context

Locate the following italicized vocabulary items in the reading and see if you can determine their meaning from the context. Then think of an example or situation to illustrate each item, using your personal experience if possible. Do not just define the italicized words and expressions. When you are done, share your answers with a partner.

1 something about a foreign culture that once *intrigued* you, and why (par. 1)

2 something you could *conceivably* see yourself doing in a new culture that would be uncommon in your culture (par. 4)

3 a reason you might want to *put* one thing *off* and call another thing off (par. 4)

4 a time when you had to accelerate or *decelerate* your pace of life, and why (par. 4)

5 something to which you *attribute* a value, belief, or behavior in a culture you once visited (par. 9)

6 whether it is common in your culture for students to *linger* after class in order to speak with a professor (par. 9)

7 an aspect of life in a new culture that once *bewildered* you (par. 14)

8 a belief that is *ingrained* in the minds of most people in your culture (par. 15)

9 an *incongruity* between a belief or behavior found in your culture and one found in a different culture (par. 15)

10 a *blunder* you once made when in a new culture or community (par. 16)

Discussion

Choose one of the following activities to do with a partner or in a small group.

1 Discuss the common perception of time in your culture and any differences you've noticed when in a new culture. Consider the general pace of life; attitude toward punctuality; and orientation to past, present, or future. Discuss your personal experiences with the different perception of time, including any problems or misunderstandings.

2 Design a brief questionnaire dealing with cultural perceptions of time. Ask several people from different cultures to respond to the questions, and then analyze their responses. What conclusions can you draw? When you are done, share your findings with the rest of the class.

3 Access the National Public Radio Web site <www.npr.org>. Click on *Archives* and search for one of the following broadcast titles (remember to include the quotation marks when you search): "A Geography of Time," "Cultural Perceptions in Time," or "Different Perceptions of Time." Listen to one of these broadcasts and list the various perceptions of time that are mentioned. Then, with your partner or a group, discuss these patterns in the context of the culture with which you are most familiar.

Writing Follow-up

Follow up the discussion activity you chose (item 1, 2, or 3) with the matching writing assignment below.

1 Imagine you are a member of an organization that is writing a brochure on cultural patterns in a particular culture or country. You are working on a section dealing with common perceptions of time: general pace of life; attitude toward punctuality; and orientation to past, present, or future. Write a brief discussion of one of these aspects of time to be included in the brochure. Your goal is to help visitors adjust to the culture or country and avoid misunderstandings that result from cultural differences in perceptions of time.

2 Write a brief report discussing the results of your questionnaire. What do people's responses have in common? What conclusions can you draw?

3 Write one paragraph summarizing the comments you heard on the radio broadcast about cultural differences in perceptions of time. In a second paragraph, discuss your reaction.

MAKING CONNECTIONS

Answer two or three of the following questions relating to the three core readings in this chapter.

1 The authors of the core readings (Althen, Davis, and Levine) describe various intercultural conflicts and misunderstandings. Although they focus on different subjects, they attribute these problems to the same cause. What is the origin of the intercultural tensions that the authors discuss?

2 All three authors either state directly or imply ways to minimize cultural misunderstanding. Are there any suggestions that are common to all three of the authors?

3 In the first reading, Althen discusses prominent values in the United States and contrasts them with values in other cultures. Which of these values, or its opposite, is reflected in the nonverbal behaviors that Davis discusses in the second reading? Give at least two examples.

4 Reread one of the following sections in Althen's chapter dealing with central U.S. values: "Individualism," "Privacy," "The Future, Change, and Progress," or "Achievement, Action, Work, and Materialism." How does this value help explain the U.S. perceptions of time that Levine discusses in the third reading?

5 How do the authors of these three readings provide detail (examples, facts, statistics, personal experiences, anecdotes, and quotations) to support their main ideas? Be as specific as possible, referring to at least two types of supporting detail that each author uses.

ADDITIONAL READING 1
Polite but Thirsty

Before You Read

With several classmates or in your journal, discuss the major challenges you have encountered while living in a new culture, including difficulties, conflicts, and misunderstandings. Then share your experiences with the rest of the class and write a list of all the challenges on the board.

Taking Notes While You Read

As you read the essay, underline or highlight the passages that describe cross-cultural differences between the United States and China. Think about the major U.S. values that Althen discusses on pages 5–13. Indicate in the margin, next to a marked passage, the value or values reflected in the cultural difference.

Polite but Thirsty
Yaping Tang

In the following essay, Yaping Tang, a native of the People's Republic of China and bilingual education teacher in the United States, discusses the culture shock she experienced when she moved to the United States. The essay initially appeared in a 1996 volume of MATSOL Currents, *a publication for teachers of English as a second language.*

Since 1979, the year in which full diplomatic relations between the People's Republic of China and the United States were established, thousands of Chinese students have come to this country for higher education or research work. Filled with enthusiasm and sincerity, they begin their new life in America.

Right after their arrival, however, these students find themselves exposed to novel, unfamiliar environments. They feel vulnerable during their first year or two. For these newcomers, life is not easy. When people suddenly find themselves in a different culture, their first and dominant experience is perhaps the feeling of inadequacy. It is not only the basic inadequacy of not knowing English fluently but also the ignorance of what is appropriate and what is not, be it in school, on the bus, in restaurants, at parties, or in stores. Newcomers, not knowing the codes of the new culture, constantly fear seeming ridiculous. As a result, there appears to be no choice but to remain silent and withdraw from others. My Chinese bilingual students, for example, who have very little or no knowledge of English when they arrive, are so shocked by the new culture, as well as by the new school system, that during their first several days at school they look like deaf mutes. Some of my students have confessed, "I feel like a baby" or "I look like an idiot." Like other Chinese students, I myself had the unforgettable experience of dealing with culture shock during my first year or so in this country. I came here in 1990 to pursue my master's degree in education, beginning my life in a place whose geography, history, language, and culture contrast markedly with those of China.

I recall my own first day at school, at Rhode Island College. When I went to my first class, I was astonished to see some of my American classmates drinking soda and eating snacks in class. I could hardly believe my eyes and said to myself, "It's like a tea-house." In China students are not allowed to drink or eat anything in class, whether in college or in elementary or high school. From that day on, I became an adventurer in a new world. Here, then, is some of what I went through, observed, and learned. 3

First, in the United States, people usually call each other by first names rather than family names. Everyone does this, including colleagues, classmates, students and teachers, friends, relatives, even children and parents. Americans don't like to be treated with special deference for age or position; it makes them uncomfortable. Being on a first-name basis is taken as a sign of acceptance and friendliness. In China, people don't call each other by their first names unless they are relatives or close friends. Rather, people use the whole name or just call you "Xiao" or "Lao" along with your family name. "Xiao" in Chinese means young or little, and "Lao" means old. Like other Chinese students, therefore, I felt very awkward in the beginning, when I was called by my first name. 4

Second, Americans are very direct. When they want something they say "yes" and when they don't they say "no." Furthermore, if they want something different from what is offered, they ask for it. But Chinese people usually respond with a "no" the first or even the second time they are offered something – even if they really want it. Being courteous requires standing on ceremony,[1] and we don't want to bother others. It's very common in China for someone to repeatedly offer something to a person and then impose it on him or her even after having had it rejected a number of times. Two days after I arrived in America, I went to visit my advisor, Dr. Green. It was a hot summer afternoon. After sitting and talking for a while, I felt very thirsty. Just then, Dr. Green asked me, "Would you like something to drink?" "Oh, no, thank you. Please don't trouble yourself," I answered. Then she said, "Are you sure you wouldn't like some orange juice, or a Coke?" Once again I refused politely: "No, really, thank you just the same." At this, she said, "OK" and walked out. A few seconds later, she returned with a Coke. She continued to talk while drinking. At that point I felt confused as well as thirsty. Later, I wrote to my husband in China about this "polite but thirsty" story and he wrote back jokingly, "Nice try but don't cry!" 5

Third, in America, when someone says to you, "That's a beautiful sweater you're wearing," you might respond, "Thank you. My mother knitted it for me two years ago." But if this conversation happens between two Chinese, the response will be, "Oh, no, I've had this ugly old thing for two years" or "No, it's already out of date." Modesty is another Chinese cultural norm. Another example: You are invited to dinner at a Chinese friend's home; the host will usually say, "Sorry, there's not much food for you. It's just a simple meal" even though the table is covered with a dozen 6

---

[1] *standing on ceremony:* Insisting on following a custom or practice – in this case, traditional acts of politeness.

dishes. What is more, in China, at the table, when someone says, "Oh the food is so good. Your wife is really a good cook," the answer is always something like, "Oh, no. The food is not good this time. She's only a so-so cook. You overpraise her." Unlike the Chinese, Americans do not consider excessive modesty a virtue. After observing and experiencing, I have gotten used to the American way of giving and receiving compliments.

Fourth, in America, if a person is given a gift, he or she will usually open it and say, "Oh, how beautiful it is! Thank you very much." In China, a person usually accepts a gift and says, "Thank you" and then leaves the gift aside, unopened. Opening the gift in front of the giver is considered impolite (so people sometimes don't know

7

STAGES OF CULTURAL ADJUSTMENT

No two people adjust to a new culture in exactly the same way. Most people, however, when living in a new culture for an extended period of time, go through five distinct stages in the adjustment process shown in the graph below.

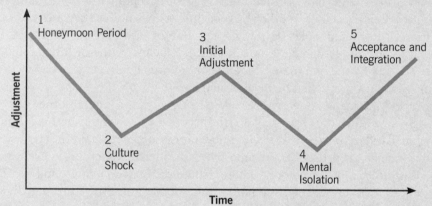

1 **Honeymoon Period:** Initially, everything seems new, intriguing, and exciting – a big adventure. People are fascinated by cultural differences and feel elated to be experiencing a new culture.

2 **Culture Shock:** After some time, people often feel tired, anxious, frustrated, and homesick (and sometimes experience physical problems, such as headaches, stomach upset, and insomnia) and are annoyed by cultural differences and everyday problems, such as language, housing, school, employment, transportation, and shopping. They also often feel disoriented and have difficulty concentrating and working well.

3 **Initial Adjustment:** As people get to know the new language and culture better, they feel more hopeful, self-confident, and connected. They have fewer problems with daily activities and can concentrate and work better.

4 **Mental Isolation:** At this point, people have been away from their family and good friends for a long time and often feel lonely, isolated, angry, and depressed and find fault with the new culture. They frequently avoid contact with people from the host culture and associate with fellow nationals and other "foreigners." The negative feelings in this stage are usually more intense than in the second stage.

5 **Acceptance and Integration:** After some time, people become more accustomed to the values, beliefs, and behaviors of the new culture; accept them as just another way of life; and often start to enjoy them. They also stop continually glorifying their native culture and criticizing the host culture. Being more familiar with the new language and way of life, and having a daily routine, they know what to expect and feel more at home.

SOURCE: Peter Gardner

what gift they have got until their friends or relatives leave!). In addition, Chinese people usually present their gifts just before they leave, while Americans usually give their gifts right after they arrive.

Fifth, in mainland China we never tip anybody. Chinese students find it hard to get used to the tipping system here and feel very embarrassed when they forget to tip a taxi driver or a waitress in a restaurant. 8

But simple embarrassment is one thing; in addition to suffering from culture shock when dealing with external matters such as differences in food, climate, language, mannerisms, and communication, newcomers also suffer psychologically from status change and status loss. Most Chinese students, for example, have been academically successful at home and are professionally well-established. They suddenly face intense academic pressure and adjustments. They also have to work hard to pay their tuition and living expenses. Some even hold two or three jobs at once. They work harder and for longer hours than most other students. Many do such jobs as taking care of the disabled or elderly, babysitting, cleaning houses, or working in restaurants. (I was a student-worker and had another job off campus taking care of a disabled girl on weekends.) Most Chinese students were university teachers, scholars, and engineers in China, where people like them would never do these kinds of jobs, so some of them feel a distinct loss of status. 9

As a result of culture shock, some Chinese students experience a painful social vulnerability. Having lost cultural and personal structures upon separating from the home country and feeling fearful about making contact with Americans, very few are successful in establishing close relationships with Americans. Instead, they often create a co-national "subculture," which recapitulates the home setting and provides necessary support but which also serves as a barrier to deep intercultural contact. Other symptoms of culture shock are the following: absent-mindedness; a feeling of hopelessness; fits of anger; excessive fear of being cheated, robbed, or injured; and, finally, that terrible longing to be back home. 10

Life is never smooth sailing. It requires a continual series of adaptations to new environments. But what should newcomers do to mitigate the shock of confronting a new culture? It's best to face unfamiliar cultural settings squarely and try to cope with them; and coping with a new culture requires the acquisition of new information and the learning of new responses and skills. But by doing so, we can broaden our perspectives, promote personal growth, gain insight into the culture of origin through a contrast with other world views, and, ultimately, successfully adapt to our new world. 11

After You Read

In your journal, write about one of the following topics.

1 Explain the main point Tang makes in the essay.
2 Discuss any experiences you may have had adjusting to a new society, including any culture shock you encountered.
3 Choose a topic of your own related to the reading.

ADDITIONAL READING 2
Friends and Strangers

Before You Read

With several classmates or in your journal, discuss what friendship means to you. What does being a friend entail? Are certain expectations, rights, and responsibilities involved in being a friend? After discussing your concept of friendship, share your ideas with the rest of the class.

Taking Notes While You Read

As you read the selection, note in the margin the cross-cultural differences between Arab and Western concepts of friendship. Also indicate which aspects of friendship are similar to and different from those in your culture.

 ## Friends and Strangers
Margaret K. (Omar) Nydell

In the following selection, Margaret K. (Omar) Nydell discusses differences between Arab and Western (North American and European) cultures in the concepts of friendship. Dr. Nydell is a cross-cultural trainer and teacher of Arabic who has lived in many Arab countries, written several books on the Arabic language, and lectured extensively on Arab culture. "Friends and Strangers" is an excerpt from a chapter of her book Understanding Arabs: A Guide for Westerners, *third edition (2002).*

THE CONCEPT OF FRIENDSHIP

Relations between people are very personalized in the Arab culture. Friendships 1 start and develop quickly. But the Arab concept of friendship, with its rights and duties, is quite different from that in the West.

Westerners, especially Americans, tend to think of a friend as someone whose 2 company they enjoy. A friend can be asked for a favor or for help if necessary, but it is considered poor form to cultivate a friendship primarily for what can be gained from that person or his or her position. Among Arabs, also, a friend is someone whose company one enjoys. *However, equally important to the relationship is the duty of a friend to give help and do favors to the best of his or her ability.*

Differences in expectations can lead to misunderstanding and, for both parties, 3 a feeling of being let down. The Westerner feels "set up" to do favors, and the Arab concludes that no Westerner can be a "true friend." In order to avoid such feelings, we must bear in mind what is meant by both sides when one person calls another "friend."

RECIPROCAL FAVORS

For an Arab, good manners require that one never openly refuse a request from a friend. This does not mean that the favor must actually be done, but rather that the response must not be stated as a direct no. If a friend asks you for a favor, do it if you can – this keeps the friendship flourishing. If it is unreasonable, illegal, or too difficult, the correct form is to listen carefully and suggest that while you are doubtful about the outcome, you will at least try to help. Later, you express your regrets and offer to do something else in the future instead. In this way you have not openly refused a favor, and your face-to-face encounters have remained pleasant. 4

I once talked to an Egyptian university student who told me that he was very disappointed in his American professor. The professor had gratefully accepted many favors while he was getting settled in Egypt, including assistance in finding a maid and buying furniture. When the Egyptian asked him to use his influence in helping him obtain a graduate fellowship in the United States, the professor told him that there was no point in trying because his grades were not high enough to be competitive. The Egyptian took this as a personal affront and felt bitter that the professor did not care about him enough to help him work toward a better future. The more appropriate cross-cultural response by the professor would have been to make helpful gestures, for example, helping the student obtain information about fellowships, assisting him with applications, and offering encouragement – even if he was not optimistic about the outcome. 5

A similar incident happened to an American military officer in Morocco, who became angry when his Moroccan neighbor asked him to buy some items from the local military exchange (PX[1]), which is illegal. When he bluntly refused, his neighbor was offended and the friendship was severely damaged. 6

In Western culture actions are far more important and more valued than words. *In the Arab culture, an oral promise has its own value as a response.* If an action does not follow, the other person cannot be held entirely responsible for a "failure." 7

If you fail to carry out a request, you will notice that no matter how hopeful your Arab friend was that you would succeed, he or she will probably accept your regrets graciously without asking precisely why the favor could not be done (which could embarrass you and possibly force you to admit a failure). You should be willing to show the same forbearance and understanding in inquiring about one of your requests. Noncommittal answers probably mean there is no hope. This is one of the most frustrating cultural patterns Westerners confront in the Arab World. You must learn to work with this idea rather than fighting against it. 8

When Arabs give a yes answer to your request, they are not necessarily certain that the action will or can be carried out. Etiquette demands that your request have a positive response. The result is a separate matter. A positive response to a request is a declaration of intention and an expression of goodwill – no more than that. Yes should not always be taken literally. You will hear phrases such as *Inshallah* (If God wills) used in connection with promised actions. This is called for culturally, and it sometimes results in lending a further degree of uncertainty to the situation. . . . 9

---

[1] *PX:* "Please exchange" or "post exchange": Store where military personnel can purchase items, usually at reduced prices.

Sometimes an Arab asks another person for something and then adds the phrase, "Do this for my sake." This phrasing sounds odd to a foreigner, especially if the persons involved do not know each other well, because it appears to imply a very close friendship. In fact, the expression means that the person requesting the action is acknowledging that he will consider himself indebted to return the favor in the future. "For my sake" is very effective in Arab culture when added to a request. 10

An Arab expects loyalty from anyone who is considered a friend. The friend is therefore not justified in becoming indignant when asked for favors, since it should be understood from the beginning that giving and receiving favors is an inherent part of the relationship. Arabs will not form or perpetuate a friendship unless they also like and respect you; their friendship is not as calculated or self-serving as it may appear. The practice of cultivating a person only in order to use him or her is no more acceptable among Arabs than it is among Westerners. 11

INTRODUCTIONS

Arabs quickly determine another person's social status and connections when they meet. They will, in addition, normally give more information about themselves than Westerners do. They may indulge in a little (or a lot of) self-praise and praise of their relatives and family and present a detailed account of their social connections. When Westerners meet someone for the first time, they tend to confine personal information to generalities about their education, profession, and interests. 12

To Arabs, information about family and social connections is important, possibly even more important than the information about themselves. Family information is also what they want from you. They may find your response so inadequate that they wonder if you are hiding something, while your impression is that much of what they say is too detailed and largely irrelevant. Both parties give the information they think the other wants to know. 13

Your Arab friends' discourse about their "influence network" is *not* bragging, and it is not irrelevant. This information may turn out to be highly useful if you are ever in need of high-level personal contacts, and you should appreciate the offer of potential assistance from insiders in the community. Listen carefully to what they have to say. 14

VISITING PATTERNS

Arabs feel that good friends should see each other often, at least every few days, and they offer many invitations to each other. Westerners who have Arab friends sometimes feel overwhelmed by the frequent contact and wonder if they will ever have any privacy. There is no concept of privacy among Arabs. In translation, the Arab word that comes closest to *privacy* means "loneliness"! 15

A British resident in Beirut once complained that he and his wife had almost no time to be alone – Arab friends and neighbors kept dropping in unexpectedly and often stayed late. He said, "I have one friend who telephoned and said, 'I haven't seen you anywhere. Where have you been for the last three days?'" 16

By far the most popular form of entertainment in the Arab World is conversation. Arabs enjoy long discussions over shared meals or many cups of coffee or tea. You will be expected to reciprocate invitations, although you do not have to keep pace precisely with the number you receive. If you plead for privacy or become too slack 17 in socializing, people will wonder if someone has offended you, if you don't like them, or if you are sick. You can say that you have been very busy, but resorting to this too often without sufficient explanation may be taken as an affront. "Perhaps," your friends may think, "you are just too busy for us."

I once experienced a classic example of the Arab (and especially Egyptian) love of companionship in Cairo. After about three hours at a party where I was surrounded by loud music and louder voices, I stepped onto the balcony for a moment of quiet and fresh air. One of the women noticed and followed immediately, asking, "Is anything wrong? Are you angry at someone?" 18

A young Arab American was quoted as saying, "In the United States you can have more personal space, I guess is about the best way to put it. You have privacy when you want privacy. And in Arab society they don't really understand the idea that you want to be alone. That means that you're mad, you're angry at something, or you're upset and you should have somebody with you."* 19

If you are not willing to increase the frequency or intensity of your personal contacts, you may hurt your friends' feelings and damage the relationship. Ritual and essentially meaningless expressions used in Western greeting and leave-taking, such as "We've got to get together sometime," may well be taken literally, and you have approximately a one-week grace period in which to follow up with an invitation before your sincerity is questioned. 20

Some Westerners, as they learn about the intricate and time-consuming relationships which develop among friends, decide that they would rather keep acquaintances at a distance. If you accept no favors, you will eventually be asked for none, and you will have much more time to yourself, but you will soon find that you have no Arab friends. Arab friends are generous with their time and efforts to help you, are willing to inconvenience themselves for you, and are concerned about your welfare. They will go to great lengths to be loyal and dependable. If you spend much time in an Arab country, it would be a great personal loss if you develop no Arab friendships. 21

* Quoted in David K. Shipler, *Arab and Jew: Wounded Spirits in a Promised Land* (New York: Penguin Books, 1986), p. 387.

After You Read

In your journal, write about one of the following topics.

1 Explain the main point you think Nydell is making in the selection.
2 Discuss a cross-cultural difference you've experienced in concepts of friendship.
3 Choose a topic of your own related to the reading.

ADDITIONAL READING 3
A Coward

Before You Read

To what extent do you agree with the following statements? Fill in each blank with SA (strongly agree), A (agree), U (undecided), D (disagree), or SD (strongly disagree). Then share your responses with several classmates.

_____ 1 I would marry someone even if my parents were against the marriage.

_____ 2 I would marry someone of a different nationality, race, religion, or social class.

_____ 3 Every country has distinct social classes that have varying degrees of status.

_____ 4 Children should follow the wishes and advice of their parents, who are wiser and more experienced.

_____ 5 Discrimination on the basis of social class is a problem in my culture.

_____ 6 Women are usually more courageous than men.

_____ 7 It is more important to follow tradition than to embrace new ideas.

_____ 8 Arranged marriages are usually stronger than those based on love.

Taking Notes While You Read

As you read the story, underline or highlight the passages that describe a conflict – for example, between two people, places, social institutions, and ideas. Then, in the margin next to the marked passage, describe the conflict in your own words.

 ## A Coward
Premchand

The following story, "A Coward," published in 1933 by the Indian writer Premchand (1881–1936), focuses on a particular type of intracultural variation in India – the caste system – and its effects on people's lives. Premchand, the pseudonym of Dhanpat Rai, is considered one of the greatest writers of modern India.

I

The boy's name was Keshav, the girl's Prema. They went to the same college and   1
they were in the same class. Keshav believed in new ways and was opposed to the old caste[1] customs. Prema adhered to the old order and fully accepted the traditions.

---

[1] *caste:* One of the social classes in Hinduism, the predominant religion in India, determined by birth and following certain rules, restrictions, and privileges. In traditional Hindu society, there were four major castes, from highest to lowest: *Brahmans* (priests and scholars), *Kshatriyas* (warriors and rulers), *Vaishyas* (merchants and farmers), and *Sudras* (artisans and laborers). Below the Sudras were the *Panchamas* – the outcasts, or untouchables – responsible for such undesirable work as slaughtering animals and sweeping streets. Today there are more than three thousand subcastes in India, ranging in size from one hundred to millions.

But all the same there was a strong attachment between them and the whole college was aware of it. Although he was a Brahman, Keshav regarded marriage with this Banya[2] girl as the culmination of his life. He didn't care a straw about his father and mother. Caste traditions he considered a fraud. If anything embodied the truth for him, it was Prema. But for Prema it was impossible to take one step in opposition to the dictates of caste and family.

One evening the two of them met in a secluded corner of Victoria Park and sat down on the grass facing one another. The strollers had gone off one by one but these two lingered on. They had got into a discussion it was impossible to end. 2

Keshav said angrily, "All it means is that you don't care about me." 3

Prema tried to calm him down. "You're being unjust to me, Keshav. It's only that I don't know how I can bring it up at home without upsetting them. They're devoted to the old traditions. If they hear anything about a matter like this from me, can't you imagine how distressed they'll be?" 4

"And aren't you a slave of those old traditions too then?" Keshav asked her sharply. 5

"No, I'm not," Prema said, her eyes tender, "but what my mother and father want is more important to me than anything." 6

"And you yourself don't count at all?" 7

"If that's how you want to understand it." 8

"I used to think those old ways were just for silly hypocrites but now it seems that educated girls like you knuckle under[3] to them too. Since I'm ready to give up everything for you, I expect the same thing from you." 9

In silence Prema wondered what authority she had over her own life. She had no right to go in any way against the mother and father who had created her from their own blood and reared her with love. To Keshav she said humbly, "Can love be considered only in terms of husband and wife and not friendship? I think of love as an attachment of the soul." 10

"You'll drive me crazy with your rationalizations," Keshav said harshly. "Just understand this – if I'm disappointed, I can't go on living. I'm a materialist and it's not possible for me to be satisfied with some intangible happiness in the world of the imagination." 11

He caught Prema's hand and tried to draw her toward him, but she broke away and said, "I told you I'm not free. Don't ask me to do something I have no right to do." 12

If she'd spoken harshly, he would not have been so hurt. For an instant he restrained himself; then he stood up and said sadly, "Just as you wish," and slowly walked away. Prema, in tears, continued to sit there. 13

II

When after supper that night Prema lay down in her mother's room, she could not sleep. Keshav had said things to her that shadowed her heart like reflections in unquiet waters, changing at every moment, and she could not calm them. How could she talk to her mother about such things? Embarrassment kept her silent. 14

---

[2] *Banya:* Hindu subcaste consisting of merchants and traders.

[3] *knuckle under:* Give in or submit to something.

She thought, "If I don't marry Keshav, what's left for me in life?" While she thought about it over and over again, her mind was made up about just one thing – if she did not marry Keshav, she would marry no one.

Her mother said, "Still not sleeping? I've told you so many times you ought to do a little work around the house. But you can never take any time off from your books. In a little while you'll be going to some strange house and who knows what sort of place it will be? If you don't get accustomed to doing housework, how are you going to manage?" 15

Naïvely Prema asked, "Why will I be going to a strange house?" Smiling, her mother said, "For a girl it's the greatest calamity, daughter. After being sheltered at home, as soon as she's grown up, off she goes to live with others. If she gets a good husband, her days pass happily, otherwise she has to go through life weeping. It all depends on fate. But in our community there's no family that appeals to me. There's no proper regard for girls anywhere. But we have to stay within our caste. Who knows how long caste marriages are going to go on?" 16

Frightened Prema said, "But here and there they're beginning to have marriages outside the caste." She'd said it for the sake of talking but she trembled lest her mother might guess something. 17

Surprised, her mother asked, "You don't mean among Hindus?" Then she answered herself. "If this has happened in a few places, then what's come of it?" 18

Prema did not reply. She was afraid her mother had understood her meaning. She saw her future in that moment before her like a great dark tunnel opening its mouth to swallow her up. It was a long time before she could fall asleep. 19

III

When she got up early in the morning, Prema was aware of a strange new courage. We all make important decisions on the spur of the moment as though some divine power impelled us toward them, and so it was with Prema. Until yesterday she'd considered her parents' ideas as unchallengeable, but facing the problem courage was born in her, much in the way a quiet breeze coming against a mountain sweeps over the summit in a violent gust. Prema thought, "Agreed, this body is my mother's and father's but whatever my own self, my soul, is to get must be got in this body. To hesitate now would not only be unfitting, it would be fatal. Why sacrifice your life for false principle? If a marriage isn't founded on love, then it's just a business bargain with the body. Could you give yourself without love?" And she rebelled against the idea that she could be married off to somebody she had never seen. 20

After breakfast she had started to read when her father called her affectionately. "Yesterday I went to see your principal and he had a lot of praise for you." 21

"You're only saying that!" 22

"No, it's true." Then he opened a drawer of his desk and took out a picture set in a velvet frame. He showed it to her and said, "This boy came out first in the Civil Service[4] examinations. You must have heard of him." 23

He had brought up the subject in such a way as not to give away his intention, but it was clear to Prema; she saw through it at once. Without looking at the picture she said, "No, I don't know who he is." 24

---

[4] *Civil Service:* Public administration.

With feigned surprise her father said, "What? You haven't even heard his name? His picture and an article about him are in today's paper." 25

"Suppose they are?" Prema said. "The examinations don't mean anything to me. I always assumed that people who took those exams must be terribly conceited. After all, what do they aim for except to lord it over their wretched, penniless brothers? – and pile up a fortune doing it. That's no great career to aspire to." 26

The objection was spiteful, unjust. Her father had assumed that after his eulogy she would be interested. When he'd listened to her answer, he said sharply, "You talk as though money and power mean nothing to you." 27

"That's right," she said, "they don't mean a thing to me. I look for self-sacrifice in a man. I know some boys who wouldn't accept that kind of position even if you tried to force it on them." 28

"Well, I've learned something new today!" he said sarcastically. "And still I see people swarming around trying to get the meanest little jobs – I'd just like to see the face of one of these fellows capable of such self-sacrifice. If I did, I'd get down on my knees to him." 29

Perhaps if she'd heard these words on another occasion, Prema might have hung her head in shame. But this time, like a soldier with a dark tunnel behind him, there was no way for her to go except forward. Scarcely controlling her anger, her eyes full of indignation, she went to her room and from among several pictures of Keshav picked out the one she considered the worst and brought it back and set it down in front of her father. He wanted to give it no more than a casual glance, but at the first glimpse he was drawn to it. Keshav was tall and even though thin one recognized a strength and discipline about him; he was not particularly handsome but his face reflected such intelligence that one felt confidence in him. 30

While he looked at it her father said, "Who is he?" 31

Prema, bowing her head, said hesitantly, "He's in my class." 32

"Is he of our community?" 33

Prema's face clouded over: her destiny was to be decided on the answer. She realized that it was useless to have brought out the picture. The firmness she had had for an instant weakened before this simple question. In a low voice she said, "No, he's not, he's a Brahman." And even while she was saying it, agitated she left the room as though the atmosphere there were suffocating her, and on the other side of the wall she began to cry. 34

Her father's anger was so great at first that he wanted to call her out again and tell her plainly it was impossible. He got as far as the door, but seeing Prema crying his anger softened. He was aware of what Prema felt for this boy and he believed in education for women but he intended to maintain the family traditions. He would have sacrificed all his property for a suitable bridegroom of his own caste. But outside the limits of his community he could not conceive of any bridegroom worthy or noble enough; he could not imagine any disgrace greater than going beyond them. 35

"From today on you'll stop going to college," he said with a harsh tone. "If education teaches you to disregard our traditions, then education is wicked." 36

Timidly Prema said, "But it's almost time for the examinations." 37

"Forget about them." 38

Then he went into his room and pondered a long time. 39

IV

One day six months later Prema's father came home and called Vriddha, his wife, 40
for a private talk.

"As far as I know," he said, "Keshav's a well-brought-up and brilliant boy. I'm 41
afraid that Prema's grieving to the point where she might take her life. You and I
have tried to explain and so have others but nobody has had the slightest effect on
her. What are we going to do about it?"

Anxiously his wife said, "Let her, but if she has her way, how can you face the 42
dishonour? How could I ever have borne a wicked girl like that!"

He frowned and said with a tone of reproach, "I've heard that a thousand times. 43
But just how long can we moan about this caste tradition business? You're mistaken
if you think the bird's going to stay hopping at home once it's spread its wings.
I've thought about the problem objectively and I've come to the conclusion that
we're obliged to face the emergency. I can't watch Prema die in the name of caste
rules. Let people laugh but the time is not far off when all these old restrictions will
be broken. Even today there have been hundreds of marriages outside the caste
limitations. If the aim of marriage is a happy life for a man and a woman together,
we can't oppose Prema."

Vriddha was angry. "If that's your intention then why ask me?" she said. "But I 44
say that I won't have anything to do with this marriage, and I'll never look at that
girl's face again, I'll consider her as dead as our sons who died."

"Well then, what else can you suggest?" 45

"What if we do let her marry this boy? He'll take his civil service examinations 46
in two years and with what he has to offer it will be a great deal if he becomes a
clerk in some office."

"But what if Prema should kill herself?" 47

"Then let her – you've encouraged her, haven't you? If she doesn't care about 48
us, why should we blacken our name for her? Anyway, suicide's no game – it's only
a threat. The heart's like a wild horse – until it's broken and bridled nobody can
touch it. If her heart stays like that, who's to say that she'll look after Keshav for
a whole life-time? The way she's in love with him today, well, she can be in love
with somebody else just as much tomorrow. And because of this you're ready to be
disgraced?"

Her husband gave her a questioning look. "And if tomorrow she should go and 49
marry Keshav, then what will you do? Then how much of your honour will be left?
Out of shyness or consideration for us she may not have done anything yet, but if
she decides to be stubborn, there's nothing you or I can do."

It had never occurred to Vriddha that the problem could have such a dreadful 50
ending. His meaning struck her with the violence of a bullet. She sat silent for a
moment as though the shock had scattered her wits. Then, backing down, she said,
"What wild ideas you have! Until today I've never heard of a decent girl marrying
according to her own wish."

"You may not have heard of it, but I have. I've seen it and it's entirely possible." 51

"The day it happens will be my last!" 52

"But if it has to be this way, isn't it preferable that we make the proper 53 arrangements? If we're to be disgraced, we may as well be efficient about it. Send for Keshav tomorrow and see what he has to say."

V

Keshav's father lived from a government pension. By nature he was ill-tempered and 54 miserly; he found satisfaction only in religious ostentation. He was totally without imagination and unable to respect the personal feelings of anybody else. At present he was still living in the same world in which he had passed his childhood and youth. The rising tide of progress he called ruination and hoped to save at least his own family from it by any means available to him. Therefore when one day Prema's father came to him and broached the prospect of her marrying Keshav, old Panditji could not control himself. Staring through eyes dim with anger he said, "Are you drunk? Whatever this relationship may be it's not marriage. It appears that you too have had your head turned by the new ideas."

"I don't like this sort of connection either," Prema's father said gently. "My ideas 55 about it are just the same as yours. But the thing is that, being helpless, I had to come to see you. You're aware too of how willful today's youngsters have become. It's getting hard for us old-timers to defend our theories. I'm afraid that if these two become desperate, they may take their lives."

Old Panditji brought his foot down with a bang and shouted, "What are you 56 saying, Sir! Aren't you ashamed? We're Brahmans and even among Brahmans we're of high rank. No matter how low a Brahman may fall, he can never be so degraded that he can countenance a marriage with a shop-keeping Banya's daughter. The day noble Brahmans run out of daughters we can discuss the problem. I say you have a fantastic nerve even to bring this matter up with me."

He was every bit as furious as Prema's father was humble, and the latter, unable 57 to bear the humiliation any longer, went off cursing his luck.

Just then Keshav returned from college. Panditji sent for him at once and said 58 severely, "I've heard that you're betrothed to some Banya girl. How far has this actually gone?"

Pretending ignorance, Keshav said, "Who told you this?" 59

"Somebody. I'm asking you, is it true or not? If it's true and you've decided to 60 go against your caste, then there's no more room for you in this house. You won't get one pice[5] of my money. Whatever is in this house I've earned, and it's my right to give it to whomever I want. If you're guilty of this wicked conduct, you won't be permitted to put your foot inside my house."

Keshav was familiar with his father's temper. He loved Prema and he intended 61 to marry her in secret. His father wouldn't always be alive and he counted on his mother's affection; sustained by that love he felt that he was ready to suffer any hardships. But Keshav was like a faint-hearted soldier who loses his courage at the sight of a gun and turns back. Like any average young fellow he would argue his theories with a passion and demonstrate his devotion with his tongue. But to suffer

---

[5] *pice:* Indian coin in existence before 1955.

for them was beyond his capacity. If he persisted and his father refused to weaken, he didn't know where he would turn; his life would be ruined.

In a low voice he said, "Whoever told you that is a complete liar and nothing else." 62

Staring at him, Panditji said, "So my information is entirely mistaken?" 63

"Yes, entirely mistaken." 64

"Then you'll write a letter to that shopkeeper this very moment and remember 65 that if there's any more of this gossip, he can regard you as his greatest enemy. Enough, go."

Keshav could say no more. He walked away but it seemed to him that his legs 66 were utterly numb.

VI

The next day Prema sent this letter to Keshav: 67

Dearest Keshav,

I was terribly upset when I heard about the rude and callous way your father treated mine. Perhaps he's threatened you too, in which case I wait anxiously to hear what your decision is. I'm ready to undergo any kind of hardship with you. I'm aware of your father's wealth but all I need is your love to content me. Come tonight and have dinner with us. My mother and father are both eager to meet you.

I'm caught up in the dream of when the two of us will be joined by that bond that cannot be broken, that remains strong no matter how great the difficulties.

Your Prema

By evening there had been no reply to this letter. Prema's mother asked over and 68 over again, "Isn't Keshav coming?" and her father kept his eyes glued on the door. By nine o'clock there was still no sign of Keshav nor any letter.

In Prema's mind all sorts of fears and hopes revolved. Perhaps Keshav had had no 69 chance to write a letter, no chance to come today so that tomorrow he would surely come. She read over again the love letters he'd written her earlier. How steeped in love was every word, how much emotion, anxiety and acute desire! Then she remembered the words he'd said a hundred times and often he'd wept before her. It was impossible to despair with so many proofs, but all the same throughout the night she was tormented by anxiety.

Early in the morning Keshav's answer came. Prema took the letter with trembling 70 hands and read it. The letter fell from her hands. It seemed to her that her blood had ceased to flow. He had written:

I'm in a terrible quandary about how to answer you. I've been desperate trying to figure out what to do and I've come to the conclusion that for the present it would be impossible for me to go against my father's orders. Don't think I'm a coward. I'm not being selfish either. But I don't have the strength to get over the obstacles facing me. Forget what I told you before. At that time I had no idea of how hard it was going to be.

Prema drew a long, painful breath, then she tore up the letter and threw it away. 71
Her eyes filled with tears. She had never had the slightest expectation that the
Keshav she had taken into her heart of hearts as her husband could be so cruel. It
was as though until now she'd been watching a golden vision but on opening her
eyes it had vanished completely. All her hope had disappeared and she was left in
darkness.

"What did Keshav write?" her mother asked. 72

Prema looked at the floor and said, "He's not feeling well." What else was there 73
to say? She could not have borne the shame of revealing Keshav's brutal disloyalty.

She spent the whole day working around the house, as though there were 74
nothing wrong. She made dinner for everyone that evening and ate with them; then
until quite late she played the harmonium[6] and sang.

In the morning they found her lying dead in her room at a moment when the 75
golden rays of dawn bestowed on her face the illusory splendour of life.

After You Read

In your journal, write about one of the following topics.

1 Explain the main point or message of "A Coward."

2 Discuss whether you would marry someone if your parents were against it.

3 Choose a topic of your own related to the story.

---

[6] *harmonium:* Small keyboard instrument similar to an organ.

ADDITIONAL READING 4
The Blind Men and the Elephant

Before You Read

With several classmates or in your journal, describe a well-known folktale or fable
that contains a lesson or moral.

Taking Notes While You Read

As you read the fable, consider how it reflects intercultural issues dealt with in the
other readings in this chapter. Note these issues in the margin.

The Blind Men and the Elephant
A Hindu Fable

John Godfrey Saxe

This well-known fable, told in poetic form by the U.S. poet John Godfrey Saxe (1816–1887), is part of the tradition of Hinduism, the dominant religion in India. Note that the poem's final two stanzas, which explain the moral, or lesson, have been omitted because you will later be asked to state what the moral is yourself.

It was six men of Indostan[1]
   To learning much inclined,
Who went to see the Elephant
   (Though all of them were blind),
That each by observation   5
   Might satisfy his mind.

The First approached the Elephant,
   And happening to fall
Against his broad and sturdy side,
   At once began to bawl: 10
"God bless me! but the Elephant
   Is very like a wall!"

The Second feeling of the tusk,
   Cried, "Ho! what have we here
So very round and smooth and sharp?   15
   To me 'tis mighty clear
This wonder of an Elephant
   Is very like a spear!"

The Third approached the animal,
   And happening to take   20
The squirming trunk within his hands,
   Thus boldly up and spake:[2]
"I see," quoth[3] he, "the Elephant
   Is very like a snake!"

The Fourth reached out an eager hand,   25
   And felt about the knee,
"What most this wondrous beast is like
   Is mighty plain," quoth he;
"'Tis clear enough the Elephant
   Is very like a tree!"   30

---

[1] *Indostan:* Indian subcontinent (India, Pakistan, Bangladesh, Nepal, Sri Lanka, Bhutan, Afghanistan, and Maldives).

[2] *boldly up and spake:* Stood up boldly and spoke.

[3] *quoth:* Said.

The Fifth who chanced to touch the ear,
　　Said: "E'en[4] the blindest man
Can tell what this resembles most;
　　Deny the fact who can,
This marvel of an Elephant   35
　　Is very like a fan!"

The Sixth no sooner had begun
　　About the beast to grope,
Than, seizing on the swinging tail
　　That fell within his scope,[5]   40
"I see," quoth he, "the Elephant
　　Is very like a rope!"

After You Read

In your journal, write about one of the following topics.

1 Explain the moral or lesson conveyed in the poem. How does this lesson relate
　to intercultural communication?
2 Discuss a fable you know that expresses a similar moral or lesson.
3 Choose a topic of your own related to the poem.

---

[4] *e'en:* Even.
[5] *scope:* Reach.

ADDITIONAL READING 5
Humor: Presidents and Gifts

With a partner, read the following joke and cartoon and discuss the issues relating
to intercultural communication, including values, behaviors, and stereotypes.

 ## Presidents and Gifts

There is a story, no doubt apocryphal, told of President John Kennedy and Mexican
president Adolfo López Mateo when the two met in Mexico in 1962. While riding
together in a car, President Kennedy noticed the beautiful wrist watch which the
Mexican President was wearing and Kennedy complimented López, saying: "What a
beautiful watch you have." Immediately the Mexican President removed the watch
from his wrist and handed it to Kennedy, saying: "It is yours." Kennedy, embarrassed

by the offer, tried to decline but the Mexican President explained that in his country when a person likes something he should be given it – ownership being a matter of human feelings or need and not private possession. Kennedy was impressed by this and received the watch with the greatest humility. A few minutes later, President López turned to the U.S. President and said: "My, what a beautiful wife you have," whereupon Kennedy replied: "Please take back your watch."

SOURCE: *An Introduction to Intercultural Communication* by John C. Condon and Fathi S. Yousef (New York: Bobbs-Merrill, 1975), p. 89.

ESSAY TOPICS

Write an essay on one of the following topics. Support your points with an appropriate combination of references to the readings in this chapter, library and Internet sources, and personal experiences and observations.

Refer to the section "The Essentials of Writing" on pages 102–132 to help you plan, draft, and revise your essay. Use this special section, too, to assist you in locating, integrating, and documenting your sources.

1 Gary Althen, the author of the first core reading, defines values as "ideas about what is right and wrong, desirable and undesirable, and so on" (par. 1). Discuss major differences you've noticed in values and assumptions while in a foreign country or community that is culturally different from where you grew up. Did anything seem "wrong" or "undesirable"?

2 Examine a cultural pattern in your country that you think a foreign visitor should be aware of in order to adjust more easily and avoid intercultural conflicts and misunderstandings. Consider such things as values, beliefs, communication styles, and concepts of time.

3 Describe the adjustment process you went through when entering a new culture or community. Did you go through any of the common stages described on page 38, including culture shock? What cross-cultural problems and challenges did you encounter? How did you deal with them? What did you learn from your stay in the new culture? Did your values, beliefs, and behaviors change in any way?

4 Explore major stumbling blocks, or obstacles, to effective intercultural communication and ways to minimize them. Focus on the origins of the barriers and methods of reducing them.

5 Discuss discrimination against a particular group of people in your culture or community. Consider stereotyping and prejudice on the basis of such factors as race, ethnicity, gender, nationality, religion, socioeconomic class, and sexual orientation. Also consider the origins and effects of the discrimination.

Education

A WRITER'S TECHNIQUE
Purpose and Audience

In this chapter, you will explore the major goals of education, the problems of educational systems in different cultures, and the roles of students and teachers. You will consider cross-cultural similarities and differences in teaching and learning styles, in the use of technology, and in definitions of intelligence.

Questions Raised in Chapter Two

Working with a partner or in a small group, discuss two or three of the following questions.

1 What does it mean to be an "educated" and "intelligent" person? Are the two the same?
2 What are the strengths and weaknesses of the educational system with which you are most familiar?
3 Are students in this educational system encouraged to express their opinions and disagree with their classmates and teachers?
4 What differences are you aware of between the educational system in the country you are studying in now and another country with which you are familiar?
5 To what extent does technology, including computers and the Internet, enhance and hinder education?

Brief Quotations

The following quotations deal with educational issues considered in this chapter. Working with a partner or in a small group, choose two or three quotations of interest and discuss them.

1 *Imagination is more important than knowledge.* (Albert Einstein, German American physicist)
2 *Give me a fish, and I will eat for a day. Teach me to fish, and I will eat for a lifetime.* (Chinese proverb)
3 *Education is an admirable thing, but it is well to remember from time to time that nothing that is worth knowing can be taught.* (Oscar Wilde, Irish writer)
4 *Teachers no longer feel that it is incumbent on them to instill patriotism or to celebrate the accomplishments of the American nation.* (Diane Ravitch, U.S. professor)
5 *The greatest danger of traditional education is that learning may remain purely verbal.* (Mirra Komarovsky, Russian American sociologist)
6 *The true test of intelligence is not how much we know how to do, but how we behave when we don't know what to do.* (John Holt, U.S. teacher)

CORE READING 1
School Is Bad for Children

Journal Writing

In your journal, write for ten to fifteen minutes about what comes to mind when you read the title of John Holt's essay, "School Is Bad for Children." Then share your thoughts with several classmates.

Previewing the Topic

Write a list of what you consider to be the major problems with the educational system in your country. Compare your ideas with those of your classmates and create a list, on the board, of all the problems the class identified.

Agreeing and Disagreeing

To what extent do you agree with the following statements? Fill in each blank with SA (strongly agree), A (agree), U (undecided), D (disagree), or SD (strongly disagree). Then share your responses with several classmates.

_____ 1 Schools should abolish compulsory attendance.

_____ 2 Tests are a good way to measure a student's mastery of course material.

_____ 3 Most students' formal education has little connection to real life.

_____ 4 High school students should be required to take courses in religion, politics, art, music, and sex education.

_____ 5 Schools should encourage creativity and originality.

_____ 6 High school students should be allowed to choose the courses they take.

_____ 7 Most real learning takes place outside of school.

_____ 8 Students should feel free to disagree with their teachers in class.

_____ 9 As part of their formal education, students should be required to do some type of socially useful work in the community.

_____ 10 Schools have many negative influences on students.

Taking Notes While You Read

As you read the following essay, note in the margin the disadvantages of formal education and the author's recommendations for improvement. Put a checkmark (✓) next to the ideas with which you agree. Put a minus sign (−) next to the ideas with which you disagree.

School Is Bad for Children
John Holt

The author of this essay, John Holt (1923–1985), was an educational theorist who taught for many years in elementary and secondary schools in the United States. A critic of formal education in general and the U.S. educational system in particular, Holt lectured nationally and internationally about school reform and wrote a number of books about the subject. The following essay dealing with the hazards of formal education first appeared in the magazine The Saturday Evening Post *in 1969.*

Almost every child, on the first day he sets foot in a school building, is smarter, more   1
curious, less afraid of what he doesn't know, better at finding and figuring things out, more confident, resourceful, persistent and independent than he will ever be again in his schooling – or, unless he is very unusual and very lucky, for the rest of his life. Already by paying close attention to and interacting with the world and people around him, and without any school-type formal instruction, he has done a task far more difficult, complicated and abstract than anything he will be asked to do in school, or than any of his teachers has done for years. He has solved the mystery of language. He has discovered it – babies don't even know that language exists – and he has found out how it works and learned to use it. He has done it by exploring, by experimenting, by developing his own model of the grammar of language, by trying it out and seeing whether it works, by gradually changing it and refining it until it does work. And while he has been doing this, he has been learning other things as well, including many of the "concepts" that the schools think only they can teach him, and many that are more complicated than the ones they do try to teach him.

In he comes, this curious, patient, determined, energetic, skillful learner. We sit   2
him down at a desk, and what do we teach him? Many things. First, that learning is separate from living. "You come to school to learn," we tell him, as if the child hadn't been learning before, as if living were out there and learning were in here, and there were no connection between the two. Secondly, that he cannot be trusted to learn and is no good at it. Everything we teach about reading, a task far simpler than many the child has already mastered, says to him, "If we don't make you read, you won't, and if you don't do it exactly the way we tell you, you can't." In short, he comes to feel that learning is a passive process, something that someone else does to you, instead of something you do for yourself.

In a great many other ways he learns that he is worthless, untrustworthy, fit only   3
to take other people's orders, a blank sheet for other people to write on. Oh, we make a lot of nice noises in school about respect for the child and individual differences, and the like. But our acts, as opposed to our talk, say to the child, "Your experience, your concerns, your curiosities, your needs, what you know, what you want, what you wonder about, what you hope for, what you fear, what you like and dislike, what you are good at or not so good at – all this is not of the slightest importance, it counts for nothing. What counts here, and the only thing that counts, is what we know, what we think is important, what we want you to do, think and be." The child soon learns not to ask questions – the teacher isn't there to satisfy his curiosity. Having learned to hide his curiosity, he later learns to be ashamed of it. Given no

chance to find out who he is – and to develop that person, whoever it is – he soon comes to accept the adults' evaluation of him.

He learns many other things. He learns that to be wrong, uncertain, confused, is a crime. Right Answers are what the school wants, and he learns countless strategies for prying these answers out of the teacher, for conning her into thinking he knows what he doesn't know. He learns to dodge, bluff, fake, cheat. He learns to be lazy. Before he came to school, he would work for hours on end, on his own, with no thought of reward, at the business of making sense of the world and gaining competence in it. In school he learns, like every buck private,[1] how to goldbrick,[2] how not to work when the sergeant isn't looking, how to know when he is looking, how to make him think you are working even when he isn't looking. He learns that in real life you don't do anything unless you are bribed, bullied, or conned into doing it, that nothing is worth doing for its own sake, or that if it is, you can't do it in school. He learns to be bored, to work with a small part of his mind, to escape from the reality around him into daydreams and fantasies – but not like the fantasies of his preschool years, in which he played a very active part.

The child comes to school curious about other people, particularly other children, and the school teaches him to be indifferent. The most interesting thing in the classroom – often the only interesting thing in it – is the other children, but he has to act as if these other children, all about him, only a few feet away, are not really there. He cannot interact with them, talk with them, smile at them. In many schools he can't talk to other children in the halls between classes; in more than a few, and some of these in stylish suburbs, he can't even talk to them at lunch. Splendid training for a world in which, when you're not studying the other person to figure out how to do him in,[3] you pay no attention to him.

In fact, he learns how to live without paying attention to anything going on around him. You might say that school is a long lesson in how to turn yourself off, which may be one reason why so many young people, seeking the awareness of the world and responsiveness to it as they had when they were little, think they can only find it in drugs. Aside from being boring, the school is almost always ugly, cold, inhuman – even the most stylish, glass-windowed $20-a-square-foot schools.

And so, in this dull and ugly place, where nobody ever says anything very truthful, where everybody is playing a kind of role, as in a charade, where the teachers are no more free to respond honestly to the students than the students are free to respond to the teachers or each other, where the air practically vibrates with suspicion and anxiety, the child learns to live in a daze, saving his energies for those small parts of his life that are too trivial for the adults to bother with, and thus remain his. It is a rare child who can come through his schooling with much left of his curiosity, his independence or sense of his own dignity, competence, and worth.

So much for criticism. What do we need to do? Many things. Some are easy – we can do them right away. Some are hard, and many take some time. Take a hard one first. We should abolish compulsory school attendance. At the very least we

---

[1] *buck private:* Person of the lowest rank in the U.S. Army and Marine Corps.

[2] *goldbrick:* To avoid assigned duties or work.

[3] *do him in:* Cheat him. (In some contexts, "to do someone in" means to kill a person.)

should modify it, perhaps by giving children every year a large number of authorized absences. Our compulsory school-attendance laws once served a humane and useful purpose. They protected children's right to some schooling, against those adults who would otherwise have denied it to them in order to exploit their labor, in farm, store, mine or factory. Today the laws help nobody, not the schools, not the teachers, not the children. To keep kids in school who would rather not be there costs the school an enormous amount of time and trouble – to say nothing of what it costs to repair the damage that these angry and resentful prisoners do every time they get a chance. Every teacher knows that any kid in class who, for whatever reason, would rather not be there not only doesn't learn anything himself, but makes it a great deal tougher for anyone else. As for protecting the children from exploitation, the chief and indeed only exploiters of children these days *are* the schools. Kids caught in the college rush more often than not work 70 hours or more a week, most of it on paper busywork. For kids who aren't going to college, school is just a useless time waster, preventing them from earning some money or doing some useful work, or even doing some true learning.

Objections. "If kids didn't have to go to school, they'd all be out in the streets." 9 No, they wouldn't. In the first place, even if schools stayed just the way they are, children would spend at least some time there because that's where they'd be likely to find friends; it's a natural meeting place for children. In the second place, schools wouldn't stay the way they are, they'd get better, because we would have to start making them what they ought to be right now – places where children would *want* to be. In the third place, those children who did not want to go to school could find, particularly if we stirred up our brains and gave them a little help, other things to do – the things many children now do during their summers and holidays.

There's something easier we could do. We need to get kids out of the school 10 buildings, give them a chance to learn about the world at first hand. It is a very recent idea, and a crazy one, that the way to teach our young people about the world they live in is to take them out of it and shut them up in brick boxes. Fortunately, educators are beginning to realize this. In Philadelphia and Portland, Oregon, to pick only two places I happen to have heard about, plans are being drawn up for public schools that won't have any school buildings at all, that will take the students out into the city and help them to use it and its people as a learning resource. In other words, students, perhaps in groups, perhaps independently, will go to libraries, museums, exhibits, courtrooms, legislatures, radio and TV stations, meetings, businesses, and laboratories to learn about their world and society at first hand. A small private school in Washington is already doing this. It makes sense. We need more of it.

As we help children get out into the world, to do their learning there, we can get 11 more of the world into the schools. Aside from their parents, most children never have any close contact with any adults except people whose sole business is children. No wonder they have no idea what adult life or work is like. We need to bring a lot more people who are not full-time teachers into the schools and into contact with the children. In New York City, under the Teachers and Writers Collaborative, real writers, working writers – novelists, poets, playwrights – come into the schools, read their work, and talk to the children about the problems of their craft. The children eat it up. In another school I know of, a practicing attorney from a nearby city comes in every month or so and talks to several classes about the law. Not the law as it is in books but as he sees it and encounters it in his cases, his problems, his work. And the children love it. It is real, grown-up, true, not *My Weekly Reader*,[4] not "social studies," not lies and baloney.

Something easier yet. Let children work together to help each other, learn from each other and each other's mistakes. We know now, from the experience of many schools, both rich-suburban and poor-city, that children are often the best teachers of other children. What is more important, we know that when a fifth- or sixth-grader who has been having trouble with reading starts helping a first-grader, his own reading sharply improves. A number of schools are beginning to use what some call Paired Learning. This means that you let children form partnerships with other children, do their work, even including their tests, together, and share whatever marks or results that this work gets – just like grown-ups in the real world. It seems to work.

Let the children learn to judge their own work. A child learning to talk does not learn by being corrected all the time – if corrected too much, he will stop talking. He compares, a thousand times a day, the difference between language as he uses it and as those around him use it. Bit by bit, he makes the necessary changes to make his language like other people's. In the same way, kids learning to do all the other things they can learn without adult teachers – to walk, run, climb, whistle, ride a bike, skate, play games, jump rope – compare their own performance with what more skilled people do, and slowly make the needed changes. But in school we never give a child a chance to detect his mistakes, let alone correct them. We do it all for him. We act as if we thought he would never notice a mistake unless it was pointed out to him, or correct it unless he was made to. Soon he becomes dependent on the expert. We should let him do it himself. Let him figure it out, with the help of other children if he wants it, what this word says, what is the answer to that problem, whether this is a good way of saying or doing this or that. If right answers are involved, as in some math or science, give him the answer book, let him correct his own papers. Why should we teachers waste time on such donkey work? Our job should be to help the kid when he tells us that he can't find a way to get the right answer. Let's get rid of all this nonsense of grades, exams, marks. We don't know now, and we never will know, how to measure what another person knows or understands. We certainly can't find out by asking him questions. All we find out is what he doesn't know – which is what most tests are for, anyway. Throw it all out, and let the child learn what every educated person must someday learn, how to measure his own understanding, how to know what he knows or does not know.

We could also abolish the fixed, required curriculum. People remember only what is interesting and useful to them, what helps them make sense of the world, or helps them get along in it. All else they quickly forget, if they ever learn it at all. The idea of a "body of knowledge," to be picked up in school and used for the rest of one's life, is nonsense in a world as complicated and rapidly changing as ours.

12

13

14

---

[4] *My Weekly Reader*: Popular weekly magazine for elementary school students.

Anyway, the most important questions and problems of our time are not *in* the curriculum, not even in the hotshot universities, let alone the schools.

Children want, more than they want anything else, and even after years of 15 miseducation, to make sense of the world, themselves, and other human beings. Let them get at this job, with our help if they ask for it, in the way that makes most sense to them.

Reading Journal

In your journal, write about one of the following topics.

1 Describe your reaction to one of Holt's major criticisms of schools or one of his recommendations for improvement.

2 Discuss whether your own education has been similar to that described in the essay.

3 Choose a topic of your own related to the reading.

Main Ideas

Answer the following questions, referring to the notes you took when reading the essay. Then share your answers with a partner.

1 What major criticisms of formal education does Holt discuss in paragraphs 1–7?

2 What are Holt's recommendations for improving the quality of schools? Summarize the suggestions presented in paragraphs 8–15.

3 What is the main point Holt is making in the essay? Summarize his central idea in one or two sentences. Use your own words. Begin with the sentence *In the essay "School Is Bad for Children," John Holt argues that . . .*

Reflecting on Content

Answer the following questions with a partner. When possible, support your answers with observations based on your own experiences.

1 What do you think might happen if compulsory school attendance were abolished?

2 What do you think of Holt's support for the notion of schools without school buildings?

3 Do you agree with Holt that schools should get rid of grades and exams?

A Writer's Technique: *Purpose and Audience*

Authors write with a purpose. As you read, ask yourself what the writer's **purpose**, or goal, is. The three most common purposes of writing are these:

To inform   The author seeks to provide readers (also called the **audience**) with information about a topic or to explain something.

To persuade   The author wishes to convince readers to believe something or to act in a certain way.

To entertain The author hopes to amuse the audience, perhaps through humor.

You can identify a writer's purpose by asking the following questions.

1 For what reasons has the author written this work?

2 What does the author want the reader to think or feel after finishing the selection?

3 Who is the author's audience, and how does the nature of the audience relate to the purpose?

4 How successful is the author in achieving his or her purpose?

Ask and answer the questions above for Holt's essay "School Is Bad for Children." Share your responses with a partner.

Vocabulary: *Synonyms*

Studying **synonyms** is a good way to develop your vocabulary. Synonyms are words or phrases that have the same or nearly the same meaning. Sometimes the vocabulary items are so close in meaning that they can be used interchangeably – for example, "*On the whole / by and large*, I feel younger than I did ten years ago." Be aware, however, that many words have more than one definition and may not function as synonyms in all contexts. For instance, we can speak of a *tender* or *caring* relationship between two people, but while we can refer to meat as *tender*, we cannot refer to it as *caring*.

Look at these sentences from Holt's essay and do the following.

• Guess the meaning of each italicized vocabulary item from the context.

• Write down two or three synonyms for each italicized word. Make sure that the synonyms you choose have the same meaning as the italicized vocabulary items and can be used in the same sentence.

• Write a sentence of your own, using the vocabulary item in such a way that its meaning is clear.

Example: *[Children learn language] by trying it out and seeing whether it works, by gradually changing it and* **refining** *it until it does work. (par. 1)*

Synonyms: *improve, perfect, develop*

Sentence: *The committee* **refined** *its proposal for a new curriculum as it got feedback from students, faculty members, and administration.*

1 *In short,* he comes to feel that learning is a passive process, something that someone else does to you, instead of something you do for yourself. (par. 2)

2 Given no chance to find out who he is – and to develop that person, whoever it is – [the student] soon comes to accept the adults' *evaluation* of him. (par. 3)

3 The child comes to school curious about other people, particularly other children, and the school teaches him to be *indifferent.* (par. 5)

4 The child learns to live in a daze, saving his energies for those small parts of his life that are too *trivial* for the adults to bother with. (par. 7)

5 We should *abolish* compulsory school attendance. At the very least we should modify it, perhaps by giving children every year a large number of authorized absences. (par. 8)

6 Our *compulsory* school-attendance laws once served a humane and useful purpose. (par. 8)

7 In Philadelphia . . . plans are being *drawn up* for public schools that won't have any school buildings at all. (par. 10)

8 In another school I know of, a practicing attorney from a nearby city comes in every month or so and talks to several classes about the law. Not the law as it is in books but as he sees it and *encounters* it in his cases, his problems, his work. (par. 11)

Vocabulary in Context

Locate the following italicized vocabulary items in the reading and see if you can determine their meaning from the context. Then think of an example or situation to illustrate each item, using your personal experience if possible. Do not just define the italicized words and expressions. When you are done, share your answers with a partner.

1 a *resourceful* approach that a student might take to a class assignment (par. 1)

2 a time during your educational career when you were *persistent* in doing something (par. 1)

3 a technique that a school administrator might use to *pry out* information from a student who has done something wrong (par. 4)

4 a student's *conning* a teacher or a teacher's *conning* a student *into* doing or believing something (par. 4)

5 a reason a student or teacher might *bluff* about something (par. 4)

6 a time when you worked on a school project for hours *on end* (par. 4)

7 something a parent might do if his or her child was being *bullied* at school (par. 4)

8 the high school classes that you think should be *compulsory*, and why (par. 8)

9 a reason a student or teacher might be *resentful* of something (par. 8)

10 an educational practice that you think should be *abolished*, and why (par. 14)

Discussion

Choose one of the following activities to do with a partner or in a small group.

1 Make a chart similar to the one on the right. Fill in the columns with at least six aspects of schooling that Holt criticizes and your reactions to these criticisms. If time allows, also consider Holt's recommendations for improvement. When you are done, share your ideas with the rest of the class.

Holt's Criticisms of Schools	My Reactions

2 Observe a class at any educational institution. Concentrate on what is being taught, how it is being taught, and the nature of the student-student and student-teacher interaction. Then share your observations, reactions, and conclusions with several classmates.

3 Access the National Public Radio Web site <www.npr.org>. Click on *Archives* and search for one of these two broadcast titles (remember to include the quotation marks when you search): "Standardized Tests: How is Testing Changing Teaching and Learning" or "Teenage Diary: Nick Epperson." While listening to the first broadcast, write a list of the advantages and disadvantages of standardized testing. If you chose to listen to the second broadcast, write a list of what Nick disliked about school and liked about home schooling. Then discuss the points on your list with your partner or group.

Writing Follow-up

Follow up the discussion activity you chose (item 1, 2, or 3) with the matching writing assignment below.

1 With a partner or by yourself, write an imagined letter to John Holt consisting of two paragraphs. In the first paragraph, respond to one of the criticisms he makes in "School Is Bad for Children." In the second paragraph, discuss one of his recommendations for improvement. In your letter, focus on why you support or oppose Holt's ideas.

2 Write a brief report of the class you observed. Describe the class and your reactions to the style of teaching that you noticed. Also consider the nature of the student-student and student-teacher interaction.

3 Write two paragraphs responding to the radio broadcast you listened to. In the first paragraph, summarize the educational issues discussed; in the second, explain your reaction to one or more of the points made.

CORE READING 2
How the Web Destroys the Quality of Students' Research Papers

Journal Writing

In your journal, write for ten to fifteen minutes about the ways you gather information for a research paper. Do you use the Internet to help you write essays and research papers? If so, what are its advantages and disadvantages? Then share your thoughts with several classmates.

Previewing the Topic

In a small group, write a list of the positive and negative consequences of increased use of the Internet as an educational tool. Does the Internet enhance learning and the development of academic skills? Does it hinder this development in any way? Compare your ideas with those of the other groups. Then, on the board, create a list of the consequences the class has come up with.

Agreeing and Disagreeing

To what extent do you agree with the following statements? Fill in each blank with SA (strongly agree), A (agree), U (undecided), D (disagree), or SD (strongly disagree). Then share your responses with several classmates.

_____ 1 In writing papers for classes, library research is more helpful than research done on the World Wide Web.

_____ 2 Use of the Internet has improved the quality of students' writing.

_____ 3 The Internet has diminished people's ability to think critically and creatively.

_____ 4 The Internet has helped improve students' attention spans and work habits.

_____ 5 The Internet is similar to television in its negative influence on children.

_____ 6 Information and knowledge are not the same thing.

_____ 7 I know how to write a bibliography for an essay, properly citing the library and Internet sources that I use.

_____ 8 When you are writing an academic paper, it is all right to copy materials from the Internet, express some of an author's ideas in your own words, and not mention the source of the material.

_____ 9 Students found guilty of plagiarism should receive a failing grade for the assignment or the course.

_____ 10 It is easier to assess the accuracy of information and ideas found in a book than the accuracy of materials found on the World Wide Web.

As you read the essay, note in the margin the hazards of using the World Wide Web according to the author. Also indicate the points with which you agree and disagree.

 # How the Web Destroys the Quality of Students' Research Papers

David Rothenberg

David Rothenberg is a professor of philosophy at the New Jersey Institute of Technology. He is the editor of the scholarly journal Terra Nova: Nature and Culture *and has written a number of books on philosophy and ecology. The following essay, which deals with the educational hazards of the World Wide Web, first appeared in 1997 in* The Chronicle of Higher Education – *a publication for college and university teachers and administrators. Following Rothenberg's essay is a letter to the editor disagreeing with aspects of his argument.*

Sometimes I look forward to the end-of-semester rush, when students' final papers come streaming into my office and mailbox. I could have hundreds of pages of original thought to read and evaluate. Once in a while, it is truly exciting, and brilliant words are typed across a page in response to a question I've asked the class to discuss.

But this past semester was different. I noticed a disturbing decline in both the quality of the writing and the originality of the thoughts expressed. What had happened since last fall? Did I ask worse questions? Were my students unusually lazy? No. My class had fallen victim to the latest easy way of writing a paper: doing their research on the World Wide Web.

It's easy to spot a research paper that is based primarily on information collected from the Web. First, the bibliography cites no books, just articles or pointers to places in that virtual land somewhere off any map: http://www.etc. Then a strange preponderance of material in the bibliography is curiously out of date. A lot of stuff on the Web that is advertised as timely is actually at least a few years old. (One student submitted a research paper last semester in which all of his sources were articles published between September and December 1995; that was probably the time span of the Web page on which he found them.)

Another clue is the beautiful pictures and graphs that are inserted neatly into the body of the student's text. They look impressive, as though they were the result of careful work and analysis, but actually they often bear little relation to the precise subject of the paper. Cut and paste from the vast realm of what's out there for the taking, they masquerade as original work.

Accompanying them are unattributed quotes (in which one can't tell who made the statement or in what context) and curiously detailed references to the kinds of things that are easy to find on the Web (pages and pages of federal documents, corporate propaganda, or snippets of commentary by people whose credibility is difficult to assess). Sadly, one finds few references to careful, in-depth commentaries

1

2

3

4

5

on the subject of the paper, the kind of analysis that requires a book, rather than an article, for its full development.

Don't get me wrong, I'm no neo-Luddite.[1] I am as enchanted as anyone else by the potential of this new technology to provide instant information. But too much of what passes for information these days is simply advertising for information. Screen after screen shows you where you can find out more, how you can connect to this place or that. The acts of linking and networking and randomly jumping from here to there become as exciting or rewarding as actually finding anything of intellectual value.

Search engines, with their half-baked algorithms,[2] are closer to slot machines than to library catalogues. You throw your query to the wind, and who knows what will come back to you? You may get 234,468 supposed references to whatever you want to know. Perhaps one in a thousand might actually help you. But it's easy to be sidetracked or frustrated as you try to go through those Web pages one by one. Unfortunately, they're not arranged in order of importance.

What I'm describing is the hunt-and-peck[3] method of writing a paper. We all know that word processing makes many first drafts look far more polished than they are. If the paper doesn't reach the assigned five pages, readjust the margin, change the font size, and . . . voilà![4] Of course, those machinations take up time that the student could have spent revising the paper. With programs to check one's spelling and grammar now standard features on most computers, one wonders why students make any mistakes at all. But errors are as prevalent as ever, no matter how crisp

---

[1] *neo-Luddite:* Someone opposed to technological change. (The Luddites were a group of British workers in the early nineteenth century who destroyed textile machinery that they thought threatened their jobs.)

[2] *algorithm:* Step-by-step procedure for solving a problem or accomplishing a task.

[3] *hunt-and-peck:* Hit or miss (random) method of a poor typist.

[4] *voilà:* French word meaning "there is / are" – used, in this case, to suggest the appearance of something as if by magic.

the typeface. Instead of becoming perfectionists, too many students have become slackers, preferring to let the machine do their work for them.

What the Web adds to the shortcuts made possible by word processing is to make research look too easy. You toss a query to the machine, wait a few minutes, and suddenly a lot of possible sources of information appear on your screen. Instead of books that you have to check out of the library, read carefully, understand, synthesize, and then tactfully excerpt, these sources are quips,[5] blips,[6] pictures, and short summaries that may be downloaded magically to the dorm-room computer screen. Fabulous! How simple! The only problem is that a paper consisting of summaries of summaries is bound to be fragmented and superficial, and to demonstrate more of a random montage than an ability to sustain an argument through 10 to 15 double-spaced pages. 9

Of course, you can't blame the students for ignoring books. When college libraries are diverting funds from books to computer technology that will be obsolete in two years at most, they send a clear message to students: Don't read, just connect. Surf. Download. Cut and paste. Originality becomes hard to separate from plagiarism if no author is cited on a Web page. Clearly, the words are up for grabs,[7] and students much prefer the fabulous jumble to the hard work of stopping to think and make sense of what they've read. 10

Libraries used to be repositories of words and ideas. Now they are seen as centers for the retrieval of information. Some of this information comes from other, bigger libraries, in the form of books that can take time to obtain through interlibrary loan. What happens to the many students (some things never change) who scramble to write a paper the night before it's due? The computer screen, the gateway to the world sitting right on their desks, promises instant access – but actually offers only a pale, two-dimensional version of a real library. 11

But it's also my fault. I take much of the blame for the decline in the quality of student research in my classes. I need to teach students how to read, to take time with language and ideas, to work through arguments, to synthesize disparate sources to come up with original thought. I need to help my students understand how to assess sources to determine their credibility, as well as to trust their own ideas more than snippets of thought that materialize on a screen. The placelessness of the Web leads to an ethereal randomness of thought. Gone are the pathways of logic and passion, the sense of the progress of an argument. Chance holds sway, and it more often misses than hits. Judgment must be taught, as well as the methods of exploration. 12

I'm seeing my students' attention spans wane and their ability to reason for themselves decline. I wish that the university's computer system would crash for a day, so that I could encourage them to go outside, sit under a tree, and read a really good book – from start to finish. I'd like them to sit for a while and ponder what it means to live in a world where some things get easier and easier so rapidly that we can hardly keep track of how easy they're getting, while other tasks remain as hard 13

---

[5] *quip:* Brief remark, often witty or sarcastic, made without preparation or forethought.

[6] *blip:* Spot on a radar screen or a very short piece of information.

[7] *up for grabs:* Available to anyone.

as ever – such as doing research and writing a good paper that teaches the writer something in the process. Knowledge does not emerge in a vacuum, but we do need silence and space for sustained thought. Next semester, I'm going to urge my students to turn off their glowing boxes and think, if only once in a while.

An Opposing View

David Rothenburg's article provoked the following letter to the editor of The Chronicle of Higher Education.

To the Editor:

1   David Rothenberg's thoughtful essay includes the common fallacy of giving the World Wide Web far too much power over our lives and consciousness. Too often, the assumption is that this technology somehow induces states of mind for which there is no remedy. But the Web is simply a tool that needs to be used strategically by teachers who have carefully thought through the outcomes they expect from their students. Even the metaphor of a web implies this, and it is up to the student to become either the spider or the fly.

2   Actually, it is often poor course design that impedes student performance to a far greater extent. Realistically, the Web no more "destroys the quality of students' research papers" than does television, the blackboard, the overhead projector, the way that poorly designed research assignments are routinely handed out to students, or the rote way that some teachers present their materials. In terms of quality, where does the buck stop?[1] I would hope at the professor's desk, where the questions about what is acceptable research need to be discussed and answered for the student's edification, while the professor makes it clear that grades will directly reflect those standards.

3   Professor Rothenberg's general points, however, are well stated, and I admire his willingness to accept the challenge of what I consider the hard job of real teaching. This includes teaching students "how to read, to take time with language and ideas, to work through arguments, to synthesize disparate sources to come up with original thought . . . [and] to assess sources to determine their credibility" [par. 12]. This is difficult and important work, and it teaches students how to sort the wheat from the chaff[2] in any kind of resource.

4   In truth, there are as many rotten books and worthless journal articles in libraries as there are rotten sources on the Internet. The particular medium will matter less and less with the preponderance of cheap printers. To suggest that the Web is solely a source of ephemeral advertisements about information is a specious generalization. It sounds great, but closer examination reveals it to be too sweeping an assessment – one that, additionally, fails to account for the Web's future development as a scholarly resource.

5   We should not allow the spider of popular culture to spin us up in a web of helplessness and despair by allowing the Internet to become so personified that it

---

[1] *where does the buck stop?:* Who takes the main responsibility? This idiom usually appears in the form "the buck stops here."

[2] *sort the wheat from the chaff:* Idiom that means "to separate what is valuable from what is worthless."

takes on extraordinary powers. It's just a bunch of interconnected computers. In addition to delineating how it may prevent students (and teachers) from thinking clearly and well, we need to place the onus of education back on the students and insist that they perform to certain standards by intelligently using available tools and technologies: books, journals, computers, and so forth.

These issues will become increasingly important as the waves of the so-called age   6
of information approach flood stage in the years ahead. Among the dikes, sandbags, and navigation equipment[3] that a college can offer are truly rigorous courses in both rhetoric and critical thinking, which all college students should be required to complete. Indeed, the Web may very well turn out to be precisely the burr under the saddle[4] that compels everyone in education to return to our mission, which is teaching people how to think in disciplined ways.

Richard Cummins
Director of IT[5] Applications
Columbia Basin College
Pasco, Washington

Reading Journal

In your journal, write about one of the following topics.

1 Discuss a point that either Rothenberg or Cummins makes about the relative value of library and Internet sources for writing a research paper.

2 Describe an experience you had in which the Internet was either helpful or not helpful as you were completing a school assignment.

3 Choose a topic of your own related to the reading.

Main Ideas

Answer the following questions, referring to the notes you took when reading the essay. Then share your answers with a partner.

1 What are Rothenberg's major criticisms of students' use of the World Wide Web in writing research papers?

2 Why does Rothenberg think that much of the fault for the declining quality of his students' research papers is his own?

3 What is the main point Rothenberg is making in the essay? Summarize his central idea in one or two sentences. Use your own words. Begin with the sentence *In the essay "How the Web Destroys the Quality of Students' Research Papers," David Rothenberg maintains that . . .*

---

[3] *dikes, sandbags, and navigation equipment:* Means of preventing or dealing with a flood. (The author is developing a metaphor, or indirect comparison between two dissimilar things, to convey his point about the flood of information on the Internet.)

[4] *burr under the saddle:* Impetus or reason to do something. (A burr is a rough or prickly covering of a certain plant. If it gets stuck under a saddle, it's very uncomfortable for a horse, which will try to shake it off.)

[5] *IT:* Abbreviation standing for Information Technology.

Reflecting on Content

Answer the following questions with a partner. When possible, support your answers with observations based on your own experiences.

1 Look back at your answer to question 1 in the exercise Main Ideas on the opposite page, and choose one or two of Rothenberg's criticisms of the World Wide Web. To what extent do you agree with him?

2 Does the "hunt-and-peck" method of writing a research paper that Rothenberg discusses in paragraphs 6–8 reflect your own experience? Do you agree that this is not an effective method of doing research for a paper?

3 In his letter to the editor, Richard Cummins says, ". . . the Web no more 'destroys the quality of students' research papers' than does television, the blackboard, the overhead projector . . ." (par. 2). What is your response to the argument that it's not the medium itself (the Internet) that is the problem but the ways in which the medium is used?

A Writer's Technique: *Purpose and Audience*

Review the three purposes of writing (page 64): to inform, to persuade, or to entertain. Answer the following questions. Then compare your responses with a partner.

1 What do you consider the major purpose of Rothenberg's essay? What does he want his readers to think or feel after finishing the selection? Support your answers with examples from the reading.

2 Who is Rothenberg's audience, and how does the nature of the audience relate to his central purpose?

3 How successful is Rothenberg in achieving his purpose?

Vocabulary: *Parts Of Speech*

A **part of speech** refers to the grammatical function a word performs in a sentence. The four major parts of speech are nouns, verbs, adjectives, and adverbs. Other parts of speech are pronouns, prepositions, and conjunctions.

The words in the chart on the next page appear in the essay "How the Web Destroys the Quality of Students' Research Papers." Fill in each box in the chart with the appropriate part of speech. If there is no corresponding form for a word, put an asterisk (✳) in the box. Try to do this exercise first without using a dictionary. The first word has been done for you as an example.

Noun	Verb	Adjective	Adverb
credibility (par. 5)	*	credible	credibly
		brilliant (par. 1)	
response (par. 1)			
decline (par. 2)			
		virtual (par. 3)	
perfectionist (par. 8)			
			tactfully (par. 9)
		fragmented (par. 9)	
	divert (par. 10)		
			rapidly (par. 13)
	reason (par. 13)		
knowledge (par. 13)			

Vocabulary in Context

Locate the following italicized vocabulary items in the reading and see if you can determine their meaning from the context. Then think of an example or situation to illustrate each item, using your personal experience if possible. Do not just define the italicized words and expressions. When you are done, share your answers with a partner.

1 the degree to which it is acceptable for a student to include materials from the World Wide Web in an essay or research paper without *citing* the source (par. 3)

2 one or two reasons why a writer should include an accurate *bibliography* at the end of a research paper (par. 3)

3 the difference between *analysis* and synthesis (par. 4)

4 a reason why it is often difficult to assess the *credibility* of people whose ideas can be found on the World Wide Web (par. 5)

5 a reason it is often easy to be *sidetracked* while doing research on the Web (par. 7)

6 a problem that is *prevalent* in the educational system of your country (par. 8)

7 an example of a teacher *tactfully* telling a student that his or her research paper needs a lot of work (par. 9)

8 an example of *plagiarism* in a written or oral project (par. 10)

9 a good way to *keep track of* the library and Web sources you find while conducting research for a paper (par. 13)

10 the degree to which *critical thinking* is encouraged in the educational system of your country (par. 6, letter to the editor)

Discussion

Choose one of the following activities to do with a partner or in a small group.

1 Make a chart similar to the one on the right. Fill in the columns with Rothenberg's major criticisms of students' use of the World Wide Web in writing research papers and your reactions to these criticisms. Consider at least five aspects of Web use that Rothenberg attacks. When you are done, share your ideas with the rest of the class.

Rothenberg's Criticisms of the World Wide Web	My Reactions

2 Discuss whether the following practices in a school essay or research paper are plagiarism and what, if any, the consequences should be for each one. Does it matter if the materials are found in a library or on the Internet? Also consider cross-cultural similarities and differences in attitudes toward plagiarism.

  • copying someone else's work, word for word, without giving the author credit
  • paraphrasing, or rewording, someone else's work without giving the author credit
  • using someone else's ideas without giving the author credit
  • using an idea that is common knowledge (e.g., found in three or more sources) without citing a source

3 Locate one or both of the following Web sites that provide information on evaluating resources on the World Wide Web: <http://lib.nmsu.edu/instruction/evalcrit.html> and <www2.widener.edu/Wolfgram-Memorial-Library/webevaluation/webeval.htm>. Make sure that you view at least one criteria checklist on either Web site. You may evaluate any Web site you like, but you might start with one of the examples on the first site. When you are finished, print out one of the criteria checklists, bring it to class, and, in a small group, describe how you conducted the online evaluation.

Follow up the discussion activity you chose (item 1, 2, or 3) with the matching writing assignment below.

1 Imagine you are writing a letter to the editor of *The Chronicle of Higher Education,* the academic publication in which Rothenberg's essay appeared. In the letter, agree and/or disagree with one or more points that Rothenberg makes in his piece. Think carefully about your *purpose* in writing the letter and your *audience.*

2 Imagine that you and several classmates are members of a college committee that is drafting a statement about plagiarism to appear in a student handbook. Write two or three paragraphs explaining what plagiarism is, why it is a serious offense, which penalties may result, and how plagiarism can be avoided.

3 Write a summary of what you learned about evaluating sources in print and on the World Wide Web. Consider both the criteria checklist you looked at and the evaluation activity you did.

CORE READING 3
Multiple Intelligences and Emotional Intelligence

Journal Writing

In your journal, use the prewriting strategy **clustering** (see page 115) to explore the meaning of intelligence. Write the word "intelligence" in the middle of a sheet of paper and draw a circle around it. Then draw a line to an idea suggested by the topic and circle that idea. Continue associating by thinking of ideas, details, and experiences. Circle each item you add to the cluster, and draw a line back to the idea that suggested it and to other related items. When you are finished, share your map of ideas with several classmates.

Previewing the Topic

In a small group, discuss what the term *intelligence* means to you. Write a list of the various components of intelligence and then share it with the rest of the class. Do most of your classmates define intelligence in a similar way?

Agreeing and Disagreeing

To what extent do you agree with the following statements? Fill in each blank with SA (strongly agree), A (agree), U (undecided), D (disagree), or SD (strongly disagree). Then share your responses with several classmates.

_____ 1 A person who hasn't attended school for many years cannot be intelligent.

_____ 2 Scores on childhood IQ tests are a reliable predictor of future success.

_____ 3 Intellectual, emotional, and moral development is stressed in the educational system of my country.

_____ 4 The definition of intelligence differs throughout the world.

_____ 5 Schools generally do a good job of developing students' intelligence.

_____ 6 Athletic skill and musical ability are types of intelligence.

_____ 7 The ability to respond to the feelings and needs of others is a better predictor of success in life than a high IQ score.

_____ 8 Certain groups of people – for example, some races, ethnicities, and nationalities – are innately more intelligent than others.

_____ 9 It is impossible to assess a person's intelligence accurately.

_____ 10 The development of verbal and mathematical skills in school is more important than that of musical, artistic, and athletic ability.

Taking Notes While You Read

As you read the selection, note in the margin the ways in which Howard Gardner and Daniel Goleman have redefined conventional theories of intelligence. Also indicate the degree to which you think you possess the various intelligences they describe.

Multiple Intelligences and Emotional Intelligence
David Miller Sadker and Myra Pollack Sadker

University professors David Miller Sadker and Myra Pollack Sadker gained a national reputation in the 1990s for their efforts to create more equitable and effective schools. In the following excerpt from their book Teachers, Schools, and Society _(2003) – aimed at future teachers – the authors discuss recent attempts by Howard Gardner and Daniel Goleman to redefine and expand traditional concepts of intelligence. Because the authors are reporting research to an academic audience, they are careful to cite their sources in the text and to include complete publication information at the close of the reading._

Learning style[1] is not the only area undergoing demystification: our understanding of intelligence is also being reconstructed. The IQ[2] score, developed early in the twentieth century, is supposed to be a measure of a person's innate intelligence, with a score of 100 defined as normal, or average. The higher the score, the brighter the person. Some of us grew up in communities where IQ was barely mentioned.

1

---

[1] _learning style:_ Way in which someone learns or understands something (all learning styles have a cognitive, emotional, and physiological component).

[2] _IQ:_ Intelligence quotient – a method of scoring or rating intelligence (intelligence tests were given much more often in the 1950s and 1960s than in later decades).

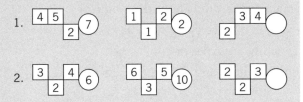
In many cases this lack of knowledge might have been a blessing. Others of us grew up with "IQ envy," in communities where IQ scores were a big part of our culture. Since the score is considered a fixed, permanent measure of intellect, like a person's physical height, the scores engendered strong feelings. Friends who scored 150 or 160 or higher on an IQ test had a secret weapon, a mysteriously wonderful brain. We were impressed. But then our friend, the "genius," was stumped trying to unpack and plug in a toaster oven or got hopelessly lost trying to follow the simplest driving directions. How could this person have such a high IQ? We may have been equally puzzled when another friend, who scored horribly low on an IQ test, went on to fame and riches (and promptly forgot that we were even their friends). What is this IQ score supposed to mean?

Also puzzled by these contradictions was Harvard professor Howard Gardner. Concerned about the traditional assessment of intelligence, with such a heavy emphasis on language and mathematical-logical skills, he broadened the concept to define intelligence as "the capacity to solve problems or to fashion products that are valued in one or more cultural settings" (1989, p. 5).

Gardner identified eight kinds of intelligence, not all of which are commonly recognized in school settings, yet Gardner believes that his theory of multiple intelligences more accurately captures the diverse nature of human capability. Consider Gardner's eight intelligences (Checkley, 1997, pp. 8–13):

1. *Logical-mathematical.* Skills related to mathematical manipulations and discerning and solving logical problems (related careers: scientist, mathematician)

2. *Linguistic.* Sensitivity to the meanings, sounds, and rhythms of words, as well as to the function of language as a whole (related careers: poet, journalist, author)

3. *Bodily-kinesthetic.* Ability to excel physically and to handle objects skillfully (related careers: athlete, dancer, surgeon)

4. *Musical.* Ability to produce pitch and rhythm, as well as to appreciate various forms of musical expression (related careers: musician, composer)

5. *Spatial.* Ability to form a mental model of the spatial world and to maneuver and operate using that model (related careers: sculptor, navigator, engineer, painter)

6. *Interpersonal.* Ability to analyze and respond to the motivations, moods, and desires of other people (related careers: psychology, sales, teaching)

7. *Intrapersonal.* Knowledge of one's feelings, needs, strengths, and weaknesses;

ability to use this knowledge to guide behavior (related benefit: accurate self-awareness)

8. *Naturalist.* (Gardner's most recently defined intelligence) Ability to discriminate among living things, to classify plants, animals and minerals; a sensitivity to the natural world (related careers: botanist, environmentalist, chef, other science- and even consumer-related careers)

Gardner and his colleagues continue to conduct research, and this list is still growing. A possible ninth intelligence being explored by Gardner concerns existential intelligence, the human inclination to formulate fundamental questions about who we are, where we come from, why we die, and the like. Gardner believes that we have yet to discover many more intelligences. (Can you think of some?)   4

The theory of multiple intelligences goes a long way in explaining why the quality of an individual's performance may vary greatly in different activities, rather than reflect a single standard of performance as indicated by an IQ score. Gardner also points out that what is considered intelligence may differ, depending on cultural values. Thus, in the Pacific Islands, intelligence is the ability to navigate among the islands. For many Muslims, the ability to memorize the Koran is a mark of intelligence. Intelligence in Balinese[3] social life is demonstrated by physical grace.   5

Gardner's theory has sparked the imaginations of many educators, some of whom are redesigning their curricula to respond to differing student intelligences. Teachers are refining their approaches in response to such questions as (Armstrong, 1994, pp. 26–28):   6

- How can I use music to emphasize key points?
- How can I promote hand and bodily movements and experiences to enhance learning?
- How can I incorporate sharing and interpersonal interactions into my lessons?
- How can I encourage students to think more deeply about their feelings and memories?
- How can I use visual organizers and visual aids to promote understanding?
- How can I encourage students to classify and appreciate the world around them?

As instruction undergoes re-examination, so does evaluation. The old pencil-and-paper tests used to assess linguistic, math, and logical intelligences seem much less appropriate for measuring these new areas identified by Gardner (1995, pp. 200–209). The portfolio approach . . . is an example of a more comprehensive assessment, which includes student artifacts (papers, projects, videotapes, exhibits) that offer tangible examples of student learning. Some schools ask students to assemble portfolios that reflect progress in Gardner's various intelligences. In other cases, rather than As and Bs or 80s and 90s, schools are using descriptions to report   7

---

[3] *Balinese:* Pertaining to the Indonesian island Bali.

Giants, Wizards, and Dwarfs was the game to play.

Being left in charge of about eighty children seven to ten years old, while their parents were off doing parent things, I mustered my troops in the church social hall and explained the game. It's a large-scale version of Rock, Paper, and Scissors, and involves some intellectual decision making. But the real purpose of the game is to make a lot of noise and run around chasing people until nobody knows which side you are on or who won.

Organizing a roomful of wired-up grade schoolers into two teams, explaining the rudiments of the game, achieving consensus on group identity – all of this is no mean accomplishment, but we did it with a right good will and were ready to go.

The excitement of the chase had reached a critical mass. I yelled out: "You have to decide now which you are – a GIANT, a WIZARD, or a DWARF!"

While the groups huddled in frenzied, whispered consultation, a tug came at my pants leg. A small child stands there looking up, and asks in a small concerned voice, "Where do the Mermaids stand?"

A long pause: A very long pause. "Where do the Mermaids stand?" says I.

"Yes. You see, I am a Mermaid."

"There are no such things as Mermaids."

"Oh, yes, I am one!"

She did not relate to being a Giant, a Wizard, or a Dwarf. She knew her category, Mermaid, and was not about to leave the game and go over and stand against the wall where a loser would stand. She intended to participate, wherever Mermaids fit into the scheme of things, without giving up dignity or identity. She took it for granted that there was a place for Mermaids and that I would know just where.

Well, where DO the Mermaids stand? All the "Mermaids" – all those who are different, who do not fit the norm and who do not accept the available boxes and pigeonholes?

Answer that question and you can build a school, a nation, or a world on it.

What was my answer at the moment? Every once in a while I say the right thing. "The Mermaid stands right here by the King of the Sea!" (Yes, right here by the King's Fool, I thought to myself.)

So we stood there hand in hand, reviewing the troops of Wizards, and Giants, and Dwarfs as they rolled by in wild disarray.

It is not true, by the way, that Mermaids do not exist. I know at least one personally. I have held her hand.

SOURCE: *All I Really Need to Know I Learned in Kindergarten* by Robert Fulghum (New York: Villard Books, 1989), pp. 81–83.

student competence. In music, for example, such descriptions might include "The student often listens to music," "She plays the piano with technical competence," "She is able to compose scores that other students and faculty enjoy," and so on. Whether the school is exploring portfolios, descriptive assessment, or another evaluation method, Gardner's multiple intelligences theory is reshaping many current assessment practices (Hoerr, 1994, pp. 29–33).

While the theory of multiple intelligences raises fundamental questions about instruction and assessment, EQ may be even more revolutionary. EQ, or the emotional intelligence quotient, is described by Daniel Goleman in his book *Emotional Intelligence*. Goleman argues that when it comes to predicting success in life, EQ may be a better predictor than IQ. How does EQ work? The "marshmallow story" may help you understand:

A researcher explains to a 4-year-old that he/she needs to run off to do an errand, but there is a marshmallow for the youngster to enjoy. The youngster can choose to eat the marshmallow immediately. But, if the 4-year-old can wait and not eat the marshmallow right away, then an extra marshmallow will be given when the researcher returns. Eat one now, or hold off and get twice the reward. (Goleman, 1995, p. 26)

What do you think you would have done as a 4-year-old? According to the social scientists who conducted the marshmallow experiment, decisions even at this age foreshadow an emotional disposition characteristic of a successful (or less successful) adult. By the time the children in the study reached high school, the now 14-year-olds were described by teachers and parents in a way that suggested their marshmallow behaviors predicted some significant differences. Students who ten years earlier were able to delay their gratification, to wait awhile and garner a second marshmallow, were reported to be better adjusted, more popular, more adventurous, and more confident in adolescence than the group who ten years earlier had gobbled down their marshmallows. The children who gave in to temptation, ate the marshmallow and abandoned their chances for a second one, were more likely to be described as stubborn, easily frustrated, and lonely teenagers. In addition to the differences between the gobblers and waiters as described by the parents and teachers, there was also a significant SAT[4] scoring gap. The students who, ten years earlier, could wait for the second marshmallow scored 210 points higher than did the gobblers. Reasoning and control, " the regulation of emotion in a way that enhances living" (Gibbs, 1995, p. 62), might be new, and perhaps better, measures of what we call smart, or intelligent.

Emotional intelligence "is a type of social intelligence that involves the ability to   9 monitor one's own and others' emotions, to discriminate among them, and to use the information to guide one's thinking and actions" (Kelly & Moon, 1998, p. 744). Goleman (1996) suggests that EQ taps into the heart, as well as the head, and introduces a new gateway for measuring intelligence, for children and adults. . . .

Goleman and Gardner are toppling educational traditions, stretching our   10 understanding of what schools are about. In a sense, they are increasing the range and diversity of educational ideas. The students you will teach will learn in diverse ways, and a single IQ or even EQ score is unlikely to capture the range of their abilities and skills. . . .

References

Armstrong, T. (1994). Multiple Intelligences: Seven Ways to Approach Curriculum. *Educational Leadership, 52,* 26–28.

Checkley, K. (1997, September). The Eight Multiple Intelligences: A Conversation with Howard Gardner. *Educational Leadership 55* (1), 8–13.

Gardner, H., & Hatch, T. (1989, November). Multiple Intelligence Goes to School: Educational Implications of the Theory of Multiple Intelligences. *Educational Researcher 18* (8), 5.

Gardner, H. (1995, November). Reflections on Multiple Intelligences: Myths and Messages. *Phi Delta Kappan 77* (3), 200–209.

Gibbs, N. (1995, October 2). The E.Q. Factor. *Time 146* (14), 60–68.

Goleman, D. (1995). *Emotional Intelligence.* New York: Bantam.

Goleman, D. (1996, May/June). Emotional Intelligence: Why It Can Matter More Than IQ. *Learning,* 49–50.

---

[4] *SAT:* Scholastic Assessment Test (admissions test for undergraduates, required by most U.S. colleges).

Hoerr, T. R. (1994, November). How the New City School Applies the Multiple Intelligences. *Educational Leadership* 52, 29–33.

Kelly, K. R. & Moon, S. M. (1998, June). Personal and Social Talents. *Phi Delta Kappan* 79 (10), 743–46.

So What's Your EQ?

Like Daniel Goleman, Yale psychologist Peter Salovey works with emotional intelligence issues, and he identifies five elements of emotional intelligence. Below is a self-assessment task that he has designed so that people can find out how high their emotional quotient is. Place a checkmark (✓) in the appropriate boxes and rate your EQ.

Knowing Emotions

The foundation of one's emotional intelligence is self-awareness. A person's ability to recognize a feeling as it happens is the essential first step in understanding the place and power of emotions. People who do not know when they are angry, jealous, or in love are at the mercy of their emotions.

Self-Rating on Knowing My Emotions
☐ Always aware of my emotions
☐ Usually aware
☐ Sometimes aware
☐ Out of touch, clueless

Managing Emotions

A person who can control and manage emotions can handle the bad times as well as the good, shake off depression, bounce back from life's setbacks, and avoid irritability. In one study, up to half of the youngsters who at age 6 were disruptive and unable to get along with others were classified as delinquents by the time they were teenagers.

Self-Rating on Managing My Emotions
☐ Always manage my emotions
☐ Usually manage
☐ Sometimes manage
☐ Emotions manage me

Motivating Oneself

Productive individuals are able to focus energy, confidence, and concentration on achieving a goal and avoid anxiety, anger, and depression. One study of 36,000 people found that "worriers" have poorer academic performance than nonworriers. (A load off your mind, no doubt!)

Self-Rating on Motivation and Focus
☐ Always self-motivated/focused
☐ Usually self-motivated/focused
☐ Sometimes self-motivated/focused
☐ Can't focus on when I was last focused (and I don't care)

Recognizing Emotions In Others

This skill is the core of empathy, the ability to pick up subtle signs of what other people need or want. Such a person always seems to "get it," even before words are spoken.

Self-Rating on Empathy
☐ Always empathetic
☐ Usually empathetic
☐ Sometimes empathetic
☐ Rarely "get it"

Handling Relationships

People whose EQ is high are the kind of people you want to be around. They are popular, are good leaders, and make you feel comfortable and connected. Children who lack social skills are often distracted from learning, and the dropout rate for children who are rejected by their peers can be two to eight times higher than for children who have friends.

Self-Rating on Relationships
- ☐ I am rich in friendship and am often asked to lead activities and events.
- ☐ I have many friends.
- ☐ I have a few friends.
- ☐ Actually, I'm pretty desperate for friends.

RATINGS

Give 4 points for each time you selected the first choice, 3 points for the "usually" or "many" second option, 2 points for the "sometimes" or third selection, and 1 point for the last choice.

18–20 points: A grade – WOW! Impressive!
14–17 points: B grade – You have considerable skills and talents.
10–13 points: C grade – Feel free to read further on this topic.
5–9 points: D grade – This may be a perfect subject to investigate in greater detail. Do you have a topic for your term project yet?

Reading Journal

In your reading journal, write about one of the following topics.

1 Describe a way in which Gardner's or Goleman's theory of intelligence might influence some aspect of formal education – for example, teaching methods, curriculum design, or assessment.

2 Consider the degree to which you possess one of Gardner's multiple intelligences or Goleman's emotional intelligence.

3 Choose a topic of your own related to the reading.

Main Ideas

Answer the following questions, referring to the notes you took when reading the essay. Then share your answers with a partner.

1 How do Gardner's and Goleman's concepts of intelligence differ from more traditional ones? Think of one or two important differences.

2 What do the authors mean in paragraph 10 when they say that "Goleman and Gardner are toppling educational traditions, stretching our understanding of what schools are about"? Give one or two examples.

3 What is the main point you think the authors are making in the reading? Summarize their central idea in one or two sentences. Use your own words. Begin with the sentence *In the chapter excerpt "Multiple Intelligences and Emotional Intelligence," Myra Sadker and David Sadker* . . .

Reflecting on Content

Answer the following questions with a partner. When possible, support your answers with observations based on your own experiences.

1 Reread Goleman's definition of emotional intelligence (par. 9). Which intelligence(s) that Gardner identifies is/are similar to the emotional abilities mentioned by Goleman? What parallels can you find between them?

2 At the beginning of paragraph 8, the authors say, "While the theory of multiple intelligences raises fundamental questions about instruction and assessment, EQ may be even more revolutionary." What do they mean by this statement?

3 Complete the EQ assessment on pages 82–83. Do you think your final rating is an accurate indication of your emotional abilities?

A Writer's Technique: *Purpose and Audience*

Review the discussion of purpose on page 64.

A writer's purpose is closely related to the **audience** who is expected to read the writer's work. Sometimes a writer has a specific reader in mind: someone from a particular age group, occupation, or educational background. At other times the audience is assumed to be the general reader.

Answer the following questions with a partner.

1 "Multiple Intelligences and Emotional Intelligence" comes from a book directed to future teachers. How does this readership help shape the authors' purpose? Consider the subject matter they discuss, the points they make, and the examples they give.

2 How successful do you think the authors are in achieving their purpose?

3 What is the authors' purpose in including the anecdote "Where Do the Mermaids Stand?" by Robert Fulghum (page 80)? How does this story relate to ideas in the reading by Sadker and Sadker?

Vocabulary: *Antonyms*

Like the study of synonyms (see page 64), the study of **antonyms** is a good way to develop your vocabulary and your ability to determine the meaning of unfamiliar words from their context – that is, from the other words in the sentence and the paragraph.

A synonym is a word that has the same or nearly the same meaning as another word (*begin* is a synonym for *start*). An antonym, in contrast, is a word with the opposite meaning (*finish* is an antonym for *begin*).

Look at these sentences from "Multiple Intelligences and Emotional Intelligence" and do the following.

- Guess the meaning of each italicized word or idiom from the context.

- Write down one or two antonyms for each vocabulary item. See if you can find words that don't just add a negative prefix to the items below. Make sure that the antonym is the same part of speech as the word given: noun, verb, adjective, or adverb.

> **Example:** *How can I promote hand and bodily movements and experiences to* **enhance** *learning? (par. 6)*
>
> **Meaning:** *improve, strengthen*
>
> **Antonyms:** *decrease, weaken*

1 The IQ score, developed early in the twentieth century, is supposed to be a measure of a person's *innate* intelligence. (par. 1)

2 Concerned about the traditional assessment of intelligence, . . . [Gardner] *broadened* the concept. (par. 2)

3 The portfolio approach . . . is an example of a more *comprehensive* assessment. (par. 7)

4 . . . student artifacts (papers, projects, videotapes, exhibits) . . . offer *tangible* examples of student learning. (par. 7)

5 She plays the piano with technical *competence.* (par. 7)

6 Eat one now, or *hold off* and get twice the reward. (par. 8)

7 The children who *gave in to* temptation, ate the marshmallow and abandoned their chances for a second one, were more likely to be described as stubborn. (par. 8)

8 Goleman and Gardner are *toppling* educational traditions, stretching our understanding of what schools are about. (par. 10)

Vocabulary in Context

Locate the following italicized vocabulary items in the reading and see if you can determine their meaning from the context. Then think of an example or situation to illustrate each item, using your personal experience if possible. Do not just define the italicized words and expressions. When you are done, share your answers with a partner.

1 a time when you were *stumped* by something at school – for example, an assignment or a question on a test (par. 1)

2 your ability to *discern* and solve logical problems (par. 3)

3 something at which you or someone you know *excels* (par. 3)

4 your ability to form a model of the spatial world and to *maneuver* and operate using that model (par. 3)

5 whether you think that most people are sensitive to the natural world and that they can *discriminate* among living things (par. 3)

6 something that *goes a long way* in enhancing academic success (par. 5)

7 someone you know with a naturally cheerful *disposition* (par. 8)

8 an academic accomplishment for which someone might *garner* praise (par. 8)

9 your ability to *monitor* your own and others' emotions (par. 9)

10 an example of someone *toppling* a traditional belief or custom (par. 10)

Discussion

Choose one of the following activities to do with a partner or in a small group.

1 Discuss whether you think Gardner's multiple intelligences and Goleman's emotional intelligence are reflected in the educational system of your country. Think especially about the curriculum and methods of assessing students' knowledge and skills. When you are finished, share your ideas with the class.

2 Imagine that you are a teacher and are designing a lesson plan for a particular class; you are using one or more of Gardner's intelligences to help you achieve your goals. Consider the following: the age group you are working with; your objectives – e.g., the knowledge and/or skills you wish to promote; the materials you will need; and your procedure (the classroom activity or task). Then share your lesson plan with the class. (If time allows, you might try executing your lesson plan with another group in the class.)

3 Access the following Web site dealing with multiple intelligences: <http://surfaquarium.com/MI/inventory.htm>. Complete the "Multiple Intelligences Inventory," calculate your score, and discuss whether you think the results are accurate.

Writing Follow-up

Follow up the discussion activity you chose (item 1, 2, or 3) with the matching writing assignment below.

1 With a partner or by yourself, write two paragraphs discussing whether you think Gardner's and Goleman's concepts of intelligence are reflected in the educational system of your country. In the first paragraph, focus on curriculum; in the second paragraph, focus on assessment of students' knowledge and skills.

2 Write up your multiple intelligences lesson plan. Write one or two sentences for each category below, except for the "procedure." There you should write one or two paragraphs to explain your classroom activity or task.
   - Title of lesson plan
   - Age group
   - Principal intelligence(s) used
   - Knowledge and/or skills promoted
   - Objectives
   - Materials needed
   - Procedure

3 Write two paragraphs discussing the online "Multiple Intelligences Survey." In the first paragraph, summarize the results of the survey. In the second paragraph, discuss whether you think the scores are an accurate reflection of your abilities.

MAKING CONNECTIONS

Answer two or three of the following questions relating to the three core readings in this chapter.

1 The authors of the core readings (Holt, Rothenberg, Sadker and Sadker) deal with traditional and nontraditional methods of education. Which of the authors advocates a relatively conventional approach to education and which a nonconventional approach? Give examples to support your answer.

2 Both Holt and Rothenberg feel that teachers are to a large degree responsible for their students' negative attitudes and poor learning habits. How does each author think that teachers contribute to their students' educational problems?

3 How do you think Holt would respond to Gardner's theory of multiple intelligences and the important role schools play in developing students' varying abilities? Think especially about Holt's criticisms of schools and his recommendations for improvement.

4 Do you think Rothenberg would see the Internet as a good tool to develop Gardner's multiple intelligences? Consider, especially, linguistic and spatial intelligence.

5 Review the three purposes of writing (page 64): to inform, to persuade, and to entertain. In which ways are the authors' purposes in the three core readings similar? In which ways are they different?

ADDITIONAL READING 1
The Teacher Who Changed My Life

Before You Read

With several classmates or in your journal, discuss a teacher who inspired you and influenced your life in some way.

Taking Notes While You Read

As you read the essay, note in the margin the special qualities the author finds in his teacher, Miss Hurd, and the things he learns from her.

The Teacher Who Changed My Life
Nicholas Gage

Nicholas Gage was born in Greece in 1939 and immigrated to the United States ten years later. In this essay, he writes about an inspirational teacher who paved the way for his career as a writer. The essay first appeared in Parade *magazine in 1989 and is adapted from Gage's book of the same year,* A Place for Us, *which focuses on his adjustment to life in the United States.*

1   The person who set the course of my life in the new land entered as a young war refugee – who, in fact, nearly dragged me on to the path that would bring all the blessings I've received in America – was a salty-tongued,[1] no-nonsense schoolteacher named Marjorie Hurd. When I entered her classroom in 1953, I had been to six schools in five years, starting in the Greek village where I was born in 1939.

2   When I stepped off a ship in New York Harbor on a gray March day in 1949, I was an undersized 9-year-old in short pants who had lost his mother and was coming to live with the father he didn't know. My mother, Eleni Gatzoyiannis, had been imprisoned, tortured, and shot by Communist guerrillas for sending me and three of my four sisters to freedom. She died so that her children could go to their father in the United States.

3   The portly, bald, well-dressed man who met me and my sisters seemed a foreign, authoritarian figure. I secretly resented him for not getting the whole family out of Greece early enough to save my mother. Ultimately, I would grow to love him and appreciate how he dealt with becoming a single parent at the age of 56, but at first our relationship was prickly, full of hostility.

4   As Father drove us to our new home – a tenement in Worcester, Mass. – and pointed out the huge brick building that would be our first school in America, I clutched my Greek notebooks from the refugee camp, hoping that my few years of schooling would impress my teachers in this cold, crowded country. They didn't. When my father led me and my 11-year-old sister to Greendale Elementary School,

---

[1] *salty-tongued:* Witty and provocative; having a mischievous charm.

the grim-faced Yankee[2] principal put the two of us in a class for the mentally retarded. There was no facility in those days for non-English-speaking children.

By the time I met Marjorie Hurd four years later, I had learned English, been placed in a normal, graded class, and had even been chosen for the college preparatory track in the Worcester public school system. I was 13 years old when our father moved us yet again, and I entered Chandler Junior High shortly after the beginning of the seventh grade. I found myself surrounded by richer, smarter, and better-dressed classmates who looked askance at my strange clothes and heavy accent. Shortly after I arrived, we were told to select a hobby to pursue during "club hour" on Fridays. The idea of hobbies and clubs made no sense to my immigrant ears, but I decided to follow the prettiest girl in my class – the blue-eyed daughter of the local Lutheran[3] minister. She led me through the door marked "Newspaper Club" and into the presence of Miss Hurd, the newspaper adviser and English teacher who would become my mentor and my muse.

A formidable, solidly built woman with salt-and-pepper hair, a steely eye, and a flat Boston accent, Miss Hurd had no patience with layabouts. "What are all you goof-offs[4] doing here?" she bellowed at the would-be journalists. "This is the Newspaper Club! We're going to put out a *newspaper*. So if there's anybody in this room who doesn't like work, I suggest you go across to the Glee Club[5] now, because you're going to work your tails off here!"

I was soon under Miss Hurd's spell. She did indeed teach us to put out a newspaper, skills I honed during my next 25 years as a journalist. Soon I asked the principal to transfer me to her English class as well. There, she drilled us on grammar until I finally began to understand the logic and structure of the English language. She assigned stories for us to read and discuss; not tales of heroes, like the Greek myths I knew, but stories of underdogs – poor people, even immigrants, who seemed ordinary until a crisis drove them to do something extraordinary. She also introduced us to the literary wealth of Greece – giving me a new perspective on my war-ravaged, impoverished homeland. I began to be proud of my origins.

One day, after discussing how writers should write about what they know, she assigned us to compose an essay from our own experience. Fixing me with a stern look, she added, "Nick, I want you to write about what happened to your family in Greece." I had been trying to put those painful memories behind me and left the assignment until the last moment. Then, on a warm spring afternoon, I sat in my room with a yellow pad and pencil and stared out the window at the buds on the trees. I wrote that the coming of spring always reminded me of the last time I said goodbye to my mother on a green and gold day in 1948.

I kept writing, one line after another, telling how the Communist guerrillas occupied our village, took our home and food, how my mother started planning our escape when she learned the children were to be sent to reeducation camps behind the Iron Curtain and how, at the last moment, she couldn't escape with us because

5

6

7

8

9

---

[2] *Yankee:* Someone born or living in New England.

[3] *Lutheran:* Relating to the Protestant churches that follow the teachings of Martin Luther (1483–1546).

[4] *goof-offs:* Those who avoid work or responsibility.

[5] *Glee Club:* Chorus that usually sings short pieces.

the guerrillas sent her with a group of women to thresh wheat in a distant village. She promised she would try to get away on her own, she told me to be brave and hung a silver cross around my neck, and then she kissed me. I watched the line of women being led down into the ravine and up the other side, until they disappeared around the bend – my mother a tiny brown figure at the end who stopped for an instant to raise her hand in one last farewell.

10   I wrote about our nighttime escape down the mountain, across the minefields and into the lines of the Nationalist soldiers, who sent us to a refugee camp. It was there that we learned of our mother's execution. I felt very lucky to have come to America, I concluded, but every year, the coming of spring made me feel sad because it reminded me of the last time I saw my mother.

11   I handed in the essay, hoping never to see it again, but Miss Hurd had it published in the school paper. This mortified me at first, until I saw that my classmates reacted with sympathy and tact to my family's story. Without telling me, Miss Hurd also submitted the essay to a contest sponsored by the Freedoms Foundation at Valley Forge, Pa., and it won a medal. The Worcester paper wrote about the award and quoted my essay at length. My father, by then a "five-and-dime-store chef,"[6] as the paper described him, was ecstatic with pride, and the Worcester Greek community celebrated the honor to one of its own.

12   For the first time I began to understand the power of the written word. A secret ambition took root in me. One day, I vowed, I would go back to Greece, find out the details of my mother's death and write about her life, so her grandchildren would know of her courage. Perhaps I would even track down the men who killed her and write of their crimes. Fulfilling that ambition would take me 30 years.

13   Meanwhile, I followed the literary path that Miss Hurd had so forcefully set me on. After junior high, I became the editor of my school paper at Classical High School and got a part-time job at the Worcester *Telegram and Gazette*. Although my father could only give me $50 and encouragement toward a college education, I managed to finance four years at Boston University with scholarships and part-time jobs in journalism. During my last year of college, an article I wrote about a friend who had died in the Philippines – the first person to lose his life working for the Peace Corps[7] – led to my winning the Hearst Award for College Journalism. And the plaque was given to me in the White House by President John F. Kennedy.

14   For a refugee who had never seen a motorized vehicle or indoor plumbing until he was 9, this was an unimaginable honor. When the Worcester paper ran a picture of me standing next to President Kennedy, my father rushed out to buy a new suit in order to properly receive the congratulations of the Worcester Greeks. He clipped out the photograph, had it laminated in plastic and carried it in his breast pocket for the rest of his life to show everyone he met. I found the much-worn photo in his pocket on the day he died 20 years later.

15   In our isolated Greek village, my mother had bribed a cousin to teach her to read, for girls were not supposed to attend school beyond a certain age. She had

---

[6] *five-and-dime-store chef:* Owner of a variety store selling inexpensive items.

[7] *Peace Corps:* Organization created by President John F. Kennedy in 1961 to train American volunteers to work with people of developing nations.

always dreamed of her children receiving an education. She couldn't be there when I graduated from Boston University, but the person who came with my father and shared our joy was my former teacher, Marjorie Hurd. We celebrated not only my bachelor's degree but also the scholarships that paid my way to Columbia's Graduate School of Journalism. There, I met the woman who wold eventually become my wife. At our wedding and at the baptisms of our three children, Marjorie Hurd was always there, dancing alongside the Greeks.

By then, she was Mrs. Rabidou, for she had married a widower when she was in   16
her early 40s. That didn't distract her from her vocation of introducing young minds to English literature, however. She taught for a total of 41 years and continually would make a "project" of some balky student in whom she spied a spark of potential. Often these were students from the most troubled homes, yet she would alternately bully and charm each one with her own special brand of tough love until the spark caught fire. She retired in 1981 at the age of 62 but still avidly follows the lives and careers of former students while overseeing her adult stepchildren and driving her husband on camping trips to New Hampshire.

Miss Hurd was one of the first to call me on Dec. 10, 1987, when President   17
Reagan,[8] in his television address after the summit meetings with Gorbachev,[9] told the nation that Eleni Gatzoyiannis' dying cry, " My children!" had helped inspire him to seek an arms agreement "for all the children of the world."

"I can't imagine a better monument for your mother," Miss Hurd said with an   18
uncharacteristic catch in her voice.

Although a bad hip makes it impossible for her to join in the Greek dancing,   19
Marjorie Hurd Rabidou is still an honored and enthusiastic guest at all family celebrations, including my 50th birthday picnic last summer, where the shish kebab[10] was cooked on spits, clarinets and *bouzoukis*[11] wailed, and costumed dancers led the guests in a serpentine line around our Colonial farmhouse, only 20 minutes from my first home in Worcester.

My sisters and I felt an aching void because my father was not there to lead the   20
line, balancing a glass of wine on his head while he danced, the way he did at every celebration during his 92 years. But Miss Hurd was there, surveying the scene with quiet satisfaction. Although my parents are gone, her presence was a consolation, because I owe her so much.

This is truly the land of opportunity, and I would have enjoyed its bounty even   21
if I hadn't walked into Miss Hurd's classroom in 1953. But she was the one who directed my grief and pain into writing, and if it weren't for her, I wouldn't have become an investigative reporter and foreign correspondent, recorded the story of my mother's life and death in *Eleni* and now my father's story in *A Place for Us*, which is also a testament to the country that took us in. She was the catalyst that sent me into journalism and indirectly caused all the good things that came after. But Miss Hurd would probably deny this emphatically.

---

8 *President Reagan:* Ronald Reagan, actor and fortieth president of the United States (1981–1989).

9 *Gorbachev:* Mikhail Gorbachev, general secretary of the Communist Party of the Soviet Union (1985–1991) and president of the Soviet Union (1990–1991).

10 *shish kebab:* Cubes of meat and often vegetables roasted on a long metal pin; popular in Turkey and Greece.

11 *bouzoukis:* Greek string instruments resembling a mandolin, or small, round-bodied guitar.

A few years ago, I answered the telephone and heard my former teacher's voice 22
telling me, in that won't-take-no-for-an-answer tone of hers, that she had decided I
was to write and deliver the eulogy at her funeral. I agreed (she didn't leave me any
choice), but that's one assignment I never want to do. I hope, Miss Hurd, that you'll
accept this remembrance instead.

After You Read

In your journal, write about one of the following topics.

1 Discuss Gage's purpose in writing the essay.
2 Explain why Gage finds Miss Hurd such an inspirational teacher.
3 Choose a topic of your own related to the reading.

ADDITIONAL READING 2
Let's Tell the Story of All America's Cultures

Before You Read

With several classmates or in your journal, discuss whether, based on your own
experiences, you agree with the following statement: "High school classes and
textbooks dealing with the history of my native country are usually very limited in
the subjects they cover. Much more attention should be paid to the contribution
of people of diverse backgrounds, including racial, ethnic, and religious, to the
formation of the nation."

As you read the essay, note in the margin the reasons the author thinks a multicultural education is important. Also indicate the points with which you agree or disagree.

Let's Tell the Story of All America's Cultures
Ji-Yeon Mary Yuhfill

The following essay, written by Ji-Yeon Mary Yuhfill, originally appeared in the daily newspaper the Philadelphia Inquirer *in 1991. Born in Seoul, Korea, in 1965, Yuhfill immigrated at the age of five with her family to the United States and went on to earn a doctorate in history from the University of Pennsylvania and to work as a reporter for several newspapers. In the essay, she discusses her personal experience with history classes that didn't recognize the contributions of various ethnic groups to the formation of the United States. The debate about the value of "multicultural education," which started in the early 1990s, continues today.*

1 I grew up hearing, seeing and almost believing that America was white – albeit with a little black tinged here and there – and that white was best.

2 The white people were everywhere in my 1970s Chicago childhood: Founding Fathers, Lewis and Clark, Lincoln, Daniel Boone, Carnegie,[1] presidents, explorers, and industrialists galore. The only black people were slaves. The only Indians were scalpers.

3 I never heard one word about how Benjamin Franklin[2] was so impressed by the Iroquois federation of nations[3] that he adapted that model into our system of state and federal government. Or that the Indian tribes were systematically betrayed and massacred by a greedy young nation that stole their land and called it the United States.

4 I never heard one word about how Asian immigrants were among the first to turn California's desert into fields of plenty. Or about Chinese immigrant Ah Bing, who bred the cherry now on sale in groceries across the nation. Or that plantation owners in Hawaii imported labor from China, Japan, Korea, and the Philippines to work the sugarcane fields. I never learned that Asian immigrants were the only immigrants denied U.S. citizenship, even though they served honorably in World War I. All the immigrants in my textbook were white.

5 I never learned about Frederick Douglass, the runaway slave who became a leading abolitionist and statesman, or about black scholar W. E. B. Du Bois. I never learned that black people rose up in arms against slavery. Nat Turner[4] wasn't one of the heroes in my childhood history class.

---

[1] *Carnegie:* Andrew Carnegie (1835–1919), U.S. manufacturer and philanthropist. (The *founding fathers* were leading figures in the formation of the United States; *Meriwether Lewis and William Clark* were American explorers in the early nineteenth century; *Abraham Lincoln* was president of the United States from 1861 to 1865; and *Daniel Boone* was an American pioneer who lived from 1734 to 1820.)

[2] *Benjamin Franklin* (1706–1790): American statesman, scientist, and writer.

[3] *Iroquis federation of nations:* Alliance of five Native American tribes living in New York State.

[4] *Nat Turner* (1800–1831): American slave who fought to lead his fellow slaves to freedom.

I never learned that the American Southwest and California were already settled   6
by Mexicans when they were annexed after the Mexican-American War.[5] I never
learned that Mexico once had a problem keeping land-hungry white men on the
U.S. side of the border.

So when other children called me a slant-eyed chink[6] and told me to go   7
back where I came from, I was ready to believe that I wasn't really an American
because I wasn't white. America's bittersweet legacy of struggling and failing and
getting another step closer to democratic ideals of liberty and equality and justice
for all wasn't for the likes of me, an immigrant child from Korea. The history
books said so.

ESTIMATES OF THE ETHNIC COMPOSITION OF THE UNITED STATES				
	1990	2005	2030	2050
White (non-Hispanic)	75%	71%	61%	53%
Hispanic	9%	13%	19%	24%
Black	12%	13%	14%	16%
Asian and Pacific Islander	3%	4%	7%	9%
American Indian and Eskimo	0.8%	0.9%	1%	1%

Hispanic refers to people with origins in Latin America; Asian, to people with origins in the Far East, Southeast Asia, and the Indian subcontinent; and Pacific Islander, to people with origins in Hawaii, Guam, Samoa, and other islands in the Pacific Ocean.

SOURCE: U.S. Census Bureau

Well, the history books   8
were wrong. Educators
around the country are
finally realizing what I
realized as a teenager in
the library, looking up the
history I wasn't getting
in school. America is
a multicultural nation,
composed of many people
with varying histories and
varying traditions who have
little in common except
their humanity, a belief in
democracy and a desire for
freedom. America changed them, but they changed America too.

A committee of scholars and teachers gathered by the New York State   9
Department of Education recognizes this in their recent report, "One Nation, Many
Peoples: A Declaration of Cultural Interdependence." They recommend that public
schools provide a "multicultural education, anchored to the shared principles of a
liberal democracy."

What that means, according to the report, is recognizing that America was shaped   10
and continues to be shaped by people of diverse backgrounds. It calls for students to
be taught that history is an ongoing process of discovery and interpretation of the
past, and that there is more than one way of viewing the world.

Thus, the westward migration of white Americans is not just a heroic settling   11
of an untamed wild, but also the conquest of indigenous peoples. Immigrants were
not just white, but Asian as well. Blacks were not merely passive slaves freed by
northern whites, but active fighters for their own liberation.

In particular, according to the report, the curriculum should help children "to   12
assess critically the reasons for the inconsistencies between the ideals of the U.S.
and social realities. It should provide information and intellectual tools that can

---

[5] Mexican-American War (1846–1848): War between the United States and Mexico resulting in U.S. acquisition of large areas of land originally inhabited by Mexicans.

[6] chink: Insulting term for a person of Chinese descent.

permit them to contribute to bringing reality closer to the ideals." In other words, show children the good with the bad, and give them the skills to help improve their country. What could be more patriotic?

Several dissenting members of the New York committee publicly worry that 13 America will splinter into ethnic fragments if this multicultural curriculum is adopted. They argue that the committee's report puts the focus on ethnicity at the expense of national unity.

But downplaying ethnicity will not bolster national unity. The history of America 14 is the story of how and why people from all over the world came to the United States, and how in struggling to make a better life for themselves, they changed each other, they changed the country, and they all came to call themselves Americans. *E pluribus unum.*[7] Out of many, one.

This is why I, with my Korean background, and my childhood tormentors, with 15 their lost-in-the-mist-of-time European backgrounds, are all Americans. It is the unique beauty of this country. It is high time we let all our children gaze upon it.

After You Read

In your journal, write about one of the following topics.

1 Examine Yuhfill's purpose in writing the essay.

2 Consider whether you agree with the argument, expressed in paragraph 13, that multicultural education weakens national unity.

3 Choose a topic of your own related to the reading.

---

[7] *E pluribus unum:* Motto appearing on U.S. documents and on several coins.

ADDITIONAL READING 3
Coyote and the Crying Song

Before You Read

With several classmates or in your journal, discuss an educational experience that you feel really taught you something. Focus on *what* you learned and *how* you learned it. Then share your experiences with the rest of the class.

While You Read

As you read the folktale, think about how it reflects the process of learning. Note in the margin what the story has to teach about the ways in which people learn or fail to learn.

Coyote and the Crying Song
Retold by Harold Courlander

This is a folktale of the Hopi Indians, a Native American people living in northeastern Arizona. The folktale appears in a book titled People of the Short Blue Corn: Tales and Legends of the Hopi Indians, *edited by Harold Courlander (1970). The main character in the fable is a coyote – a common figure in Native American folklore that is usually portrayed as a trickster and a troublemaker.*

Coyote once lived on Second Mesa[1] near the village of Shipaulovi. The dove also 1
lived near Shipaulovi. It was harvest time, and the dove was in the field collecting
the seeds of the kwakwi grass.[2] To separate the seeds from the stalks, she had to
rub the tassels vigorously. But the kwakwi grass was very sharp and the dove cut
her hands. She began to moan: "Hu-hu-huuu! Hu-hu-huuu! Ho-uuu, ho-uuu,
ho-uuu!"

It happened that Coyote was out hunting, and he heard the voice of the dove. 2
To Coyote, the moaning sounded like music. "What a fine voice," he said to himself,
approaching the place where the dove was working. He stopped nearby, listening
with admiration as the dove moaned again: "Hu-hu-huuu! Hu-hu-huuu! Ho-uuu,
ho-uuu, ho-uuu!"

Coyote spoke, saying, "The song is beautiful. Sing it again." 3

The dove said, "I am not singing; I am crying." 4

Coyote said, "I know a song when I hear one. Sing it once more." 5

"I am not singing," the dove said. "I was gathering seeds from the kwakwi grass 6
and I cut myself. Therefore, I am crying."

Coyote became angry. "I was hunting," he said, "and I heard your song. I came 7
here thinking, 'The music is beautiful.' I stood and listened. And now you tell me
you are not singing. You do not respect my intelligence. Sing! It is only your voice
that keeps me from eating you. Sing again!"

And now, because she feared for her life, the dove began once more to moan: 8
"Hu-hu-huuu! Hu-hu-huuu! Ho-uuu, ho-uuu, ho-uuu!"

Coyote listened carefully. He memorized the song. And when he thought he had 9
it in mind, he said, "First I will take the song home and leave it there safely. Then
I will continue hunting."

He turned and ran, saying the words over and over so that he would not forget 10
them. He came to a place where he had to leap from one rock to another, but he
missed his footing and fell. He got to his feet. He was annoyed. He said, "Now I have
lost the song." He tried to remember it, but all he could think of was "Hu-hu."

So he went back and said angrily to the dove, "I was taking the song home, but 11
I fell and lost it. So you must give it to me again."

The dove said, "I did not sing; I only cried." 12

Coyote bared his teeth. He said, "Do you prefer to be eaten?" 13

The dove quickly began to moan: "Hu-hu-huuu! Hu-hu-huuu! Ho-uuu, ho-uuu, 14
ho-uuu!"

---

[1] *Mesa:* Hill with a flat top and one or more steep sides, common in the southwestern United States.

[2] *kwakwi grass:* Hopi name for a common type of grass in the southwestern United States.

"Ah, now I have it," Coyote said, and once more he started for home. In his 15
haste he slipped and tumbled into a gully. When he regained his footing, the song
was gone. Again he had lost it. So he returned to the place where the dove was
working.

"Your song is very slippery," he said. "It keeps getting away. Sing it again. This 16
time I shall grasp it firmly. If I can't hold on to it this time, I shall come and take
you instead."

"I was not singing; I was crying," the dove said, but seeing the Coyote's anger she 17
repeated her moaning sounds.

And this time Coyote grasped the song firmly as he ran toward his home near 18
Shipaulovi. When he was out of sight, the dove thought that it would be best for
her to leave the kwakwi field. But before she left, she found a stone that looked like
a bird. She painted eyes on it and placed it where she had been working. Then she
gathered up her kwakwi seeds and went away.

Coyote was tired from so much running back and forth. When he was almost 19
home, he had to jump over a small ravine, but he misjudged the distance and fell.
Now Coyote was truly angry, for the song had been lost again. He went back to the
kwakwi field. He saw the stone that the dove had placed there. He saw the painted
eyes looking at him.

"Now you have done it," he said. "There is no purpose in looking at me that way. 20
I am a hunter. Therefore, I hunt." He leaped forward and his jaws snapped. But the
stone bird was very hard. Coyote's teeth broke and his mouth began to bleed. "Hu-
hu-huuu!" he moaned. "Hu-hu-huuu! Ho-uuu, ho-uuu, ho-uuu!"

Just at that moment a crow alighted in the kwakwi field. He said, "Coyote, that 21
is a beautiful song you are singing."

Coyote replied, "How stupid the crow people are that they can't tell the 22
difference between singing and crying!"

After You Read

In your journal, write about one of the following topics.

1 Explain how "Coyote and the Crying Song" can be related to education – for
   example, goals, teaching and learning styles, and factors that enhance and
   obstruct learning.

2 Discuss a folktale in your culture that teaches a lesson about human experience.

3 Choose a topic of your own related to the story.

ADDITIONAL READING 4
First Grade – Standing in the Hall

Before You Read

With several classmates or in your journal, discuss your earliest reading experiences. How and when did you learn to read? Who first got you interested in reading? What was the experience like?

Taking Notes While You Read

As you read the poem, note in the margin the points you think poet Cheryl Savageau is making about students, teachers, and education in general.

 ## First Grade – Standing in the Hall
Cheryl Savageau

The following poem by Cheryl Savageau appears in her book Dirt Road Home *(1995). This collection of poetry dealing with poverty, mixed ancestry, nature, and family is rooted in Savageau's Native American and French Canadian ancestry.*

Because he can't read
the teacher makes him stand
in the hall. He can sing
all his letters, knows
what they look like. He knows   5
that out of books come stories,
like the ones his Gramma told him.
Now she is in the hospital.
He wonders if she is sleeping,
when she will come home.   10

The letters do not
talk to him.
They keep their stories
to themselves.

He is hopeless, he is stupid,   15
he is standing in the hall.
He is waiting in the hall
for the principal
to see him, for the bell to ring,
for the teacher   20
to call him back inside.

After a while
when no one comes
he stops crying.
A spider is webbing   25
the pie-shaped window pane
and outside,
the sun is making fire
in the yellow leaves.

If he listens closely   30
a song will begin in him
that the teachers
can't silence.

After You Read

In your journal, write about one of the following topics.

1 Discuss the main point or points you think Savageau is making about students, teachers, and education in general.

2 Describe an experience you have had that is similar in some way to that of the boy in the poem.

3 Choose a topic of your own related to the poem.

ADDITIONAL READING 5
Humor: The Test

With a partner, read the following joke and cartoon and discuss the issues relating to education.

 The Test

At the University of Minnesota, there were four sophomores taking organic   1
chemistry. They did so well on all the quizzes, midterms, and labs that each had an
"A" so far for the semester. These four friends were so confident that, the weekend
before the final exam, they decided to go up to the University of Michigan and party
with some friends there. They had a great time; however, after all the hard partying,
they slept all day Sunday and didn't make it back to Minnesota until early Monday
morning.

Rather than taking the final exam then, they decided to find their professor after   2
the exam and explain to her why they had missed it. They told her that they had

gone to the University of Michigan for the weekend planning to come back in time to study, but, unfortunately, they had a flat tire on the way back, didn't have a spare, and couldn't get help for a long time. As a result, they missed the final.

The professor thought it over and then agreed they could make up the final the 3 following day. The students were elated and relieved. They studied that night and went in the next day at the time the professor had told them. She placed them in separate rooms, handed each of them a test booklet, and told them to begin.

The students looked at the first problem, worth five points. It was a problem they 4 had studied before. "Cool," they thought at the same time, each one in his separate room. "This is going to be easy." Each finished the problem and then turned the page. On the second page was written: "(For 95 points): Which tire?"

ESSAY TOPICS

Write an essay on one of the following topics. Support your points with an appropriate combination of references to the readings in this chapter, library and Internet sources, and personal experiences and observations.

Refer to the section "The Essentials of Writing" on pages 102–132 to help you plan, draft, and revise your essay. Use this special section, too, to assist you in locating, integrating, and documenting your sources.

1 Discuss the extent to which you agree with one of the following quotations:

"What I wish for all students is some release from the clammy grip of the future. I wish them a chance to savor each segment of their education as an experience in itself and not as a grim preparation for the next step. I wish them the right to experiment, to trip and fall, to learn that defeat is as instructive as victory and is not the end of the world." (William Zinsser, U.S. writer and educator)

"The purpose of education, finally, is to create in a person the ability to look at the world for himself, to make his own decisions, to say to himself this is black or this is white, to decide for himself whether there is a God in heaven or not." (James Baldwin, U.S. author)

2 Explore any major differences between the educational system of your country and that of another country with which you are familiar. Consider educational practices and the values reflected in them.

3 Analyze the qualities of good teachers and/or good students. Consider such things as goals, values, teaching and learning styles, behaviors, and character traits.

4 Explain how well the educational system in your country prepares students for the challenges they will face in the real world. What are the strengths and weaknesses of the education students receive? Do you have any recommendations for its improvement?

5 Examine the pros and cons of using the Internet, especially the World Wide Web, as an educational tool. To what degree does this mass medium enhance, and to what degree does it obstruct, students' learning?

The Essentials of Writing

As a student, you will encounter many types of writing assignments in college and university classes: essays, research papers, reports, summaries of articles, paraphrases of reading passages, journal entries, and other formal and informal types of writing. This section of your book will help you complete these assignments. In the first part, you will learn about the typical structure of a piece of academic writing; in the second part, you will learn about the stages of the writing process; and, in the third part, you will learn how to use library, Internet, and other sources in your writing.

PART ONE

The Structure of an Essay

All essays consist of three major parts: the *introduction* (beginning), *body* (middle), and *conclusion* (end).

Figure 1.1 Structure of an Essay

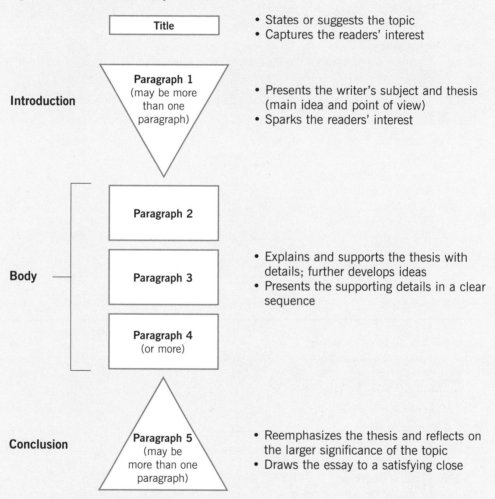

Title
- States or suggests the topic
- Captures the readers' interest

Introduction

Paragraph 1
(may be more than one paragraph)
- Presents the writer's subject and thesis (main idea and point of view)
- Sparks the readers' interest

Body

Paragraph 2

Paragraph 3
- Explains and supports the thesis with details; further develops ideas
- Presents the supporting details in a clear sequence

Paragraph 4
(or more)

Conclusion

Paragraph 5
(may be more than one paragraph)
- Reemphasizes the thesis and reflects on the larger significance of the topic
- Draws the essay to a satisfying close

1 The Introduction

An effective introduction captures your readers' interest and gives them a sense of your topic and purpose. There are many ways to write an introduction, depending on your subject, audience, and intent. The opening paragraph, however, is always an essential component of any writing, since it is the first thing your readers will see and will often determine whether they continue reading.

Thesis Statement

A *thesis statement* expresses the main idea in an essay and the writer's point of view. This statement is usually one sentence long and consists of two parts. In the first part, the writer states the topic of the essay and, in the second part, the writer makes a point about the topic. In much college writing, students are expected to include a thesis statement in their introduction and to support the thesis in the body of the essay. By placing this statement of the main idea and purpose in the introduction, usually at the end, the writer indicates to the reader what to focus on and what to expect in the rest of the essay.

When writing a thesis statement, try to express a point of view or take a stand on an issue rather than merely state a fact. Be as specific as possible; limit the topic to make it manageable in the space allowed. A thesis that is overly general is not effective.

Following are three examples of thesis statements. Notice how the first part of each statement identifies the topic and the second part expresses the writer's position or focus.

- The advantages of living in a new culture far exceed the disadvantages.

- The most effective way to reduce discrimination is to teach young children to be open-minded and tolerant of differences.

- The study of cultural differences in verbal communication style involves three main types of expression: direct vs. indirect, formal vs. informal, and logical vs. emotional.

The Most Common Type of Introduction

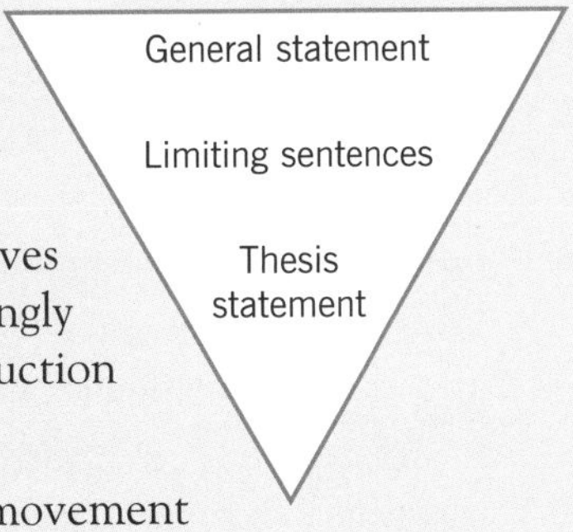

There are many ways to introduce a topic. The most common type of introduction starts with a general statement about the subject, clarifies or limits the topic in one or more sentences, and then states the thesis of the essay in the final sentence. As the introduction moves from general to specific, the sentences become increasingly focused on the topic. You might picture such an introduction as shaped like a funnel or an inverted triangle.

Figure 1.2 Introduction

General statement

Limiting sentences

Thesis statement

Following is an example of an introduction where the movement is from general to specific.

The ways in which people communicate differ significantly around the world. What people say, how they say it, and what they mean when they say it depend on the standards and customs of their society. People in some cultures, for example, tend to say things directly, whereas those in other cultures speak indirectly. Some cultures value formal means of communication, while other societies prefer the informal; some cultures stress emotional expression, and others emphasize logical expression. These variations in the forms and functions of verbal communication, reflecting culturally learned values, often lead to intercultural conflict and misunderstanding.

general statement

limiting sentences

thesis statement

Ways to Capture Your Readers' Interest

One of the most important functions of an introduction is to capture your readers' interest. The following is a list of possible ways to achieve this. You can use one or more of these strategies in your introduction. Experiment; try out different techniques. The most suitable will depend on your particular topic, audience, and purpose.

1 Ask a provocative question or short series of related questions.
2 Use an engaging quotation.
3 Make an unexpected or controversial statement.
4 State a common belief and then declare a contrary view.
5 Offer a striking example or description of something.
6 Provide an unusual fact or statistic.
7 Tell a brief story or anecdote, perhaps involving a personal experience.
8 Pose a hypothetical situation.
9 Define an important term.
10 Make an interesting analogy – a comparison between two things of a different kind or quality.

What to Avoid in an Introduction

Inexperienced writers often have difficulty creating effective introductions. The following is a list of things that you should avoid in your introduction.

1 **Don't blatantly announce your intent.** Avoid such statements as "In this essay, I will analyze . . ." and "The intent of this essay is to . . ." Simply state your thesis and purpose, without such prefatory comments. (See the thesis statement in the introductory paragraph on page 105.)
2 **Don't apologize.** Avoid statements such as "I am not an expert in this subject, but I will try my best to . . ." Apologizing starts the essay on a weak note.
3 **Don't make a promise that you don't fulfill in the essay.** Unfulfilled promises are often annoying and confusing.
4 **Don't create an introduction that is too long or too short.** A very long introduction for a short essay will probably feel out of balance. A very short introduction for a long essay might also seem unbalanced.

Writing Introductions: *The Essentials*

- Give a sense, in one or two paragraphs, of your subject and the aspect of it you are focusing on.
- Provide an overview of the topic and any background information that will help the reader understand your purpose.
- Include a thesis statement, or sentence expressing the main idea of the essay and your point of view.

- Attract the attention of your readers.
- Establish your tone, or attitude toward the topic – for example, formal, confident, playful, or angry.

2 Body Paragraphs

In the body, or central part, of the essay, you present and develop your main points. Each of the body paragraphs explains, clarifies, or illustrates the thesis in some way. Each body paragraph focuses on one main point – either a previous point that you want to explore further or a new point supporting the thesis.

Topic Sentences

Every paragraph in an essay has a main idea – the central point about the topic that the writer wants the reader to understand. Often the writer will include a sentence that clearly states the main idea of the paragraph. This sentence is called the *topic sentence*. It usually appears at the beginning of the paragraph but can be in the middle or at the end. The other sentences in the paragraph develop the main idea expressed in the topic sentence. The topic sentence of each body paragraph supports the thesis of the essay.

Not every paragraph will have a topic sentence. Sometimes a writer omits a direct statement and implies, or suggests, the main idea through details. In college writing, however, instructors will often expect students to include a topic sentence in each paragraph to help focus their ideas. It is, therefore, probably best if you formulate a topic sentence in your body paragraphs, at least until you become an accomplished writer.

Look at the following example of a topic sentence from the opening reading in this book. Here you will see that the topic sentence is stated directly and is followed by the supporting details.

> The premium Americans place on *efficiency* is closely related to their concepts of the future, change, and time. To do something efficiently is to do it in the way that is quickest and requires the smallest expenditure of resources. . . . American businesses sometimes hire "efficiency experts" to review their operations and to suggest ways in which they could accomplish more with the resources they are investing. Popular magazines offer suggestions for more efficient ways to shop, cook, clean house, do errands, raise children, tend the yard, and on and on. . . . (Althen, pages 10–11, par. 33)

topic sentence

supporting details

Characteristics of Body Paragraphs

Each paragraph in the body of an essay should be clearly expressed; well unified, developed, and organized; and coherent. Body paragraphs, in other words, should have the following characteristics.

1 **Clarity.** The main point and supporting details of the paragraph are clear.

2 **Unity.** All the sentences clearly relate to the main idea of the paragraph and support the topic sentence.

3 **Development.** The paragraph provides sufficient detail, including examples, facts, statistics, reasons, anecdotes, quotations, and definitions, to explain or support the main idea.

4 **Organization.** The ideas and supporting details have a logical pattern of arrangement, such as time, space, or emphasis (for example, from most to least important, from least to most important, or from simplest to most complex).

5 **Coherence.** The sentences are logically connected to each other, and the ideas flow smoothly.

What to Avoid in Body Paragraphs

Inexperienced writers often have difficulty creating body paragraphs. The following is a list of what to avoid in your body paragraphs.

1 **Don't write paragraphs that are overly long or short.** Consider developing a very short paragraph or dividing a very long paragraph into two.

2 **Don't include more than one main idea in each paragraph.** Multiple ideas weaken your focus and often confuse your readers.

3 **Don't include general statements that are not supported with specific detail.** Unsupported generalizations result in abstract and unconvincing writing.

4 **Don't repeat ideas or details unnecessarily in a paragraph.** Unnecessary repetition is annoying and distracting.

Writing Body Paragraphs: *The Essentials*

- Include a topic sentence, which states the main idea of the paragraph and supports the thesis of the essay. If you choose not to include a direct topic sentence, make sure that the main idea of the paragraph is implied through the supporting details.
- Explain or support the topic sentence with details, including examples, facts, statistics, quotations, and anecdotes.
- Arrange the supporting details in a clear sequence, such as time, space, or emphasis.
- Make a new point or expand on a point made in the previous paragraph.
- Be sure that each paragraph is clear, unified, well developed, organized, and coherent.

3 The Conclusion

An effective conclusion reemphasizes the importance of your thesis, reflects on the larger significance of your topic, and brings the essay to a logical and satisfying close.

The Most Common Type of Conclusion

Whereas an introduction typically moves from the general to the specific and can thus be diagrammed as an inverted triangle (see page 105), a conclusion usually proceeds from the specific to the general and can be visually represented by a regular triangle with the broad base at the bottom. Sometimes (as in Figure 1.3) writers summarize their main point at the beginning of the conclusion and then present their major deduction and make a final statement, such as a prediction, recommendation, or quotation. At other times, writers leave out the opening summary and start right in with their deduction, followed by a final statement. In either case, an effective conclusion looks back to the essay, echoing the main point; and looks forward, directing your readers' attention to future areas of exploration.

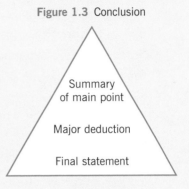

Figure 1.3 Conclusion

Summary of main point

Major deduction

Final statement

The following is an example of a conclusion in which the writer summarizes the main point at the beginning and then presents the deduction and final statement. You can read the introduction to the essay that includes this conclusion on page 105. (For an example of another conclusion with the same three-part structure, see the revised conclusion in the section Revising on page 120.)

> The forms and functions of verbal communication vary significantly around the world and reflect striking differences in values and beliefs. These culturally learned patterns usually function on a highly unconscious level and can result in serious conflict, misunderstanding, and negative stereotyping when people from different cultures interact. *— summary of main point*
>
> To minimize such tensions and problems and to enhance intercultural communication, international travelers should be aware of their own speaking style and the ways it differs from that of the culture they are visiting. *— major deduction*
>
> By increasing their knowledge of what people in the host country tend to say and how they tend to say it, international visitors will be able to traverse the minefield of cultural differences and adjust to the new environment more easily. *— final statement*

Ways to Conclude an Essay

Whatever type of ending you choose, the conclusion is an essential element of any writing, since it is the last part of your work that the readers will see. Think carefully about the impression with which you wish to leave your audience. The following is a list of ways you can effectively end an essay.

1 Summarize the main point of the essay.

2 Discuss the broader implications of your topic and encourage your readers to consider your topic from a new perspective.

3 Make a prediction.

4 Offer a recommendation or a suggested course of action.

5 Use an engaging quotation that reinforces your main point.

6 Ask a provocative question or short series of related questions.

7 End with a brief anecdote that reflects your main point.

8 State your personal opinion or position on the topic.

9 Invite your readers to relate the topic to their own lives.

10 Return to the beginning. Refer to an anecdote, quotation, analogy, question, or example that appears in the introduction or other early part of the essay.

What to Avoid in a Conclusion

Inexperienced writers often have difficulty creating a conclusion because they either repeat word for word ideas in the body of the essay or they end abruptly. The following is a list of what to avoid when writing a conclusion.

1 **Don't simply repeat or restate your thesis.** It is usually more effective to leave your readers with one or two provocative thoughts to ponder than with merely a summary of your main point.

2 **Don't introduce a new idea that needs further development.** The insertion of a totally new idea will lead your audience to wonder why that point wasn't developed in the body of the essay.

3 **Don't announce what you have done.** Avoid statements like "In this essay I have tried to show . . ." Such announcements may sound mechanical.

4 **Don't apologize.** Avoid statements such as "I may not have considered every argument, but . . ." Apologies weaken the impact of your ending.

5 **Don't create a conclusion that is too long or too short.** A very long conclusion for a short essay will probably feel out of balance. A very short conclusion for a long essay might also seem unbalanced.

6 **Don't end in an abrupt manner.** Your conclusion should flow smoothly from the rest of the essay and not come to a sudden stop.

Writing Conclusions: *The Essentials*

■ Reinforce, in one or two paragraphs, the importance of your topic and bring the essay to a logical and satisfying close.

■ Reflect on the broader implications of your topic.

■ Encourage your readers to think about the topic in a fresh way.

■ Think about the tone with which you want to end the essay – for example, optimistic, assertive, intimate, or cautionary.

PART TWO

The Writing Process

Experienced writers do not approach the task of writing in a simple, linear manner. Writing is a whole process of discovering ideas, developing and organizing them, and revising material to achieve the best effect. Writers do not wave a magic wand and create a polished composition out of thin air. Good writing takes time and practice.

No two people write in the same way. Some like to outline their ideas before writing about them; others don't. Some write their introduction first, some at the end. Some revise their writing as they go along, some at a later point. Not all authors follow the same method, and individual authors often write in different ways for different purposes. Every writer must discover the approach that works best on any particular occasion. Still, most experienced writers find that they pass through the following stages while composing an essay, research paper, or other formal writing assignment.

1 **Assessing the writing situation:** reflecting on the subject, one's attitude toward the subject, purpose, audience, sources of available information, and the writing assignment

2 **Exploring and planning:** discovering, refining, finding support for, and organizing ideas

3 **Drafting:** expressing and developing ideas and supporting details in rough form

4 **Revising:** rethinking and rewriting drafts to improve the content, focus, and structure

5 **Editing and proofreading:** checking for effective word choice and sentence structure and for correct grammar, spelling, punctuation, and mechanics

Figure 2.1
The Writing Process

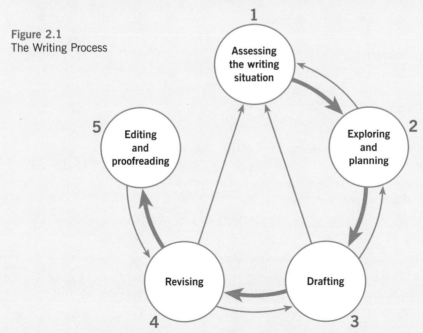

As Figure 2.1 shows, the five stages of the writing process overlap; that is, writers go back and forth, assessing the writing situation and planning, drafting, and revising material. Assessing the writing situation is not over when planning begins; planning is not over when drafting begins; drafting is not over when revision begins; and revision is not necessarily over when editing begins.

1 Assessing the Writing Situation

For any writing assignment, especially essays and research papers, you will have several choices to make, depending on the writing situation you face. The central elements of the writing situation include your subject, attitude toward the subject, purpose, audience, sources of available information, and the writing assignment. Reflecting briefly on these broad areas before you start writing can help clarify your ideas and shape the content, organization, and style of your text. Of course, you will not be able to answer all of the questions in the checklist below when you start because some of the issues become clear only later in the writing process. Yet thinking about these elements in advance will help you draft your paper and save time later.

Checklist for Assessing the Writing Situation

1 **Subject**
   - ☐ Is your subject interesting and important to you? Will it be interesting to your readers?
   - ☐ Is your topic too broad or too narrow? Is it focused enough for you to do justice to it in the time and space allowed?

2 **Writer's attitude toward the subject**
   - ☐ What is your overall attitude toward the subject? Is it positive? Negative? Curious? Indifferent?
   - ☐ What questions do you have about the subject, and what types of conclusions do you think you will reach? Do you have any preconceptions about the topic?

3 **Purpose**
   - ☐ What is your main purpose in writing the essay? Is your goal to provide information or to explain something; to persuade your readers to believe something or to take a certain course of action; to entertain the readers; or some combination of the three?
   - ☐ What do you want your audience to think or feel after reading the essay?

4 **Audience**
   - ☐ Who is going to read your essay, and what is your relationship to your audience? Is the relationship student to instructor; expert to novice; or citizen to citizen? What attitude will you take toward your readers, for example, formal, informal, sarcastic, angry, or confident?

☐ What are your readers likely to know about your topic already, and what might they want or need to know?

5 **Sources of available information**

☐ What type of evidence will you use to support and illustrate your points: personal experience, direct observation, interviews, questionnaires, library, or Internet research?

☐ How will you evaluate the usefulness of your sources?

6 **Writing assignment**

☐ What specifically does the assignment ask you to do? What are the instructor's goals and expectations? Do you see key words such as *analyze, synthesize, evaluate, interpret, argue, discuss, explain, compare, contrast, classify, define, summarize*?

☐ Can you limit or broaden the assignment or the topic to make it more interesting?

2 Exploring and Planning

After assessing the writing situation and before starting your first draft, experiment with one or more of the following prewriting strategies. These strategies can help you to discover ideas, determine which aspect of a subject will be your focus, and find details to support your points.

Prewriting is an important stage in the writing process. Don't shut off this exploratory stage too early and rush into drafting your essay.

Brainstorming

To help them discover ideas and the relationships among them, many writers *brainstorm* a topic – they make a list of everything that comes to mind when they think about a subject and then group the items in the list.

The following is an example of a brainstormed list on the topic of culture shock. In the first list, ideas are in random order. In the second, ideas are grouped into categories, and an asterisk appears next to the items that the writer finds most interesting or important.

Culture shock (*random list*)
- homesick, lonely
- symptoms: physical (insomnia, upset stomach) and emotional (boredom, tension, depression)
- language difficulty
- different values, customs, and expectations: religion, education, food, family
- criticizing the new culture
- daily problems: finances, finding an apartment, work, school, making friends

Culture shock (*grouped list*)

1. Causes of culture shock
   - homesick, lonely
   - language difficulty
   - *different values, customs, and expectations: religion, education, food, family
   - *daily problems: finances, finding an apartment, work, school, making friends
2. Effects of culture shock
   - *symptoms: physical (insomnia, upset stomach) and emotional (boredom, tension, depression)
   - criticizing the new culture

Brainstorming: *The Essentials*

- Write a list of everything you can think of – ideas, impressions, experiences, examples, facts, and associations – related to a particular topic.
- Don't be concerned about the order of ideas or how important they seem. Use words and phrases, rather than sentences, to create your list.
- Read through your list and look for patterns. Try to make connections among items by grouping them into categories.
- Put an asterisk (*) next to the ideas that seem the most interesting or important.
- After brainstorming your topic, explore it further by using one of the other prewriting strategies.

Freewriting

One of the best ways to generate ideas for an essay is to *freewrite*. When you freewrite, you write nonstop for a certain amount of time, usually five to ten minutes, about anything that comes to mind when you think about a subject.

The following is an example of the use of freewriting to explore the topic of culture shock.

When I think of culture shock, I imagine a roller coaster ride – up and down, faster and slower, going around and around. Sometimes I feel this way – one moment happy and excited and the next lonely and depressed. Some of my friends have told me they feel the same way too. I thought I was the only one. It makes me feel better to know that other people are having the same problems. Culture shock. Culture shock. I think of a flower in a small pot that's placed in a bigger one. I come from a small town of 30,000 people, and now I'm living in a big city of 2 million. I'm a little flower in a big pot.

Freewriting: *The Essentials*

- Write down your ideas in whatever manner and order they come. Don't worry about complete sentences, grammar, spelling, or punctuation.
- Continue writing for the entire amount of time; don't stop at all. If you can't think of anything to say, just keep repeating a word or writing something like "I'm sure I have more ideas." Usually while you're doing this, another idea will come, and you'll be able to continue.
- When your time is up, read what you've written and underline an idea that you'd like to pursue. Then freewrite on this idea or use one of the other prewriting strategies to explore the idea further.

Clustering

Like freewriting and brainstorming, *clustering* is a means of rapidly generating ideas and discovering relationships among them. Unlike the first two exploratory techniques, though, clustering provides a sketch or visual map of the connections among ideas and details. Many writers find that this process of graphically exploring a subject helps them think more creatively and associate ideas more freely.

The following is an example of the use of clustering to explore the topic of culture shock.

Figure 2.2 An Example of a Clustering Diagram

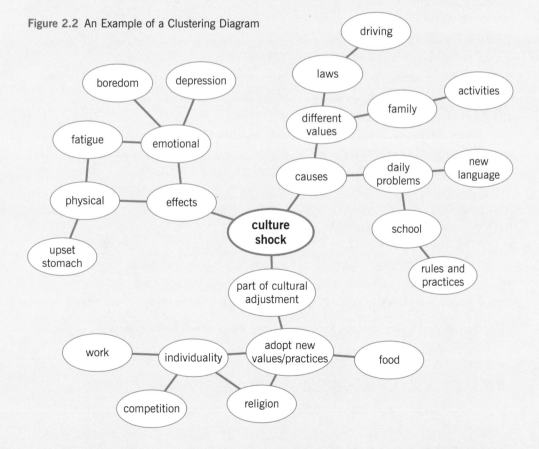

Clustering: *The Essentials*

- Write your topic in the middle of an unlined sheet of paper and draw a circle around it.
- Draw a line from your topic to an idea suggested by it and circle this idea.
- Continue associating to further ideas, details, and experiences. Circle each item and draw a line back to the idea that suggested it and to other related ideas.
- When you finish with one major division, or branch, of your topic, return to the center and start again with another idea. Repeat the process until you run out of ideas.
- When you are done, look over your diagram and decide which chains of ideas seem the most intriguing. Consider analyzing these ideas further by using one of the other prewriting strategies.

The Journalist's Questions

To view a topic from different perspectives, many writers ask the questions journalists use when reporting an event: *who, what, when, where, why,* and *how.*

The following is an example of the use of the journalist's questions to explore the topic of culture shock.

1 Who experiences culture shock?
   - people living in a new culture with different values, beliefs, and behaviors
2 What is culture shock?
   - emotional disorientation that results from living in a new culture
3 When does culture shock occur?
   - after an initial stage of excitement about being in a new culture
4 Where does culture shock occur?
   - in a foreign country or in a part of your own country that is culturally different from where you grew up
5 Why does culture shock occur?
   - feelings of being cut off from your own country, family, friends, language, and customs
6 How does culture shock affect people?
   - emotionally (homesickness, frustration, anger) and physically (upset stomach, disrupted sleep)

The Journalist's Questions: *The Essentials*

- When asking the questions journalists use, think of as many questions as you can about your topic.
- Don't stop until you have considered all six perspectives.
- After you have written the questions, answer each one using brief notes.

Outlining

Outlining is one of the most frequent techniques writers use to discover ideas and the relationships among them. An outline is a list of a writer's main points in the order they will appear in an essay or other written work. Usually the *thesis statement* – a sentence stating the writer's main idea and point of view – and major supporting details for each point are also included. Many writers find that outlines are very helpful in clarifying and organizing their ideas.

There are two types of outlines: informal and formal. An *informal outline* is a brief list of the main points in an essay in the order they will appear and the major supporting details. It is usually written in phrases, not complete sentences. A *formal outline* is generally more detailed than an informal one and has a specific pattern of presentation. Most writers use an informal outline to help organize their ideas.

The following is an informal outline of an essay about culture shock. (For an example of a formal outline, refer to a writing style manual.)

Informal Outline

Thesis: *There are ways to minimize the effects of culture shock and to turn a potentially negative experience into a positive one.*

1. Definition of culture shock
   * psychological disorientation that results from living in a new culture
   * emotional symptoms: angry, homesick, frustrated
   * physical symptoms: upset stomach, too much or too little sleep
2. Causes of culture shock
   * cut off from one's own culture, family, friends, language
   * exposure to different values, beliefs, customs: education, religion, gender roles
3. Ways to minimize culture shock
   * learn about the new culture before and after arrival
   * improve language skills

Outlining: *The Essentials*

■ Write a thesis statement at the top of the outline.
■ Create a list of the major points you intend to make in the essay, in the order they will appear.
■ Under each point, write the main detail(s) you will use to support it, including examples, statistics, anecdotes, quotations, and/or definitions.
■ You may choose to write the outline in complete sentences or you may use words and phrases, whichever you prefer.

Keeping a Journal

To help generate ideas and explore relationships among them, many writers keep a journal – a notebook in which you record your ideas and reactions to various issues.

The following is an example of a journal entry by Yoshi, a student from Japan, in response to the essay "Polite but Thirsty" in Chapter 1.

> In the essay "Polite but Thirsty," Yaping Tang says that "Americans are very direct. When they want something, they say 'yes,' and when they don't, they say 'no.'" I had a similar experience revising my essay. I had to rewrite a lot of things because of the differences between the style of an American essay and the style of a Japanese essay. Japanese don't write essays clearly compared to Americans, such as this is the introduction, this is the main point, this is the conclusion, this is this, this is that. In a Japanese essay, much effort is required to create the proper atmosphere, and this also requires the reader's effort to make his own interpretations. The plain, outspoken essay is the worst type in Japan; no Japanese would enjoy reading an essay like that. But now I understand the way of writing an American essay a little bit. I can write a better one next time.

Keeping a Journal: *The Essentials*

- Write in your journal as often as you can, ideally, every day.
- Write freely and informally, without worrying about grammar, spelling, and punctuation. Try, however, to express your ideas in complete sentences and paragraphs.
- Consider the following possibilities for journal entries:
  - Reflect on personal experiences, observations, feelings, and opinions about issues, events, and readings.
  - Discuss what you like or dislike about an issue or reading, what you agree or disagree with, or what you find clear or unclear.
  - Explore relationships among people, issues, or readings, commenting on similarities and differences.
  - Reflect on your own writing process, including strengths, weaknesses, challenges, and strategies.

3 Drafting

When you write a first draft of an essay or research paper, either on paper or on the computer, you express your ideas in rough form without worrying too much about what is correct, appropriate, or relevant. Your aim in this stage is not to produce a perfect composition but to get down, in full sentences and paragraphs, your main ideas and supporting details, realizing that you will later revise them. As a result, your first, or rough, draft will often have many mistakes in grammar, spelling, punctuation, and mechanics and include many ideas and details you will later change. Your goal, at this point, is to discover and express meaning, to find connections among ideas, and to seek an effective structure for what you want to say.

Drafting: *The Essentials*

- As you write your first draft, keep your exploring and planning materials – including outlines, diagrams, and lists – nearby so that you can easily refer to them. If you find, however, that your initial organizational plan doesn't seem to work, try another one. If you have a new idea, write it down and don't be overly concerned with where it goes or whether it fits with the other ideas. You can work on this later.
- Start by writing an introduction in which you present your subject and thesis statement, or sentence stating your main idea and point of view. If you have problems, move on to the body, or middle, of the essay and return to the introduction later. (See the section The Introduction on page 104.)
- Next, write the body paragraphs, in which you present your major points and the details that will support or illustrate them, including examples, facts, quotations, and/or personal experiences. (See the section Body Paragraphs on page 107.)
- Finally, write a conclusion, in which you reflect on your topic and bring the essay to a logical close. If you're not sure what to write at this point, you can return to the conclusion later. (See the section The Conclusion on page 109.)

4 Revising

After drafting the first version of their essay, most experienced writers revise their work several times, to sharpen their focus and to show more clearly how each of the main points supports the thesis. Revision means much more than correcting grammar, spelling, punctuation, and mechanics. It involves a whole process of "re-vision," or seeing again – rethinking and reshaping the content and structure of a draft to improve it at all levels: word, sentence, paragraph, and essay. To revise an essay, a writer adds, deletes, rearranges, and rewords material.

The following is an example of an original conclusion in an essay by a South Korean student, Dalkyun Im, and the revised version of the paragraph. The topic of the essay is cultural differences in verbal communication style. In the revision, notice how Dalkyun has developed the middle part of his conclusion in order to discuss his major deduction in greater depth, created a more personal tone, and added a final statement for greater impact.

Original Conclusion

There are so many people from other countries in America and there are so many international students at Berklee College of Music. I have experienced cross-cultural communication with students from many different countries.

Through this process of cross-cultural communication, I believe that we can learn a lot of things beyond language. We can get to understand the unfamiliar culture, and we can have a deeper understanding of our own culture. Of course, this requires a great effort.

Revised Conclusion

There are so many people from different countries in America and so many international students at Berklee College of Music. I have often spoken with these students, and sometimes this cross-cultural communication has led to misunderstandings. However, today I experience less stress and fewer language problems than I did during my first year in this country. I have become more aware of the cultural values and patterns reflected in language differences, and this has helped me to learn the language better and to avoid problems. Through the process of cross-cultural communication, I believe that we can learn a lot of things beyond language. We can come to understand the unfamiliar culture better and also have a deeper understanding of our own culture. Of course, this requires a great deal of effort, but no one ever said that cross-cultural communication was easy!

There are many factors to take into account when revising an essay. It is, therefore, a good idea to use a revision checklist to help you evaluate and revise your writing. Answer the questions in the following checklist when you revise your work.

Revision Checklist

1 **Content**
   ☐ Do I need to add, delete, rearrange, or reword any material?
   ☐ Do I omit any important points or repeat any material unnecessarily?

2 **Audience**
   ☐ Have I taken into account the expectations, interests, and needs of my readers?
   ☐ Are my topic, purpose, and tone appropriate for this particular audience?

3 **Purpose**
   ☐ Is my purpose clear, for example, to inform, persuade, or entertain?
   ☐ Do I want my audience to think or act in a certain way after reading the essay? If so, have I accomplished my purpose?

4 **Tone**
   ☐ Is the tone of the essay appropriate for my topic, audience, and purpose?
   ☐ Is the tone consistent throughout the essay? If not, are the variations intentional?

5 **Title**
   ☐ Do I have an effective title that states or suggests my topic and sparks the readers' interest?
   ☐ Is the title vague, obscure, or inappropriate?

6 **Clarity**
   ☐ Is the thesis, or main idea, clear?
   ☐ Are all of my points and supporting details clear?

7 **Unity**
- ☐ Do all of the sentences in each paragraph clearly relate to the main idea of the paragraph?
- ☐ Do all of the paragraphs clearly support the thesis of the essay?

8 **Coherence**
- ☐ Are all of the sentences, paragraphs, and larger divisions of my essay logically connected?
- ☐ Are there smooth transitions among paragraphs, and do these connections help to develop my points?

9 **Development**
- ☐ Do I support my thesis and main points with sufficient detail, such as examples, facts, statistics, reasons, anecdotes, quotations, and definitions?
- ☐ Does each body paragraph explain, clarify, or illustrate the thesis and make a new point or expand on a point already made?

10 **Organization**
- ☐ Does the introduction give my readers a sense of the topic and engage their interest?
- ☐ Do the body paragraphs and the essay as a whole have a logical pattern of organization? Should I rearrange any material?
- ☐ Does the conclusion explore the broader implications of my topic and bring the essay to a satisfying close?

Revising: *The Essentials*

- Leave enough time to revise your essay. Few writers produce polished first drafts of their essays; they usually need to make significant changes. Don't cut short this important stage of the writing process.
- Ask someone to read your essay and to respond to any aspect of the content, organization, or development. Encourage your reader to ask questions and to tell you if anything is unclear.
- Read your rough draft aloud. As you do so, you may notice ideas that are not clearly stated or are not adequately supported by details.
- Start with large revisions – those dealing with content, organization, and development – and later focus on sentence-level changes, including words and phrases.
- Keep revising your essay until you are satisfied with the content, clarity, unity, coherence, development, and organization.

5 Editing and Proofreading

When you feel that the revised draft of your essay has suitable content, clarity, unity, coherence, development, and organization, you are ready for the final stage of the writing process: editing and proofreading. Editing involves looking closely at individual sentences for technical correctness – grammar, spelling, punctuation, mechanics – and effective structure and word choice. Proofreading involves reading the final draft of the essay for any typing errors. Some writers like to combine the revising and editing stages of writing; others prefer to keep them separate.

Your point in editing the revised draft is not to produce a "perfect" essay but to make your meaning clearer and your language more forceful. Making mistakes is a natural part of learning how to write well. However, even the most engaging essay will lose force if your readers are distracted and annoyed by incorrect grammar, misspelled words, misleading punctuation, and repetitious language.

The following is the original introductory paragraph from the essay mentioned on page 119 by Dalkyun Im and the revised version with the editorial changes he has made to individual words and sentences. In the revision, notice how Dalkyun has clarified the meaning of certain sentences; eliminated redundancy (unnecessary repetition) whenever possible; combined two sentences to make the style smoother; and corrected mistakes in grammar, spelling, and punctuation.

Original Introduction

There are hundreds of countries in the world, and also hundreds of languages. Some of them have a very similar structure and vocablary. Some languages are totally different from other ones. It is said that the language reflect the thought process of people who use it, and is the accumulation of thoughts, cultures, and habits. This aspect of culture result in a lot of differences in language; for instance the different order of vocablary and different concept of adjectives. Sometime this result in problems in communication and sometime it just represents a difference. So people from different countries that has a very different culture and different language tends to encounter problem in communicating, although one has been trained to use the language for a long time.

Edited Introduction

There are almost two hundred countries in the world and also hundreds of languages. Some of these languages have a similar structure and vocablary, and others don't. It is often said that a language reflects the thought process of the people who use it and the values, expectations, and habits of the culture. Differences in cultural patterns result in many differences in language; for instance, the word order and the concept of adjectives. Sometimes these language variations lead to problems in communication, and other times they don't. In general, people from countries that have a very different culture and language tend to encounter problems in communicating, even if they have been trained for a long time to use the new language.

Use the following checklist of questions to help you edit the revised draft of your essay.

Editing Checklist

1 Word choice

☐ Do I use the most accurate, effective words to convey my meaning?

☐ Do I avoid redundancy by not using two or three words when one would be enough (for example, *green*, not *green in color*)?

2 Sentence structure

☐ Do I avoid sentence fragments and run-on sentences?

☐ Do I vary the sentence structure and length? Can I make a very long sentence into two shorter ones? Can two short sentences be combined?

3 Grammar

☐ Is the grammar correct? Are all the sentences grammatically complete?

☐ Is my use of parts of speech (nouns, verbs, adjectives, adverbs, pronouns, articles, prepositions, conjunctions) and word order correct?

4 Usage

☐ Do I spell all words correctly and use proper punctuation, including periods, commas, semicolons, colons, quotation marks, and apostrophes?

☐ Do I use capital letters, hyphens, italics, abbreviations, and paragraph indentation correctly?

5 Citation of sources

☐ If I have taken ideas and information from sources through summary, paraphrase, or quotation, have I cited, or given credit to, these sources? (See the section Documenting Sources on pages 128–131.)

☐ Have I been careful not to plagiarize any material – that is, to present someone else's work as my own – through proper source citation? (See the section Avoiding Plagiarism on page 132.)

6 Essay format

☐ Have I followed any formatting requirements for the essay by using a specified typeface and type size, line spacing, margins, and page numbering?

Editing and Proofreading: *The Essentials*

■ After finishing your revisions, allow some time before the final editing and proofreading step. Briefly setting aside your work will help you to examine your writing more objectively and to detect mistakes.

■ Leave enough time to edit and proofread your essay. This is an important stage in the writing process.

■ Strengthen individual sentences wherever possible, focusing on structure, grammar, word choice, spelling, punctuation, and mechanics. Concentrate on changes that will make your meaning clear, concise, and engaging.

■ Read your final draft aloud and at a slow rate. As you do so, you can more readily check that the sentences flow smoothly, and you can spot mistakes, including omitted words.

PART THREE

Writing with Sources

Some college writing assignments are based solely on your personal knowledge and experience. Others require some type of research. In these kinds of assignments, you will have to analyze and synthesize several sources of information and draw conclusions that are supported by convincing and well-documented evidence.

The amount and type of source material you will use depends on your topic, audience, and purpose; there is no magic number of sources to include. Try not to use too much or too little source material or to rely excessively on any one source. Also be careful that your final paper is not simply a collection of summaries, paraphrases, and quotations of material conceived by others. Choose carefully the sources that will best help you make your points, and be sure that your own voice, or perspective, is present throughout the paper.

When integrating a source into a paper through summary, paraphrase, or quotation, precede or follow it with an explanation of its relevance to your argument or an interpretation of its meaning. Do not refer to a source without some commentary of your own, and make sure that your commentary doesn't simply echo the source. A source should not substitute for a point you are making; it should help convey and support a point.

There are many good reasons for including references to source material in your college writing assignments:

1 They give background information to help the readers understand your ideas.
2 They provide examples and other details to support a point you are making or to counter an argument.
3 They enhance your credibility by providing evidence from specialists in your subject area, demonstrating that you are aware of previous thinking about your topic.
4 They indicate to your reader where to find further information about your subject.

1 Types of Sources

Sources are either primary or secondary. *Primary sources* are firsthand, or original materials, including eyewitness accounts of events, historical documents, diaries, letters, speeches, TV shows, movies, photographs, literary works (novels, stories, poems, plays), and original research, such as interviews, surveys, and reports of experiments. *Secondary sources* include materials – such as books, journal articles, encyclopedia entries, and reviews of books and films – that describe, analyze, or comment on primary sources. Depending on the kind of research you are doing, you will sometimes use only primary sources, sometimes only secondary sources, but most often, you will use a combination of the two. The following sources may be primary or secondary, depending on their content.

1 **Print sources:** books and periodicals (professional journals, popular magazines, newspapers)
2 **Electronic sources:** Internet and CD-ROM
3 **Media sources:** television, radio, film, sound recordings
4 **Graphic sources:** drawings, photographs, maps, cartoons, tables, graphs, charts
5 **Field sources:** interviews, surveys, and personal observation

2 Locating Sources

The two main places to find primary and secondary sources are libraries and the Internet.

Library Sources

University and public libraries are excellent places to start your research; they contain extensive collections of print, electronic, media, graphic, and field sources in various disciplines. Before starting your research, familiarize yourself with the resources of the library by looking at its Web site, speaking with a reference librarian, or taking a tour of the facility. You'll learn how to use the library's electronic catalog and databases (online collections of information) and to locate relevant, reliable sources, including books; articles in newspapers, magazines, and academic journals; and videotapes.

Internet Sources

The Internet offers a wide range of multi-media sources for research. However, despite the wealth of information and primary sources that are available on the Internet, this type of research will not help you with all assignments. Historical analysis, literary criticism, scientific reports, and secondary sources of scholarly information and in-depth research, including books and articles, are often best found in a library or on its electronic databases, rather than on the Web.

The following list shows the main ways you can find sources on the Internet.

1 **World Wide Web:** a global network of online sites created by individuals, organizations, and government agencies that provide information in textual, graphic, audio, and video form
2 **E-mail:** an application that enables you to send requests for information to individuals and organizations; conduct interviews; transmit and receive files; and subscribe to online newspapers and magazines
3 **Listservs and newsgroups:** electronic discussions on a broad spectrum of topics

3 Evaluating Sources

You must carefully evaluate all primary and secondary sources you find in the library and on the Internet. Keep in mind that there is a deluge of information on the Web, much of it changing from one day to the next, and that most of the information is not assessed for quality and organization in the same way library sources are. Although you can find many excellent, reliable sources on the Web, you will also encounter plenty of inaccurate, incomplete, and biased information.

To help you evaluate the usefulness and credibility of library – and especially Internet – sources, here is a checklist of questions to consider.

Checklist for Evaluating Sources

1 **Relevance**
   - ☐ How closely related is the source to the focus of your topic?
   - ☐ Is the source too general or too specialized for the topic, purpose, or audience of your paper?

2 **Reliability**
   - ☐ How accurate, complete, and unbiased is the source information?
   - ☐ Does the source present opposing viewpoints and do so in a fair manner?

3 **Currency**
   - ☐ How recent is the information in the source, and is there any indication of how often the information is updated?
   - ☐ If you are using a relatively old source, is it still relevant to your research?

4 **Authorship**
   - ☐ Who is the author of the source, and what are his or her qualifications for writing about the subject?
   - ☐ Is the author associated with a special-interest group that might compromise his or her objectivity?

5 **Purpose and Audience**
   - ☐ What is the purpose of the source – to inform, persuade, or entertain the audience?
   - ☐ Who is the intended audience for the source, and what are the attitudes, expectations, and preconceptions of this group?

4 Taking Notes from Sources

While conducting your research, take good notes on any materials you might use in your paper, including notes on the content of the materials and on publication information about the sources. Effective note taking will help you integrate your sources into your paper and avoid plagiarizing material. (For a discussion of plagiarism, or using a source without giving appropriate credit, see page 132.)

Taking effective notes – on paper, index cards, or the computer – involves compiling a working bibliography, with complete publication information for each source (see the section Documenting Sources on pages 128–131); it also entails highlighting and annotating relevant material, writing summaries or paraphrases of passages, and transcribing quotations accurately.

Highlighting and Annotating Sources

To help with your note taking, make photocopies of print sources and printouts of electronic sources whenever possible. Then, on your copy of the source (never on the original!), highlight or underline the main ideas and key supporting details. You can use different colors to indicate main ideas or supporting details. Be selective in this process; don't highlight or underline excessively. Then, in the margins, annotate relevant passages by writing personal impressions, critical responses – including points of agreement and disagreement – and questions.

Taking Summary Notes

Much of your note taking will involve summarizing source material. A *summary* is a brief restatement, in your own words, of the main ideas of a reading passage or other type of source. For a paragraph in an article or a book, the restatement might be only a sentence; for a whole work, a paragraph. (See the discussion and examples of summarizing on pages 196 and 214.) Condensing information and ideas will help you to understand the content of the sources, convey your understanding to your audience, and establish the ideas you will explore in your paper.

When writing a summary, include only the author's ideas and not your own opinions and judgments. Also don't just copy statements from the original source and put them together. To summarize effectively, you need to restate the main ideas in your own words and to synthesize the material – to combine information and to group ideas in a way that shows the relationships among them.

Taking Paraphrase Notes

Paraphrasing a reading passage is similar to summarizing it: both involve restating someone else's ideas in your own words. But whereas a summary is a condensed version of the original, a *paraphrase* is a complete restatement, including all of the writer's main ideas and key supporting details. Thus a paraphrase is usually as long as, or longer than, the original. Your goal in paraphrasing a passage is to give your reader an accurate sense of its meaning, tone, and emphasis.

Like summarizing, paraphrasing information and ideas helps you to understand the content of a source, demonstrate your understanding to your audience, and establish the ideas you will explore in your paper. A paraphrase, however, is different from a summary in that it gives the reader a detailed account of the source material and not a brief overview. As a result, you will usually paraphrase relatively short passages and never an entire article. (See the discussion and examples of paraphrasing on page 197.)

Taking Quotation Notes

For certain types of research, you may wish to write down direct quotations (the exact words of a source) instead of summarizing or paraphrasing the material. A quotation can be used to introduce a passage that you will analyze, interpret, or comment on critically. It may also be helpful in presenting language that is vivid, striking, precise, or unique; which would be lost in a summary or paraphrase.

When you copy a quotation, do so carefully; use the same spelling, punctuation, and capitalization as in the original. Use quotation marks at the beginning and at the end of the original passage; ellipses (. . .) to indicate any words you omit; and brackets ([ ]) to add any necessary clarification.

> Studies of the nonverbal behavior patterns of the French show that ". . . they [the French] . . . can tolerate constant interruptions and . . . maintain direct eye contact. . . ." (Hall and Hall 88–89)

5 Documenting Sources

An essential part of researched writing is the careful documentation of all the sources you've used in composing your paper. The origin of all information, ideas, opinions, and judgments in your paper must be cited, or acknowledged, properly. Material you must cite includes any summary, paraphrase, or quotation; photograph, diagram, chart, or other work of art; video, DVD, or sound recording; statistic; survey; system of organization or structure; and anything else you take from any source other than your own knowledge. The only exception is common knowledge – information, such as a fact, that is well known or found in a number of sources. If you are uncertain about whether or not to acknowledge a source, it is better to be cautious and cite the material. It is wiser to document too much rather than too little and risk being guilty of plagiarism.

Keeping a Working Bibliography

One way to help you to keep track of the works that you cite in your paper is, while you are taking notes, to create a *working bibliography*; that is, a list of all the primary and secondary sources – including articles, books, and Web sites – that you might use for your paper. This initial bibliography will help you to organize your research and later to integrate your sources and prepare the list of works cited at the end of your paper. If you know ahead of time what the particular documentation style will be for your paper, you will save yourself time later by using this format for the working bibliography. (See the section Selecting a Documentation Style on the next page.)

While compiling your working bibliography, you should keep a careful record of the following information for books; articles from journals, magazines, and newspapers; and World Wide Web sites. (For Web sites, record as much of the information as is available.)

Figure 3.1 Information to Record in a Working Bibliography

Book	Article	Web Site
• Name of author(s) or editors(s) • Title of book • Place of publication • Name of publisher • Year of publication • Volume, edition, and translator's name, if relevant	• Name of author(s) • Title of article • Name of publication • Volume and issue number of publication • Date of publication • Page numbers on which article appears	• Name of author(s) • Title of document • Name of Web site • Date of publication or last update • Page, paragraph, or section number(s) • Editor or sponsoring organization of site • Date on which Web site was accessed • Full electronic address, or URL

Selecting a Documentation Style

Various academic disciplines use their own style of documentation to cite print and electronic sources within a paper, to list these sources at the end of the paper, and to write footnotes and endnotes. Although there are many documentation styles, the two most common are the MLA (Modern Language Association), used widely in the humanities, and the APA (American Psychological Association), used widely in the social sciences. Both MLA and APA style cite sources within the text of a paper in parentheses and list these sources alphabetically by the authors' last names at the end of the paper. Although the two styles differ in their documentation of source information, their purpose is the same: to let the audience know, in a complete and accurate manner, the origin of every quotation, paraphrase, or summary of source material a writer has used.

Following is a brief discussion of MLA and APA documentation style, with several examples of in-text citations and the entries for these citations in the list of sources at the end of the paper. If you have any questions about which documentation style to use or how to cite sources in either of these styles, ask your instructor or refer to a writing style manual.

MLA Documentation Style

MLA is an author-page system that cites a writer's sources parenthetically in the paper and includes the full publication information for each source at the end of the paper in a Works Cited list arranged alphabetically by the authors' last names.

For an example of sources documented in MLA style, see the article "Sex Roles" on pages 189–195.

MLA Citations in the Text

1 Author named in a signal phrase

Start with a signal phrase that mentions the author's last name. Also indicate the page number(s) in parentheses at the end of the citation. (Examples of signal phrases are "According to Johnson" and "Raemy indicates/maintains/claims/asserts/argues that . . .")

> Althen contends that people's communication style is "strongly influenced by cultural values, assumptions, and beliefs" (33).

2 Author named in parentheses

If you do not begin with a signal phrase that mentions the author, place the author's last name and the page number in parentheses at the end of the citation.

> There is a strong need for educational training that helps new teachers work in culturally diverse classrooms (Grisham 190).

3 World Wide Web sources

With online sources, it is often difficult to find all of the information you would use to cite a print source. Many Web sources, for example, lack a clear author and page numbers. Whenever possible, however, cite an online source in the same way you would a print source, using the author-page style. If a Web source does not have an individual author but is sponsored by an organization, use the organization's name as the author.

> HIV testing and counselling in populations at risk are essential in preventing transmission of the infection (World Health Organization 1).

MLA List of Works Cited

A Works Cited list at the end of your paper, arranged alphabetically by the authors' last names, includes the full publication information for each source cited in the text (see Figure 3.1 on page 129). Do not include any sources in your final list that aren't cited in the paper, even if you have read them.

Works Cited

Althen, Gary. *American Ways: A Guide for Foreigners in the United States.* 2nd ed. Yarmouth: Intercultural P, 2003.

Grisham, Dana L., et. al. "Connecting Communities of Practice Through Professional Development School Activities." *Journal of Teacher Education* 50.3 (1999): 182–191.

World Health Organization. "Testing and Counselling." 2004. 11 Nov. 2004 <http://www.who.int/hiv/topics/vct/testing/en/#why>.

APA Documentation Style

APA is an author-year system that cites a writer's sources parenthetically in the paper and includes the full publication information for each source at the end of the paper in a References list arranged alphabetically by the authors' last names. For an example of APA documentation style, see the article "Multiple Intelligences and Emotional Intelligence" on pages 77–82.

APA Citations in the Text

1 **Author named in a signal phrase**

Start with a signal phrase that mentions the author's last name and indicate the date, in parentheses, immediately after the author's name. For quoted material, place the page number in parentheses at the end of the quotation and precede it with "p.". Note that APA style requires the use of the past tense or the present perfect tense in signal phrases.

> Althen (2003) has contended that people's communication style is "strongly influenced by cultural values, assumptions, and beliefs" (p. 33).

2 **Author named in parentheses**

If you do not begin with a signal phrase that mentions the author, place the author's last name and the date in parentheses at the end of the citation. For a quotation, include the page number after the date.

> There is a strong need for educational training that helps new teachers work in culturally diverse classrooms (Grisham, 1999).

3 **World Wide Web sources**

Whenever possible, cite an online source in the same way you would a print source, using the author-year style. If a Web source does not have an individual author but is sponsored by an organization, use the organization's name as the author.

> HIV testing and counselling in populations at risk are essential in preventing transmission of the infection (World Health Orgranization, 2004).

APA List of References

A list of references at the end of your paper, arranged alphabetically by the authors' last names, includes the full publication information for each source cited in the text (see Figure 3.1 on page 129). Do not include any sources in your final list that aren't cited in the paper, even if you have read them.

When listing your sources in any documentation style, it is important to follow the exact use of underlining, italics, parentheses, abbreviations, periods, commas, colons, etc. If you compare the APA References list on the next page with the Works Cited list in MLA style on page 130, you will see several such differences in the two systems.

References

Althen, G. (2003). *American ways: A guide for foreigners in the United States* (2nd ed.). Yarmouth: Intercultural Press.

Grisham, D. L., et. al. (1999). Connecting communities of practice through professional development school activities. *Journal of Teacher Education, 50* (3), 182–191.

World Health Organization. (2004). Testing and counselling. Retrieved November 11, 2004, from http://www.who.int/hiv/topics/vct/testing/en/#why

Avoiding Plagiarism

When integrating source material into a paper, it is very easy to borrow too many ideas and too much language from the original, unintentionally committing *plagiarism* – the academic offense of using information from a source without giving proper credit to the author or other owner of the intellectual property. Plagiarism, intentional or unintentional, is a type of intellectual theft (presenting someone else's material as your own) and can have serious consequences ranging from failure on an assignment to expulsion from school.

If you have any questions about what plagiarism is and how to avoid it, you should consult your instructor or a librarian, or refer to a writing style manual. Meanwhile, if you follow the guidelines below, it will reduce the chance of your plagiarizing.

1 **Take accurate summary and paraphrase notes.** To be sure that your language is not too close to that of the original, change both the wording and the sentence structure. Use your own words whenever possible, and don't mix the author's language with your own unless you place the original material in quotation marks.

2 **Take accurate quotation notes.** Use quotation marks for all phrases and sentences you copy directly from a source. Be especially careful not to cut and paste any online material into your paper without putting it in quotation marks and fully citing the source.

3 **Document completely all summaries, paraphrases, and quotations of source material in your paper.** Acknowledge all ideas, information, visuals, and other materials taken from any print, electronic, or other source. (See the information required for accurate documentation in the section Keeping a Working Bibliography on pages 128–129.)

Mass Media and Technology

A WRITER'S TECHNIQUE
Figures of Speech

In this chapter, you will explore the content, functions, and effects of the mass media, especially the Internet. In addition, you will consider the possibilities and limitations of technology and the ways in which it shapes how people view themselves, others, and the world at large.

Questions Raised in Chapter Three

Working with a partner or in a small group, discuss two or three of the following questions.

1 What role do the mass media and other forms of technology play in people's lives?

2 What are the advantages and disadvantages of various mass media?

3 Do the media and other technologies influence people's lives positively, negatively, or both?

4 How do e-mail and other forms of online communication affect the ways in which people interact?

5 Do the mass media merely reflect cultural values, attitudes, and stereotypes, or do they help shape, reinforce, and change them?

Brief Quotations

The following quotations deal with issues, relating to the mass media and technology, that are considered in this chapter. Working with a partner or in a small group, choose two or three quotations and discuss them.

1 *TV captures the imagination, but does not liberate it. A good book at once stimulates and frees the mind.* (Bruno Bettelheim, Austrian-born U.S. psychologist and author)

2 *The Internet is a tool that can be used for good or evil. It can misinform as easily as it enlightens and offend as quickly as it entertains. Its potential is as limitless as human curiosity.* (H. D. Greenway, U.S. journalist)

3 *Cinema, radio, television, magazines are a school of inattention; people look without seeing.* (Christine McQuade, U.S. modern dancer)

4 *Were it left to me to decide whether we should have a government without newspapers or newspapers without government, I should not hesitate a moment to prefer the latter.* (Thomas Jefferson, third president of the United States)

5 *Rapidly our technology is creating a new type of human being, one who is plugged into machines instead of relationships, one who lives in a virtual reality rather than a family.* (Mary Pipher, U.S. professor and author)

6 *Without question, the most important invention in human history, next to frozen yogurt, is the computer.* (Dave Barry, U.S. humor columnist)

CORE READING 1
Computers and the Pursuit of Happiness

Journal Writing

In your journal, write for ten to fifteen minutes about the following statement: "The Internet is one of the greatest technological developments in human history." Do you agree or disagree? Then share your thoughts with several classmates.

Previewing the Topic

Write a list of the positive and negative consequences of increasing global use of the Internet. Consider both individual and social influences. Discuss your list in a small group. Then create a list, on the board, of all the consequences identified by the group.

Agreeing and Disagreeing

To what extent do you agree with the following statements? Fill in each blank with SA (strongly agree), A (agree), U (undecided), D (disagree), or SD (strongly disagree). Then share your responses with several classmates.

_____ 1 The Internet is one of the most revolutionary achievements in human history.

_____ 2 Because of the use of computers and the Internet, most people are better informed than they were fifty years ago.

_____ 3 The present "information age" is unlike any period in the past.

_____ 4 Computers and the Internet have significantly increased human happiness.

_____ 5 For everything gained from technology, something is lost.

_____ 6 The Internet is a powerful tool in fostering global democracy.

_____ 7 The quality of my life would be greatly diminished without the Internet.

_____ 8 Television is a more influential mass medium than the Internet.

_____ 9 Online shopping will largely replace real stores in the future.

_____ 10 If I could have access to only one mass medium, it would be the Internet.

At the end of the first paragraph of "Computers and the Pursuit of Happiness," the author asks three questions, which he then attempts to answer in the essay. As you read the selection, note in the margin Gelernter's answers to these questions.

 # Computers and the Pursuit of Happiness
David Gelernter

David Gelernter, a professor of computer science at Yale University, has written many books and articles on the role of technology in people's lives. The following reading is an excerpt from his essay "Computers and the Pursuit of Happiness," which deals with the influence, on individuals and on society, of computers and the Internet. The essay first appeared in the journal Commentary in 2001. Included with Gelernter's essay is a letter to the editor disagreeing with various aspects of his argument.

In recent years we have been notified almost continuously that we are living in an "information age." Mankind (it is suggested) has completed a sort of phase shift: the solid agricultural age was replaced two centuries ago by the liquid industrial age, which has now given way to the gaseous (so to speak) age of information. Everyone says so, but is it true? *Has* an old age ended, and are we, thanks to computers and the Internet, living in a new one? A related question: computers have been around for roughly a half-century; have they been good or bad for mankind? And finally: are they likely to do good or bad over the next half-century?

I

We are *not* in an information age, and computers and the Internet are not a revolutionary development in human history.

In the old industrial age (people say) coal, steel, and concrete mattered; in the new age, information counts. Yet it is obvious that coal, steel, and concrete still count just as much as they ever did. We have always needed food, clothing, shelter, possessions, and above all each other. We always *will* need those things, and the "information revolution" will never lessen our needs by half a hair's breadth. So whom are we kidding? What nouveau[1] cyber-billionaire ever used his billions to buy *information*? Who ever worried about poverty because he would be unable to keep his family well-informed?

Not long ago I saw a rented U-Haul trailer[2] with the inevitable Web address in big letters on the side, "uhaul.com" – the information age in nine easy characters. Yes, it is convenient to check a Web site for information about trailers for rent; but the Internet will never (*can* never) change our need for physical stuff, or for trailers to haul it around in. Fifty years from now, it may be possible to download artistically

---

[1] *nouveau:* Newly arrived or developed (from the French word for "new").

[2] *U-Haul trailer:* Vehicle attached to the back of a car that is used to haul, or transport, furniture and other items.

designed experiences and beam them via trick signals into your brain. (To many people this will sound like a junior grade of hell, but some technologists think of it as a Coming Attraction.³) The interesting fact remains: virtual gourmet food will make you feel full but will not keep you from starving. Virtual heat will make you feel warm but will not keep you from freezing. Virtual sex will make you feel satisfied in the sense that a pig feels satisfied.

About computers in particular, believers in a new information age make three arguments. They say it is a new age because we now have sophisticated machines to create, store, and deliver information; because computer networks can overcome geography; and because machines (in their own special areas) can act intelligently. All three claims are wrong. Computers have done marvelous deeds – but in each case, their great deeds are in keeping with the long-established patterns of the industrial age. Computation today is a dusting of snow that makes everything look different – on the surface.

Fancy machines to create, move, and store information were a main preoccupation of the whole 20th century, not just the computerized part of it. Movies, phonographs, color photography and color printing, the electronic transmission of photos, the invention of radio and radio networks and international radio hookups, newsreels,⁴ television, transistorized electronics, long-distance phone networks, communication satellites, fax machines, photocopiers, audio and video tapes, compact disks, cell phones, cable TV – and then, with the emergence of PC's and the Internet, suddenly we are in an information age? The 20th century was one information-gusher after another; information pouring into people's lives through more and more stuck-open faucets.

The defeat of geography? In *Cyberspace and the American Dream* (1994), distributed electronically by the Progress and Freedom Foundation, a distinguished group of authors argued that "we constitute the final generation of an old civilization and, at the very same time, the first generation of a new one." Their claim centered on the idea that, thanks to computer networks, geography had (in effect) been overcome; henceforth, shared interests and not physical proximity would shape community and society.

But using technology to defeat distance has been another goal of the industrial revolution from the start, from railroads through the Panama Canal⁵ and onward. Rail networks, telegraph networks, air and phone and highway and radio and TV networks – the Internet is the latest in a long line.

The 20th century teemed with smart machines, too, long before the computer showed up – simple ones like the thermostat or a car's electrical system (with automatic spark-advance); complex, sophisticated ones like automatic transmissions or the Norden bombsight⁶ in World War II. Granted, computers are a huge advance over the machines that came before, but huge advances are the stuff of the industrial

---

³ *Coming Attraction:* Exciting event in the near future to be looked forward to (a coming attraction is a film that will soon appear in a movie theater).

⁴ *newsreels:* Short movies dealing with current events, especially popular in the 1930s and 1940s.

⁵ *Panama Canal:* Waterway across Panama built by U.S. military engineers (1904–1914) to connect the Atlantic and the Pacific Oceans.

⁶ *Norden bombsight:* Device used in U.S. military airplanes to help guide bombs.

age. The Web is a big deal, but flying machines were a pretty big deal, too. Radio and TV changed the nature of American democracy. The electric-power industry turned society inside out.

The cost of not knowing history is not ignorance so much as arrogance. A 10 popular book about the Internet and the Web begins with this "personal note" from the author:

> The Internet is, by far, the greatest and most significant achievement in the history of mankind. What? Am I saying that the Internet is more impressive than the pyramids? More beautiful than Michelangelo's *David?*[7] More important to mankind than the wondrous inventions of the industrial revolution? Yes, yes, and yes.

That sort of statement suggests that technologists are fundamentally unserious. 11 By the way: it is a useful and interesting book. But the author protests too much. It is hard to picture comparable statements greeting the airplane's or the electric-power industry's emergence; they were too big and too obviously important to need this sort of cheerleading. What the author is really announcing is not a new age of information but a new age of hype, a new age of new ages.

Computers and the Internet *have* made a revolution in science and engineering. 12 Studying computational models of reality can be cheaper and better than studying reality. Sometimes reality is impossible to measure or too steep to scale, and computational models are the only way to get any purchase on[8] it. Those are the *actual* computer revolutions; the others are mostly potential and not real, locked up in awe-inspiring icebergs that just float around eliciting admiration and making trouble. The computer revolution is still frozen, latent, waiting to happen.

As for the information age, it must have begun at least a hundred years ago if 13 it exists at all. *Are* we better informed than we used to be? I doubt it. Is anyone prepared to assert that the U.S. electorate is better informed today than it was at the time of (say) the 1960 presidential election? That our fifth graders are better informed about reading, writing, history, or arithmetic? That our fifth-grade *teachers* are better informed? (Recently my fifth-grade son learned from his English teacher that "incredible" and "incredulous" are synonyms. That's the information age for you.)

II

Have computers been good or bad for mankind since they were invented roughly 14 50 years ago?

Other things being equal, information is good. Wealth is good. Computers have 15 supplied lots of information, and generated much wealth.

But we are marvelously adaptable. We can take miserable conditions in stride 16 and triumph over them; we can take wonderful conditions in stride and triumph over *them.* Humanity in any given age has a wealth threshold and an information threshold. If you are below either one, living in poverty or ignorance, you need more

---

[7] *Michelangelo's* David: Statue of the biblical hero David, made by Michelangelo (1475–1564), a famous Italian sculptor, painter, and architect.

[8] *get any purchase on:* Have an accurate indication or measurement of.

wealth or information. But once you are over the threshold, only the rate of change matters. Acquire more wealth or information, and presumably you will be happier; then you stabilize at your new, higher level, and chances are you are no happier than before. It is not exactly a deep or novel observation that money doesn't buy happiness. Neither does information.

In this country, the majority – obviously not everyone, but most of us – have 17 been over-threshold in wealth and information for several generations, roughly since the end of World War II. That is a remarkable achievement; it ought to make us proud and thankful. But it follows that increasing our level of wealth or information is unlikely to count terribly much in the larger scheme of things. The increase itself will feel good, but the substance of our new wealth or information won't matter much.

Here is a small case in point. My two boys, who are ten and thirteen, love 18 playing with computers, like most children nowadays. The computer is their favorite toy, and unquestionably it makes them happy. Computer play as it is practiced in real life, at least at our house, is a mindless activity; like many families, we have to limit the time our boys are allowed at it or they would spend all day wrecking pretend Porsches and blowing up enemy airplanes. But mindless activities are fine in reasonable doses. It's good for children to have fun, and I'm glad ours have so much fun with computers.

When my wife and I were children, we didn't have computers to play with. We 19 lacked these wonderful, happiness-generating devices. But – so what? Other things made us happy. We never felt deprived on account of our lack of computer power. It would be crazy to deny that computers are great toys, but it would be equally crazy to argue that they have made children any happier, on the whole, than children used to be. Fifty years from now, the computer-based toys will make today's look pathetic, and children will love all their snazzy new stuff – just as much, probably, as children loved their bats and balls and blocks and trains and jump ropes and dollhouses in 1900.

What we ordinarily fail to take into account when we are adding up the score 20 is the nature of technological change. Technology is a tool for building social structures. Granted, each new technology is better than the one it replaces. But new technologies engender new social structures, and the important question is not whether the new technology is better but whether the new structure is better. Except in the case of medical technologies, the answer will nearly always be debatable; nearly always *must* be debatable. We can easily show that, with each passing generation, paints have improved. It is much harder to show that art has improved.

Human nature does not change; human needs and wants remain basically the 21 same. Human ingenuity dreams up a new technology, and we put it to use – doing in a new way something we have always done in some other way. In years past, many towns had shared public wells. They were communal gathering places: you met neighbors, heard the news, checked out strangers, sized up the competition, made deals, dates, matches. Plumbing was a great leap forward, which few of us (certainly not me) would be willing to trade in. The old system was a nuisance, especially if *you* were the one carrying the water; but it was neighborly. The new, plumbing-induced social structure was far more convenient, not to say healthier. It was also lonelier. The old and new structures excelled in different ways, and cannot be directly compared.

The Web is an improvement much like plumbing, without the health benefits. 22 Fifty years ago, most shopping was face to face. In the Internet age, face-to-face stores will not survive long, any more than communal wells survived the advent of plumbing. To our great-grandchildren, shopping will mean "online," as it meant "face to face" to our great-grandparents. Future generations will look back wistfully but probably not unhappily. On the whole, their happiness and their ancestors' will probably be about the same. To the extent future generations are happier or unhappier than we – and "national happiness" does change; it's hard to doubt that America in 1950 was a happier country than America today – we can be fairly sure of one thing. The net change will have nothing to do with technology.

A major new technology remakes society – picks up the shoebox, shakes it hard, 23 puts it back. The new social structures we build almost always incorporate less human labor than the old ones. The old structures (in other words) have a larger "human ingredient," the new ones a larger "machine ingredient." It is nearly always impossible to compare the two directly. And in the meantime the old ones have disappeared. Where technology is concerned, we demolish the past and live in a permanent present.

In the lush technological future, we will be kids in a candy store. The old zero- 24 sum economics of Malthus[9] and his modern disciples has long since been discredited; we will swagger into that Candy Store of the Future with more money all the time, and find more and fancier candy in there every day. Our inventiveness, productivity, and potential wealth are all unlimited. Only our appetite for candy is not.

III

If mankind were somehow prevented from continuing to invent technology, 25 continuing to develop computers and software – that would be a tragedy, and the world would suffer. Nothing comes more naturally to us than building and playing with machines. Inventing technology is the intellectual equivalent of breathing.

Is breathing helpful? Yes. Will it conduce to a better world in 2050? Right again! 26 But only in a certain sense.

In 1991, I published a book called *Mirror Worlds;* in a way, it was a celebration 27 of computing technology (although it was ambivalent about computers in the end). It predicted the emergence of software versions of real-world institutions that you would "tune in" by means of a global network. It claimed that this would be a good development: you would be able to tour the world "without changing out of your pajamas." These mirror worlds would be "the new public square," would "monopolize the energy and attention of thousands . . . , broadcast an aesthetic and a worldview to millions, mold behavior and epitomize the age."

Talk about modest claims – although in looking back at the Web boom that 28 began in 1994, they seem, if anything, too modest. In predicting that "the software

---

[9] *zero-sum economics of Malthus:* Belief that when one person or group gets more, there is less for other people or groups. (Thomas Robert Malthus, 1766–1834, was an English economist who studied the causes and effects of rapid population growth.)

revolution hasn't begun yet, but it will soon," I was basically right. The industrial age ushered in new categories and possibilities, and computers and software are creating new possibilities, too: new types of structures that are just as unprecedented as the Eiffel Tower.[10]

Consider an online school. Such a school might offer guided nature walks through teeming, chattering, blossoming rain forests of the intellect where your guide knows exactly what you are capable of, can make the path expand or shrink to suit you, can point out the biggest vistas or the tiniest orchid – and the whole structure can be moored in cyberspace, where anyone who likes can climb aboard. Instead of merely reteaching the same class year after year, we could make the path better every year. As a student follows a trail, we could turn that trail into his personal diary, for review or revisiting whenever he likes; he could keep his whole school career in his back pocket. We could plant pictures or maps at the center of lessons if they belonged there, instead of pasting them in as afterthoughts. 29

And these new software structures could be world-spanning switchboards, connecting the right student to the right teacher. If Mrs. Feinstein is the English teacher for little Kate Smith, then wherever Mrs. Feinstein lives (Auckland, Nome, Passaic),[11] whatever hours she keeps, whatever her formal qualifications, we could patch her into the system. 30

I would rather put Kate in an actual school where actual teachers could look her in the face when they are trying to teach her something. But American education is in desperate trouble – and under the circumstances, software-based teaching is probably our best hope. In the future we will compare our ubiquitous software schools to the face-to-face education of the pre-1970s the way we compare online shopping to long-ago Main Streets: we will be wistful, as usual, but not wistful enough to do anything about it. On the whole, we will be content. 31

Of course, we are talking about new software *structures* – not mere computers, not mere information. And we are talking about something that *could* happen, but hasn't yet. 32

Human beings are mainly interested in human beings. If computers do good in the next 50 years, the good they are most likely to do lies in helping mankind know itself better. . . . 33

Machines can move faster than we do; so it cannot be that the important thing (the distinguishing thing) about humans is how fast we are. Cannot be how strong we are. Cannot be how well we do arithmetic. It might easily be that in 50 years, machines will be smarter than we are, too. . . . 34

But I do not think we will conclude that to be human is no big deal after all. I have heard one of technology's most honored, distinguished men tell a large audience how he wished human beings would stop thinking that they are somehow different from animals; it pained him to hear the old canard about man's "uniqueness." He is offering us an easy out: it is simple to be an animal and complicated (Lord knows) to be a man. Should we stop trying, call it a day, and relocate to the barnyard? 35

---

[10] *Eiffel Tower:* Structure designed for the Paris Exposition of 1889 by the French engineer Gustave Eiffel (it was the world's tallest building until 1930).

[11] *Aukland, Nome, Passaic:* Cities in New Zealand, Alaska, and New Jersey.

Not yet. Most of us are not quite ready to toss out the scraps of morality and 36
sanctity we have pieced together over the long, hard centuries; they may look
shabby but they are the best clothes we own. They might even be as important as
the Internet. I think we will decide not that we are merely animals after all but that
our uniqueness lies beyond strength, speed, and *intellect.*

People have said so for a long time, of course. . . . Chances are that, 50 years from 37
now – thanks to computers – many more people will believe it. Chances are that,
50 years from now, we will be grateful to computer technology for showing us what
marvelously powerful machines we can build – and how little they mean after all.

An Opposing View

Gelernter's article provoked the following letter to the editor of the journal Commentary.

To the Editor:

In his article, "Computers and the Pursuit of Happiness," David Gelernter 1
completely misses the key points. For one thing, while it is true, as he writes, that
our need for food, shelter, and clothing has not changed significantly because of
technology, the methods of acquiring these goods certainly have. I do not have to
hunt for lunch with a spear; rather, it is produced and distributed very efficiently
with the help of computers.

For another thing, and of far greater importance, the Internet extends the very 2
substantial changes in Western civilization brought about by the printing press. The
printed word enabled Western civilization's overthrow of the monarchical systems of
government,[1] certainly a sea change[2] in the way we once lived and thought. In our
own lifetime, television was the pivotal factor in the overthrow of the Soviet regime,
accomplishing quietly what all of America's missiles could not. Today, the Internet is
challenging China's ability to repress the development of ideas in that culture, too.

To suggest that a worldwide, person-to-person medium will have little or no 3
impact, as Mr. Gelernter does, is to be an extreme Luddite.[3] The Web holds the
potential of increasing our ability to deal with our own government's bureaucratic
complex, which is the greatest threat to individual freedom today. We, the electorate,
can follow bills through committee,[4] through debate, and correspond directly with
our representatives and their staff. Ultimately, the Internet may help facilitate direct
voting on important issues such as taxes and government spending.

Most important, the Internet will bring comprehensive education to more and 4
more people throughout the world. Marshall McLuhan[5] gave us the startling image
of a camel driver listening to a radio in the desert – no longer separated from the
rest of the world. The Internet will extend not just communication but a universe

---

[1] *monarchical systems of government:* Governments with a monarch, or single ruler with absolute power.

[2] *sea change:* Distinct change or transformation.

[3] *Luddite:* Someone opposed to technological change. (The Luddites were a group of British workers in the early
nineteenth century who destroyed textile machinery that they thought threatened their jobs.)

[4] *follow bills through committee:* Follow the making of laws by a group of elected representatives.

[5] *Marshall McLuhan* (1911–1980): Well-known Canadian educator and commentator on communications
technology.

of educational experience to all the remote peoples of the world, even if their remoteness is the result of economic rather than geographical factors. The impact of this spreading education is unpredictable, but, if history is any example, it will be used to enhance freedom.

Winn F. Martin
Atlanta, Georgia

Reading Journal

In your journal, write about one of the following topics.

1 Discuss a point that David Gelernter or Winn F. Martin makes about the positive influence of the Internet on people's lives.

2 Describe the importance of computers and the Internet in your own life.

3 Choose a topic of your own related to the reading.

Main Ideas

Answer the following questions, referring to the notes you took when reading the essay. Then share your answers with a partner.

1 Choose one of the three questions that Gelernter asks at the end of the first paragraph of his essay. How does he answer this question? Use your own words in summarizing Gelernter's response.

2 In paragraph 20, Gelernter says, "But new technologies engender new social structures, and the important question is not whether the new technology is better but whether the new structure is better." What does Gelernter mean by this statement? Looking at his examples in paragraphs 21–22, explain his idea in your own words.

3 What is the main point Gelernter makes in the reading? Summarize his central idea in one or two sentences. Use your own words. Begin with the sentence *In his essay "Computers and the Pursuit of Happiness," David Gelernter argues that . . .*

Reflecting on Content

Answer the following questions with a partner. When possible, support your answers with observations based on your own experiences.

1 To what extent do you agree with Gelernter's answer to one of the questions he asks at the end of the first paragraph?

2 Do you agree with any of the criticisms of Gelernter's argument that Winn F. Martin makes in his letter to the editor? Why or why not?

3 In the essay, Gelernter uses several types of evidence to support his points (see the discussion of supporting detail on page 14). What types of evidence does Gelernter provide, and how effective do you think the evidence is?

A Writer's Technique: *Figures of Speech*

Authors often use **figurative language**, or **figures of speech**, to make their writing lively and memorable. Figures of speech are imaginative comparisons between two dissimilar things. Such comparisons help readers visualize, identify with, and understand ideas by looking at familiar topics in new ways or at new topics in familiar ways.

The two most common types of figurative, or nonliteral, language are **similes** and **metaphors**. A simile is a comparison between two dissimilar things, using the words *like* or *as*. A metaphor is a comparison between two dissimilar things, without using *like* or *as*.

Similes	Metaphors
Their marriage is *like* a storm.	Their marriage is a storm.
Their marriage is *as* rough *as* a storm.	Their stormy marriage led to a divorce.

With a partner, decide whether the following sentences from Gelernter's essay contain a simile or a metaphor. Identify the two things being compared and the main idea the author expresses.

> **Example:** *Inventing technology is the intellectual equivalent of breathing. (par. 25)*
>
> **Figure of Speech:** *Metaphor*
>
> **Comparison:** *Invention of technology and the process of breathing.*
>
> **Main Idea:** *Inventing technology is one of the most natural things that humans do.*

1 Computation today is a dusting of snow that makes everything look different – on the surface. (par. 5)

2 Those [computational models of reality] are the *actual* computer revolutions; the others are mostly potential and not real, locked up in awe-inspiring icebergs that just float around eliciting admiration and making trouble. (par. 12)

3 The Web is an improvement much like plumbing, without the health benefits. (par. 22)

4 In the lush technological future we will be kids in a candy store. . . . we will swagger into that Candy Store of the Future with more money all the time, and find more and fancier candy in there every day. (par. 24)

5 The industrial age ushered in new categories and possibilities, and computers and software are creating new possibilities, too: new types of structures that are just as unprecedented as the Eiffel Tower. (par. 28)

Vocabulary: *Phrasal Verbs*

Often in English a verb is combined with a preposition to form a new vocabulary item – one that functions as an idiom. These verb-preposition combinations are called **phrasal verbs** or **two-word verbs**.

> *Look* my friend *up* when you have a chance. (*look up* = go and visit)
>
> I hope you *get over* your cold soon. (*get over* = recover from)

Note that some phrasal verbs are **separable**; that is, a noun may come either between the verb and the preposition or after the preposition:

> *Look* my friend *up* or *Look up* my friend.

Other phrasal verbs are **nonseparable**; the noun always comes after the preposition:

> I *got over* my cold.
>
> **X** I *got* my cold *over* (not grammatical)

In the following sentences from "Computers and the Pursuit of Happiness," fill in each blank with the appropriate preposition. Then give the meaning of the phrasal verb and write a sentence of your own using it correctly.

> **Example:** *The 20th century teemed with smart machines, too, long before the computer* showed ___*up*___. *(par. 9)*
>
> **Meaning:** *appear (often unexpectedly or late)*
>
> **Sentence:** *Renée* showed up *after the meeting had started and was reprimanded by her boss.*

1 We have to limit the time our boys are allowed at it or they would spend all day wrecking Porsches and blowing _____ enemy airplanes. (par. 18)

2 What we ordinarily fail to take into account when we are adding _____ the score is the nature of technological change. (par. 20)

3 Human ingenuity dreams _____ a new technology, and we put it to use. (par. 21)

4 They were communal gathering places: you met neighbors, heard the news, checked out strangers, sized _____ the competition, made deals, dates, matches. (par. 21)

5 Plumbing was a great leap forward, which few of us (certainly not me) would be willing to trade _____. (par. 21)

6 It [the book *Mirror Worlds*] predicted the emergence of software versions of real-world institutions that you would "tune _____" by means of a global network. (par. 27)

7 The industrial age ushered _____ new categories and possibilities. (par. 28)

8 Most of us are not ready to toss _____ the scraps of morality and sanctity we have pieced together over the long, hard centuries. (par. 36)

Vocabulary in Context

Locate the following italicized vocabulary items in the reading and see if you can determine their meaning from the context. Then think of an example or situation to illustrate each item, using your personal experience if possible. Do not just define the italicized words and expressions. When you are done, share your answers with a partner.

1 one form of technology that has *given way* to another, and why (par. 1).

2 a positive or negative aspect of the mass media that often *elicits* a strong response from people (par. 12).

3 the difference in meaning between *incredible* and *incredulous* (par. 13).

4 a situation in which someone might *take something in stride* (par. 16).

5 an example of technological *ingenuity* (par. 21).

6 a form of technology or mass media that you think humanity has *put to good use* (par. 21).

7 an aspect of the mass media that you feel *ambivalent* about, and why (par. 27).

8 an aspect of technology or the mass media that you think *epitomizes* the early twenty-first century (par. 27).

9 a form of technology that is *ubiquitous*, and the degree to which you think its influence is positive or negative (par. 31).

10 a situation in which you might say to someone, "Let's *call it a day*" (par. 35).

Discussion

Choose one of the following activities to do with a partner or in a small group.

1 Reread paragraphs 20–24 of Gelernter's essay, in which the writer discusses the nature of technological change. Then give your own example of a technology and the social structure or structures it creates. Discuss the ways in which the technology has influenced social interaction positively and negatively. When you are done, share your example with the class.

2 Set up a class debate in which one side argues that computers and the Internet have had a positive influence on society and the other side maintains that the technology has had a negative influence. To prepare for the debate, think about the arguments in favor of your position and the counterarguments. (If time allows, research your topic in the library and on the Internet.)

3 Access the National Public Radio Web site <www.npr.org>. Click on *Archives* and search for one of the following broadcast titles (remember to include the quotation marks when you search): "20th Anniversary of Personal Computers" or "Pop Culture Values." Listen to one of these broadcasts and write a list of the positive and negative influences that people mention. Then, with your partner or group, discuss your list of influences and share it with the rest of the class.

Writing Follow-up

Follow up the discussion activity you chose (item 1, 2, or 3) with the matching writing assignment below.

1   With your partner or group, write two or three paragraphs discussing your example of a technology and the social structure it has created. Consider the positive and negative influences of the technology on social interaction. Use one or two figures of speech (see page 145) to help convey your ideas.

2   Imagine that you are writing a letter to the editor of *Commentary*, the journal in which Gelernter's essay appeared. In the letter, one to three paragraphs in length, agree or disagree with one or two points that Gelernter makes. Try to use a simile and a metaphor to help make your points.

3   Write two paragraphs responding to the radio broadcast to which you listened. In the first paragraph, summarize the issues discussed; in the second, describe your personal reaction to the main points.

CORE READING 2
We've Got Mail – Always

Journal Writing

In your journal, spend ten to fifteen minutes **brainstorming** the advantages and disadvantages of using e-mail on a regular basis. Write a list of the benefits and drawbacks of e-mail that come to mind. Then look for connections among items in your list by grouping them into categories. (See the discussion of brainstorming, a prewriting strategy, on page 113.) When you are finished, share your ideas with several classmates.

Previewing the Topic

In a small group, write a list of ways in which online communication – including e-mail, instant messaging, and chat rooms – has influenced people's lives positively and negatively. Compare your ideas with those of the rest of the class. Then list the pros and cons on the board.

Agreeing and Disagreeing

To what extent do you agree with the following statements? Fill in each blank with SA (strongly agree), A (agree), U (undecided), D (disagree), or SD (strongly disagree). Then share your responses with several classmates.

_____ 1 People spend most of their time on the Internet, using e-mail and other forms of online communication.

_____ 2 There are as many disadvantages as advantages to using e-mail in one's daily life.

_____ 3 The time and energy that people spend on the Internet could often be used in better ways.

_____ 4 I prefer communicating with friends and family through letters rather than communicating by e-mail.

_____ 5 E-mail has helped improve people's writing skills.

_____ 6 Online communication encourages shallow interactions among people.

_____ 7 The quality of my life would be significantly diminished without e-mail.

_____ 8 Because of the Internet, the attention spans of people of all ages are decreasing.

_____ 9 Online dating services are an effective way to meet people.

_____ 10 More and more, people's personal lives are being controlled by technology.

Taking Notes While You Read

As you read the essay, underline or highlight the arguments the author makes about the pros and cons of using e-mail. In the margin, indicate whether you agree or disagree with these points.

 # We've Got Mail – Always[1]
Andrew Leonard

Andrew Leonard is a freelance writer in the United States and senior technology correspondent for the online magazine Salon.com. In the following article, which appeared in Newsweek _magazine in 1999, Leonard explores the positive and negative effects of e-mail and other relatively new forms of online communication, especially the ways in which people interact with each other._

Is e-mail a blessing or a curse? Last month, after a week's vacation, I discovered 1,218 unread e-mail messages waiting in my IN box. I pretended to be dismayed, but secretly I was pleased. This is how we measure our wired worth in the late 1990s. If you aren't overwhelmed by e-mail, you must be doing something wrong. 1

Never mind that after subtracting the stale office chit-chat, spam, flame wars,[2] dumb jokes forwarded by friends who should have known better, and other e-mail detritus, there were perhaps seven messages actually worth reading. I was doomed to spend half my workday just deleting junk. E-mail sucks. 2

---

[1] _We've Got Mail – Always:_ A play on, or humorous treatment of, _You've Got Mail_ (1998), the title of a film about anonymous e-mail friends who fall in love.

[2] _flame wars:_ Angry or hostile e-mail messages meant to insult, provoke, or rebuke someone.

But wait – what about those seven? A close friend in Taipei I haven't seen in five years tells me he's planning to start a family. A complete stranger in Belgium sends me a hot story tip. Another stranger offers me a job. I'd rather lose an eye than lose my e-mail account. E-mail rocks!

3

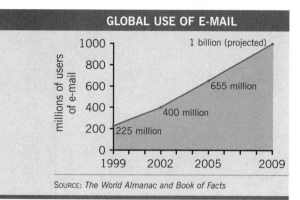

GLOBAL USE OF E-MAIL

millions of users of e-mail

1000
800
600 — 655 million
400 — 400 million
200 — 225 million
0
1 billion (projected)

1999   2002   2005   2009

SOURCE: *The World Almanac and Book of Facts*

E-mail. Can't live with it, can't live without it. Con artists and real artists, advertisers and freedom fighters, lovers and sworn enemies – they've all flocked to e-mail as they would to any medium of expression. E-mail is convenient, saves time, brings us closer to one another, helps us manage our ever-more-complex lives. Books are written, campaigns conducted, crimes committed – all via e-mail. But it is also inconvenient, wastes our time, isolates us in front of our computers and introduces more complexity into our already too-harried lives. To skeptics, e-mail is just the latest chapter in the evolving history of human communication. A snooping husband now discovers his wife's affair by reading her private e-mail – but he could've uncovered the same sin by finding letters a generation ago.

4

Yet e-mail – and all online communication – is in fact something truly different; it captures the essence of life at the close of the twentieth century with an authority that few other products of digital technology can claim. Does the pace of life seem ever faster? E-mail simultaneously allows us to cope with that acceleration and contributes to it. Are our attention spans shriveling under barrages of new, improved forms of stimulation? The quick and dirty e-mail is made to order for those whose ability to concentrate is measured in nanoseconds.[3] If we accept that the creation of the globe-spanning Internet is one of the most important technological innovations of the last half of this century, then we must give e-mail – the living embodiment of human connection across the Net – pride of place. The way we interact with each other is changing; e-mail is both the catalyst and the instrument of that change.

5

The scope of the phenomenon is mind-boggling. Worldwide, 225 million people can send and receive e-mail. Forget about the Web or e-commerce or even online pornography: e-mail is the Internet's true killer app – the software application that we simply must have, even if it means buying a $2000 computer and plunking down $20 a month to America Online. According to Donna Hoffman, a professor of marketing at Vanderbilt University, one survey after another finds that when online users are asked what they do on the Net, "e-mail is always No. 1."

6

Oddly enough, no one planned it, and no one predicted it. When research scientists first began cooking up the Internet's predecessor, the Arpanet,[4] in 1968, their primary goal was to enable disparate computing centers to share resources. "But it didn't take very long before they discovered that the most important thing was the ability to send mail around, which they had not anticipated at all," says

7

---

[3] *nanosecond:* One billionth of a second (measurement used in digital technology).

[4] *Arpanet:* The Advanced Research Programs Agency of the U.S. Department of Defense.

Eric Alden, chief technical officer of Sendmail, Inc. and the primary author of a 20-year-old program – Sendmail – that still transports the vast majority of the world's e-mail across the Internet. It seems that what all those top computer scientists really wanted to use the Internet for was as a place to debate, via e-mail, such crucially important topics as the best science-fiction novel of all time. Even though Alden is now quite proud that his software helps hundreds of millions of people communicate, he says he didn't set out originally to change the world. As a systems administrator at the University of California, Berkeley in the late 1970s, he was constantly hassled by computer-science researchers in one building who wanted to get their e-mail from machines in another location. "I just wanted to make my life easier," says Alden.

Don't we all? When my first child was born in 1994, e-mail seemed to me some 8 kind of Promethean[5] gift perfectly designed to help me cope with the irreconcilable pressures of new fatherhood and full-time freelance writing. It saved me time and money without ever requiring me to leave the house; it salvaged my social life, allowed me to conduct interviews as a reporter and kept a lifeline open to my far-flung extended family. Indeed, I finally knew for sure that the digital world was viscerally potent when I found myself in the middle of a bitter fight with my mother – on e-mail. Again, new medium, old story.

My mother had given me an e-mail head start. In 1988, she bought me a 9 modem so I could create a CompuServe account. The reason? Her younger brother had contracted a rapidly worsening case of Parkinson's disease. He wasn't able to talk clearly, and could hardly scrawl his name with a pen or pencil. But he had a computer, and could peck out words on a keyboard. My mom figured that if the family all had CompuServe accounts, we could send him e-mail. She grasped, long before the Internet became a household word, how online communication offered new possibilities for transcending physical limitations, how as simple a thing as e-mail could bring us closer to those whom we love.

It may even help us find those whom we want to love in the first place. Jenn 10 Shreve is a freelance writer in the San Francisco Bay area who keeps a close eye on the emerging culture of the new online generation. For the last couple of years, she's seen what she considers to be a positive change in online dating habits. E-mail, she argues, encourages the shy. "It offers a semi-risk-free environment to initiate romance," says Shreve. "Because it lacks the immediate threat of physical rejection, people who are perhaps shy or had painful romantic failures in the past can use the Internet as a way to build a relationship in the early romantic stages."

But it's not just about lust. E-mail also flattens hierarchies within the bounds of 11 an office. It is far easier, Shreve notes, to make a suggestion to your superiors and colleagues via e-mail than it is to do so in a pressure-filled meeting room. "Any time when you have something that is difficult to say, e-mail can make it easier," she says. "It serves as a buffer zone."

Of course, e-mail's uses as a social lubricant can be taken to extremes. There is 12 little point in denying the obvious dark side to the lack of self-constraint encouraged

---

[5] *Promethean*: Boldly creative or original. (In Greek mythology, Prometheus was a giant who stole fire from the heavens and gave it to humans.)

by e-mail. Purveyors of pornography rarely call us on the phone and suggest out loud that we check out some "hot teen action." But they don't think twice about jamming our e-mail boxes full of outrageously prurient advertisements. People who would never insult us face to face will spew the vilest, most objectionable, most appalling rhetoric imaginable via e-mail or an instant message, or in the no-holds-barred confines of a chat room.

Cyberspace's lapses in gentility underscore a central contradiction inherent in 13 online communication. If it is true that hours spent on the Net are often hours subtracted from watching television, one could argue that the digital era has raised the curtains on a new age of literacy – more people are writing more words than ever before! But what kind of words are we writing? Are we really more literate, or are we sliding ever faster into a quicksand of meaningless irrelevance, of pop-cultural triviality – expressed usually in lower case letters – run amok? E-mail is actually too easy, too casual. Gone are the days when one would worry over a letter to a lover or relative or colleague. Now there's just time for that quick e-mail, a few hastily cobbled together thoughts written in a colloquial style that usually borders on unedited stream of consciousness.[6] The dangerous obvious: snippy comments to a friend, overly sharp retorts to one's boss, insults mistakenly sent to the target, not the intended audience. E-mail allows us to act before we can think – the perfect tool for a culture of hyperstimulation.

So instead of creating something new, we forward something old. Instead 14 of crafting the perfect phrase, we use a brain-dead abbreviation: IMHO for In My Humble Opinion, or ROTFLMAO, for Rolling On The Floor Laughing My A— Off.[7] Got a rumor? E-mail 50 people! Instant messaging and chat rooms just accentuate the casual negative. If e-mail requires little thought, then instant messaging – flashing a message directly onto a recipient's computer monitor – is so insubstantial as to be practically nonexistent.

E-mail, ultimately, is a fragile thing, easy to forge, easy to corrupt, easy to destroy. 15 A few weeks ago a co-worker of mine accidentally and irretrievably wiped out 1,500 of his own saved messages. For a person who conducts the bulk of his life online, such a digital tragedy is a kin to erasing part of your own memory. Suddenly, nothing's left. It is comforting to think that, if preserved in a retrievable way, all the notes the world is passing back and forth today may constitute a vast historical archive, but the opposite may also be true. Earlier this summer, I visited some curators at the Stanford University Library who are hard at work compiling a digital archive of Silicon Valley[8] history. They bemoaned a new, fast-spreading corporate policy that requires the deletion of all corporate e-mails after every 60 or 90 days. As Microsoft and Netscape[9] have learned to their dismay, old e-mails, however trivial

---

[6] *stream of consciousness:* Spontaneous flow of thoughts and feelings that may not be well connected to each other.

[7] *Laughing My A— Off:* Vulgar expression meaning to laugh very hard (a more polite expression is *to laugh one's head off*).

[8] *Silicon Valley:* Region of California southeast of San Francisco known for its high-tech design and manufacturing industries.

[9] *Microsoft and Netscape:* World's largest supplier of operations systems and other software for personal computers (Microsoft) and popular World Wide Web browser (Netscape). During an antitrust trial (1998–2000), damaging e-mails were discovered showing that Microsoft chairman Bill Gates had illegally used his monopoly position to suppress competition with Netscape.

they seem when they are written, can and will come back to haunt you. It is best, say the lawyers, to just wipe them all out.

Still, e-mail is enabling radically new forms of worldwide human collaboration. 16 Those 225 million people who can send and receive it represent a network of potentially cooperating individuals dwarfing anything that even the mightiest corporation or government can muster. Mailing-list discussion groups and online conferencing allow us to gather together to work on a multitude of projects that are interesting or helpful to us – to pool our collective efforts in a fashion never before possible. The most obvious place to see this collaboration right now is in the world of software. For decades, programmers have used e-mail to collaborate on projects. With increasing frequency, this collaboration is occurring across company lines, and often without even the spur of commercial incentives. It's happening largely because it can – it's relatively easy for a thousand programmers to collectively contribute to a project using e-mail and the Internet. Perhaps each individual contribution is small, but the scale of the Internet multiplies all efforts dramatically.

Meanwhile, now that we are all connected, day and night, across time zones and 17 oceans and corporate firewalls,[10] we are beginning to lose sight of the distinction between what is work and what is play.

Six years after I logged onto CompuServe for the first time, I went to Australia 18 for three weeks. Midway through my visit, I ended up in Alice Springs, a fraying-at-the-edges frontier town about a thousand miles away from anywhere, in the middle of the great Australian outback. An exotic place, nestled among the oldest mountain remnants of the world, where flocks of parrots swoop and flutter through the downtown shopping district. But instead of wandering through the desert seeking out wallabies and feral camels, I found myself dialing long distance to a friend's University of Melbourne Internet account, and transferring from there via a telnet program to my own account at the Well in San Francisco. Once on the Well, I checked my mail to see if a fact checker for *Wired* magazine had any fresh queries for me concerning the story I had recently submitted.

I was on the job – in large part because I had an e-mail address and had made 19 the Devil's bargain[11] with the wired world. As I listened for the sound of the modem connecting in Alice Springs, I felt in the pit of my stomach that I had lost control over some valuable part of my life. Your employer will refrain from calling you at 11:30 at night, but not from sending an inquiring, hectoring, must-be-promptly-answered-as-soon-as-you-log-on e-mail. E-mail doesn't just collapse distance; it demolishes all boundaries. And that can be, depending on the moment, either a blessing or a curse.

---

10 *corporate firewall:* Security system used to protect computer network connections, especially the Internet.

11 *Devil's bargain* (or Faustian bargain): Situation that results in one's gaining and losing something at the same time. (From the medieval legend of Doctor Faustus, who is seduced by the Devil into giving up his immortal soul in exchange for secret knowledge.)

Reading Journal

In your journal, write about one of the following topics.

1 Are there more advantages or disadvantages to using e-mail on a daily basis?

2 Describe how your life would be different without the Internet.

3 Choose a topic of your own related to the reading.

Main Ideas

Answer the following questions, referring to the notes you took when reading the selection. Then share your answers with a partner.

1 A contradiction is a statement expressing opposite points of view about something. In the article, Leonard discusses several contradictions involving the use of e-mail. What is one of the contradictions that he mentions?

2 What point is Leonard making in his personal story at the end of the essay (paragraphs 18–19)? Use your own words to explain the meaning of the anecdote.

3 What is the main point Leonard makes in the reading? Summarize his central idea in one or two sentences. Use your own words. Begin with the sentence *In his article "We've Got Mail – Always," Andrew Leonard maintains that . . .*

Reflecting on Content

Answer the following questions with a partner. When possible, support your answers with observations based on your own experiences.

1 How does Leonard answer the question that he starts his article with: "Is e-mail a blessing or a curse?" How would you answer this question yourself?

2 Do you think that e-mail, instant messaging, chat rooms, and other forms of online communication can bring people closer together?

3 In paragraph 19, Leonard describes the "Devil's bargain" (see footnote 11 on page 153). Can you think of another form of technology that has resulted in society's gaining and losing something at the same time?

A Writer's Technique: *Figures of Speech*

Review the discussion of figures of speech on page 145.

Working with a partner, consider the metaphors in the following sentences. Identify the two things being compared and the main idea the author is expressing.

> **Example:** *. . . the digital era has raised the curtains on a new age of literacy. (par. 13)*
>
> **Comparison:** *A new period of literacy and the beginning of a play on the stage.*
>
> **Main Idea:** *The computer age has led to a new period of literacy.*

1 [E-mail] . . . kept a lifeline open to my far-flung extended family. (par. 8)

2 Of course, e-mail's uses as a social lubricant can be taken to extremes. (par. 12)

3 Are we really more literate, or are we sliding ever faster into a quicksand of meaningless irrelevance? (par. 13)

4 . . . all the notes the world is passing back and forth today may constitute a vast historical archive. (par. 15)

5 E-mail doesn't just collapse distance; it demolishes all boundaries. (par. 19)

Vocabulary: *Verb-Preposition Combinations*

In English there are many **verb-preposition combinations** which, unlike phrasal verbs (see page 146), do not form a new vocabulary item. Examples of such combinations are *rely on, consist of, deal with,* and *recover from.*

In the following sentences from "We've Got Mail – Always," fill in each blank with the correct preposition. Then use the verb-preposition combination in a sentence of your own.

Example: *Six years after I* logged ___*onto*___ *CompuServe for the first time, I went to Australia for three weeks. (par. 18)*

Sentence: *Because the computer network at my college was being repaired yesterday, I couldn't* **log onto** *the Internet.*

1 But it [e-mail] is also inconvenient, wastes our time, isolates us in front of our computers and *introduces* more complexity _____ our already too-harried lives. (par. 4)

2 E-mail simultaneously allows us to *cope* _____ that acceleration [of the pace of life] and contributes to it. (par. 5)

3 The way we *interact* _____ each other is changing; e-mail is both the catalyst and the instrument of that change. (par. 5)

4 Gone are the days when one would *worry* _____ a letter to a lover or a relative or colleague. (par. 13)

5 Now there's just time for that quick e-mail, a few . . . thoughts written in a colloquial style that usually borders _____ unedited stream of consciousness. (par. 13)

6 For decades, programmers have used e-mail to *collaborate* _____ projects. (par. 16)

7 . . . it's relatively easy for a thousand programmers to collectively *contribute* _____ a project using e-mail and the Internet. (par. 16)

8 Your employer will *refrain* _____ calling you at 11:30 at night, but not from sending an inquiring, hectoring . . . e-mail. (par. 19)

Vocabulary in Context

Locate the following italicized vocabulary items in the reading and see if you can determine their meanings from the context. Then think of an example or situation to illustrate each item, using your personal experience if possible. Do not just define the italicized words and expressions. When you are done, share your idea with a partner.

1 an aspect of today's technology about which many people are *dismayed* (par. 1)

2 a possible result of the *barrage* of information that people receive from the mass media (par. 5)

3 a form of technology that has served as a *catalyst* of social change (par. 5)

4 an aspect of the mass media that someone might find *mind-boggling,* and why (par. 6)

5 two aspects of contemporary society that you find *irreconcilable,* and why (par. 8)

6 an aspect of technology or science that you think is important to *keep a close eye on* (par. 10)

7 an *appalling* situation or condition today that the Internet might help improve (par. 12)

8 something *inherent* in the use of online communication (par. 13)

9 something about communications technology that we can easily *lose sight of* (par. 17)

10 a reason someone might *refrain from* doing something on the Internet (par. 19)

Discussion

Choose one of the following activities to do with a partner or in a small group.

1 Make a chart similar to the one on the right. Fill in the columns with the benefits and drawbacks of e-mail and other forms of online communication mentioned in Leonard's article (and any other pros and cons you can think of). When you are done, share your ideas with the class.

Benefits of Online Communication	Drawbacks of Online Communication

2 Set up a class debate in which one side argues the advantages of e-mail and other forms of online communication, and the other side presents the disadvantages. To prepare for the debate, think about the arguments in favor of your position and the counterarguments.

3 Access one of the following Web sites: <www.idemployee.id.tue.nl/ g.w.m.rauterberg/ibq/ibq_engl.html> or <www.haverford.edu/psych/ddavis/ webforms/p214.03.ql.html>. Complete the questionnaire about personal use of the Internet. Then share your answers with several classmates. How do your responses compare?

Writing Follow-up

Follow up the discussion activity you chose (item 1, 2, or 3) with the matching writing assignment below.

1 Write two similes, one conveying an advantage of e-mail or other form of online communication and the other a disadvantage. For one simile use the form "*a is like b*" and for the other, "*a is as _____ as b.*" Then write two metaphors, one conveying a benefit and the other a drawback of online communication. (See the discussion of figures of speech on page 145.) Use your imagination to come up with original comparisons that evoke vivid images. Two possible answers are provided below to help give you ideas.

> Simile: *Looking at one's e-mail is like walking through a junkyard filled with valuable and worthless items. (a is like b)*
>
> Metaphor: *Instant messaging provides appetizers for discussion but not a full meal.*

2 Imagine that you and your group are drafting the opening statement for your debate on the advantages or disadvantages of e-mail and other forms of online communication. Write a paragraph explaining the position your team is taking.

3 Briefly discuss the results of the online questionnaire dealing with personal use of the Internet. What conclusions can you draw about your own use of this mass medium? What are your attitudes toward the issues raised in the survey?

CORE READING 3
Propaganda Techniques in Today's Advertising

Journal Writing

Choose one of the advertisements on pages 159 and 160 and examine the picture and the text. In your journal, write for ten to fifteen minutes about one or two techniques that you think the advertiser uses to market its product or service. Then share your thoughts with several classmates.

Previewing the Topic

Think of a magazine advertisement or a television commercial that seems to be especially effective. In a small group, describe the ad or commercial and explain why you find it successful. Then write a list of the reasons on the board.

Agreeing and Disagreeing

To what extent do you agree with the following statements? Fill in each blank with SA (strongly agree), A (agree), U (undecided), D (disagree), or SD (strongly disagree). Then share your responses with several classmates.

_____ 1 Consumers selecting products are not usually influenced by advertising.

_____ 2 Most people are unaware of the propaganda they encounter in their daily lives.

_____ 3 Advertisements do not merely reflect social attitudes and behaviors; they help shape, reinforce, and change them.

_____ 4 Most people are exposed to hundreds of advertising messages every day.

_____ 5 A TV commercial dealing with the dangers of drunk driving or cigarette smoking is a form of propaganda.

_____ 6 Most advertising tries to influence people by appealing to their logic.

_____ 7 TV commercials are usually more effective than print ads.

_____ 8 People are limited in the ways they can combat the negative effects of propaganda.

_____ 9 Governments should ban white supremacist and other hate-group Web sites on the Internet.

_____ 10 Every government uses propaganda to shape its citizens' values, beliefs, and behaviors.

Taking Notes While You Read

As you read the article, look for the different propaganda techniques that are mentioned. When you find one, restate it in the margin, using your own words.

Propaganda Techniques in Today's Advertising
Ann McClintock

In the following article, Ann McClintock, a freelance writer, focuses on the propaganda techniques that advertisers and political candidates use in an effort to sway people's opinions. She stresses the need for consumers and voters to be aware of these tactics. The article originally appeared in a college reading and writing textbook in 1998.

Americans, adults and children alike, are being seduced. They are being brainwashed. And few of us protest. Why? Because the seducers and the brainwashers are the advertisers we willingly invite into our homes. We are victims, content – even eager – to be victimized. We read advertisers' propaganda messages in newspapers and magazines; we watch their alluring images on television. We absorb their messages and images into our subconscious. We all do it – even those of us who claim to see through advertisers' tricks and therefore feel immune to advertising's charm.

1

Advertisers lean heavily on propaganda to sell products, whether the "products" are a brand of toothpaste, a candidate for office, or a particular political viewpoint.

Propaganda is a systematic effort to influence people's opinions, to win them over to a certain view or side. Propaganda is not necessarily concerned with what is true or false, good or bad. Propagandists simply want people to believe the messages being sent. Often, propagandists will use outright lies or more subtle deceptions to sway people's opinions. In a propaganda war, any tactic is considered fair.

2

Stop sleeping on a dinosaur!

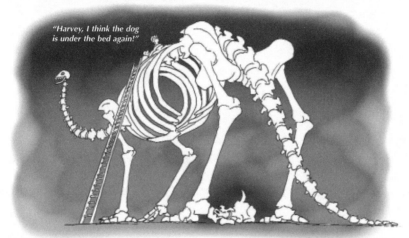

"Harvey, I think the dog is under the bed again!"

Switch to a Tempur-Pedic bed.

You have a nice home...drive a fine car...enjoy the good things of life. But you're *still* sleeping on an uncomfortable *outmoded* bed.

That's where *we* come in...

Seven years ago, we brought the famous Tempur-Pedic SWEDISH SLEEP SYSTEM to America. Since then, millions have discovered our new

fatigue-fighting, energy-elevating *weightless sleep* phenomenon.

- A marvel of molecular physics!
- Drastically cuts tossing & turning.
- No air, water, or steel springs.
- Adjusts its shape automatically.
- Only one moving part—*you.*

We expanded NASA's anti-G-force research to invent a new weightless sleep material. Our technology is recognized by NASA, the U.S. Space

Foundation—and certified by the Space Awareness Alliance.

Other beds are fancy on the outside. Ours is a *miracle* on the inside —where billions of self-ventilating viscoelastic microcells cuddle your body with *perfect* support!

Thousands of sleep clinics and health professionals recommend us. TV, radio, magazines, newspapers give us rave reviews!

Call or fax now for a free sample, free video, and free information. We'll also send you a **FREE HOME TRYOUT CERTIFICATE.**

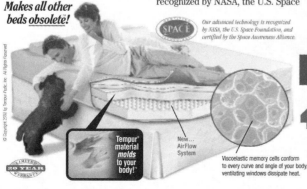

Makes all other beds obsolete!

© Copyright 2000 by Tempur-Pedic Inc. All Rights Reserved

Our advanced technology is recognized by NASA, the U.S. Space Foundation, and certified by the Space Awareness Alliance.

Tempur® material *molds* to your body!™

New... AirFlow System

Viscoelastic memory cells conform to every curve and angle of your body, ventilating windows dissipate heat.

20 YEAR LIMITED WARRANTY

FREE DEMONSTRATION KIT is now yours for the asking!

✚ **TEMPUR**-PEDIC®
PRESSURE RELIEVING
SWEDISH MATTRESS AND PILLOW

FREE SAMPLE / FREE VIDEO / FREE INFO

1-888-242-3885
OR SEND FAX TO 1-859-259-9843
Tempur-Pedic, Inc., 1713 Jaggie Fox Way, Lexington, KY 40511

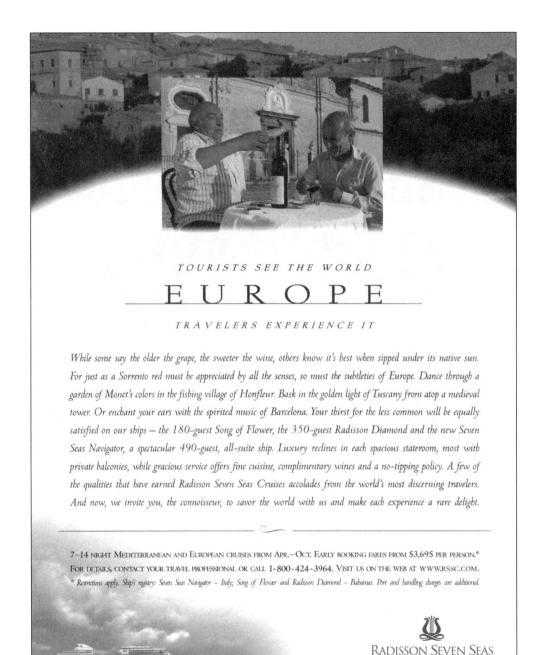

TOURISTS SEE THE WORLD

EUROPE

TRAVELERS EXPERIENCE IT

While some say the older the grape, the sweeter the wine, others know it's best when sipped under its native sun. For just as a Sorrento red must be appreciated by all the senses, so must the subtleties of Europe. Dance through a garden of Monet's colors in the fishing village of Honfleur. Bask in the golden light of Tuscany from atop a medieval tower. Or enchant your ears with the spirited music of Barcelona. Your thirst for the less common will be equally satisfied on our ships — the 180-guest Song of Flower, the 350-guest Radisson Diamond and the new Seven Seas Navigator, a spectacular 490-guest, all-suite ship. Luxury reclines in each spacious stateroom, most with private balconies, while gracious service offers fine cuisine, complimentary wines and a no-tipping policy. A few of the qualities that have earned Radisson Seven Seas Cruises accolades from the world's most discerning travelers. And now, we invite you, the connoisseur, to savor the world with us and make each experience a rare delight.

7–14 NIGHT MEDITERRANEAN AND EUROPEAN CRUISES FROM APR.–OCT. EARLY BOOKING FARES FROM $3,695 PER PERSON.*
FOR DETAILS, CONTACT YOUR TRAVEL PROFESSIONAL OR CALL 1-800-424-3964. VISIT US ON THE WEB AT WWW.RSSC.COM.
* Restrictions apply. Ship's registry: Seven Seas Navigator - Italy; Song of Flower and Radisson Diamond - Bahamas. Port and handling charges are additional.

RADISSON SEVEN SEAS
CRUISES

When we hear the word "propaganda," we usually think of a foreign menace: anti-American radio programs broadcast by a totalitarian regime or brainwashing tactics practiced on hostages. Although propaganda may seem relevant only in the political arena, the concept can be applied fruitfully to the way products and ideas are sold in advertising. Indeed, the vast majority of us are targets in advertisers' propaganda war. Every day, we are bombarded with slogans, print ads, commercials, packaging claims, billboards, trademarks, logos, and designer brands – all forms of propaganda. One study reports that each of us, during an average day, is exposed to over *five hundred* advertising claims of various types. This saturation may even increase in the future, since current trends include ads on movie screens, shopping carts, videocassettes, even public television.

What kind of propaganda techniques do advertisers use? There are seven basic types.

4

NAME CALLING

Name calling is a propaganda tactic in which negatively charged names are hurled against the opposing side or competitor. By using such names, propagandists try to arouse feelings of mistrust, fear, and hate in their audiences. For example, a political advertisement may label an opposing candidate a "loser," "fence-sitter," or "warmonger." Depending on the advertiser's target market, labels such as "a friend of big business" or "a dues-paying member of the party in power"[1] can be the epithets that damage an opponent. Ads for products may also use name calling. An American manufacturer may refer, for instance, to a "foreign car" in its commercial – not an "imported" one. The label of foreignness will have unpleasant connotations in many people's minds. A childhood rhyme claims that "names can never hurt me,"[2] but name calling is an effective way to damage the opposition, whether it is another car maker or a congressional candidate.

5

GLITTERING GENERALITIES

Using glittering generalities is the opposite of name calling. In this case, advertisers surround their products with attractive – and slippery – words and phrases. They use vague terms that are difficult to define and that may have different meanings to different people: *freedom, democratic, all-American, progressive, Christian, justice.* Many such words have strong affirmative overtones. This kind of language stirs positive feelings in people, feelings that may spill over to the product. After all, how can anyone oppose "truth, justice, and the American way"?[3]

6

The ads for politicians and political causes often use glittering generalities because such buzz words can influence votes. Election slogans include high-sounding but basically empty phrases like the following:

7

- "He cares about people." (That's nice, but is he a better candidate than his opponent?)
- "Vote for progress." (Progress by *whose* standards?)
- "They'll make this country great again." (What does "great" mean? Does "great" mean the same thing to others as it does to me?)
- "Vote for the future." (What kind of future?)
- "If you love America, vote for Phyllis Smith." (If I don't vote for Smith, does that mean I don't love America?)

---

[1] *dues-paying member of the party in power:* Supporter of the political party in power – Democrat or Republican. (Some organizations charge their members yearly dues, or fees.)

[2] *names can never hurt me:* Part of the children's saying "Sticks and stones can break my bones, but names can never hurt me."

[3] *truth, justice, and the American way:* The values that Batman fights for in the popular comic strip, TV series, and film.

Ads for consumer goods are also sprinkled with glittering generalities. Product 8 names, for instance, are supposed to evoke good feelings: *Luvs* diapers, *New Freedom* feminine hygiene products, *Joy* liquid detergent, *Loving Care* hair color, *Almost Home* cookies, *Yankee Doodle*[4] pastries. Product slogans lean heavily on vague but comforting phrases: Kinney is "The Great American Shoe Store," General Electric "brings good things to life," and Dow Chemical "lets you do great things." Chevrolet, we are told, is the "heartbeat of America," and Chrysler boasts cars that are "built by Americans for Americans."

TRANSFER[5]

In transfer, advertisers try to improve the image of a product by associating it with a 9 symbol most people respect, like the American flag or Uncle Sam.[6] The advertisers hope that the prestige attached to the symbol will carry over to the product. Many companies use transfer devices to identify their products: Lincoln Insurance shows a profile of the president; Continental Insurance portrays a Revolutionary War minuteman;[7] Amtrak's[8] logo is red, white, and blue; Liberty Mutual's[9] corporate symbol is the Statue of Liberty; Allstate's[10] name is cradled by a pair of protective, fatherly hands.

Corporations also use the transfer technique when they sponsor prestigious shows 10 on radio and television. These shows function as symbols of dignity and class. Kraft Corporation,[11] for instance, sponsored a "Leonard Bernstein[12] Conducts Beethoven" concert, while Gulf Oil is the sponsor of *National Geographic*[13] specials and Mobil supports public television's *Masterpiece Theater.*[14] In this way, corporations can reach an educated, influential audience and, perhaps, improve their public image by associating themselves with quality programming.

Political ads, of course, practically wrap themselves in the flag. Ads for a political 11 candidate often show either the Washington Monument, a Fourth of July parade, the Stars and Stripes,[15] a bald eagle[16] soaring over the mountains, or a white-steepled church on the village green. The national anthem or "America the Beautiful" may play softly in the background. Such appeals to Americans' love of country can surround the candidate with an aura of patriotism and integrity.

---

[4] *Yankee Doodle:* Name of a popular song that goes back to the American Revolution (1775–1783).

[5] *Transfer:* In addition to the type of positive transfer discussed in this section, advertisers and politicians often use *negative* transfer: an attack on a person or thing through association with someone or something most people dislike.

[6] *Uncle Sam:* U.S. government (also the American nation or people).

[7] *Minuteman:* Member of a group of armed citizens, during the American Revolution, who were ready to fight in a minute.

[8] *Amtrak:* U.S. national passenger train company. (Red, white, and blue are the colors of the U.S. flag.)

[9] *Liberty Mutual:* Large U.S. investment and insurance company.

[10] *Allstate:* One of the largest insurance companies in the United States.

[11] *Kraft Corporation:* Large U.S. producer of food products.

[12] *Leonard Bernstein* (1918–1990): Well-known U.S. conductor and composer.

[13] *National Geographic specials:* TV programs, produced by the National Geographic Society, focusing on scientific research and nature expeditions.

[14] *Masterpiece Theater:* Theater or film productions for TV, sometimes adapted from literary classics.

[15] *Stars and Stripes:* Nickname for the U.S. flag.

[16] *bald eagle:* U.S. national bird.

TESTIMONIAL

The testimonial is one of advertisers' most-loved and most-used propaganda [12] techniques. Similar to the transfer device, the testimonial capitalizes on the admiration people have for a celebrity, to make the product shine more brightly – even though the celebrity is not an expert on the product being sold.

Print and television ads offer a nonstop parade of testimonials: here's Cher [13] for Holiday Spas; here's basketball star Michael Jordan eating Wheaties; Michael Jackson sings about Pepsi; American Express features a slew of well-known people who assure us that they never go anywhere without their American Express card. Testimonials can sell movies, too; newspaper ads for films often feature favorable comments by well-known reviewers. And, in recent years, testimonials have played an important role in pitching books; the backs of paperbacks frequently list complimentary blurbs by celebrities.

Political candidates, as well as their ad agencies, know the value of testimonials. [14] Barbra Streisand lent her star appeal to the presidential campaign of Bill Clinton, while Arnold Schwarzenegger endorsed George Bush.[17] Even controversial social issues are debated by celebrities. The nuclear freeze, for instance, starred Paul Newman for the pro side and Charlton Heston for the con.

As illogical as testimonials sometimes are (Pepsi's Michael Jackson, for instance, [15] is a health-food adherent who does not drink soft drinks), they are effective propaganda. We like the *person* so much that we like the *product* too.

PLAIN FOLKS

The plain folks approach says, in effect, "Buy me or vote for me. I'm just like you." [16] Regular folks will surely like Bob Evans's Down on the Farm Country Sausage or good old-fashioned Countrytime Lemonade. Some ads emphasize the idea that "we're all in the same boat." We see people making long-distance calls for just the reasons we do – to put the baby on the phone to Grandma or to tell Mom we love her. And how do these folksy, warmhearted (usually saccharine) scenes affect us? They're supposed to make us feel that AT&T – the multinational corporate giant – has the same values we do. Similarly, we are introduced to the little people at Ford, the ordinary folks who work on the assembly line, not to bigwigs in their executive offices. What's the purpose of such an approach? To encourage us to buy a car built by these honest, hardworking "everyday Joes" who care about quality as much as we do.

Political advertisements make almost as much use of the "plain folks" appeal as [17] they do of transfer devices. Candidates wear hard hats, farmers' caps, and assembly-line coveralls. They jog around the block and carry their own luggage through the airport. The idea is to convince voters that the candidates are average people, not the elite – not wealthy lawyers or executives but common citizens.

CARD STACKING

When people say that "the cards were stacked against me," they mean that they [18] were never given a fair chance. Applied to propaganda, card stacking means that one side may suppress or distort evidence, tell half-truths, oversimplify the facts, or

---

[17] *Bill Clinton . . . George Bush:* Clinton challenged and defeated George H. W. Bush, who ran for reelection, in 1992.

set up a "straw man" – a false target – to divert attention from the issue at hand. Card stacking is a difficult form of propaganda both to detect and to combat. When a candidate claims that an opponent has "changed his mind five times on this important issue," we tend to accept the claim without investigating whether the candidate had good reasons for changing his mind. Many people are simply swayed by the distorted claim that the candidate is "waffling" on the issue.

Advertisers often stack the cards in favor of the products they are pushing. They 19 may, for instance, use what are called "weasel words." These are small words that usually slip right past us, but that make the difference between reality and illusion. The weasel words are underlined in the following claims:

- "Helps control dandruff symptoms." (The audience usually interprets this as *stops* dandruff.)
- "Most dentists surveyed recommend sugarless gum for their patients who chew gum." (We hear the "most dentists" and "for their patients," but we don't think about how many were surveyed or whether the dentists first recommended that the patients not chew gum at all.)
- "Sticker price $1,000 lower than most comparable cars." (How many is "most"? What car does the advertiser consider "comparable"?)

Advertisers also use a card-stacking trick when they make an unfinished claim. 20 For example, they will say that their product has "twice as much pain reliever." We are left with a favorable impression. We don't usually ask, "Twice as much pain reliever as what?" Or advertisers may make extremely vague claims that sound alluring but have no substance: Toyota's "Oh, what a feeling!"; Vantage cigarettes' "the taste of success"; "the spirit of Marlboro"; Coke's "the real thing." Another way to stack the cards in favor of a certain product is to use scientific-sounding claims that are not supported by sound research. When Ford claimed that its LTD model was "400% quieter," many people assumed that the LTD must be quieter than all other cars. When taken to court, however, Ford admitted that the phrase referred to the difference between the noise level inside and outside the LTD. Other scientific-sounding claims use mysterious ingredients that are never explained as selling points: "Retsyn," "special whitening agents," "the ingredient doctors recommend."

BANDWAGON

In the bandwagon technique, advertisers pressure, "Everyone's doing it. Why don't 21 you?" This kind of propaganda often succeeds because many people have a deep desire not to be different. Political ads tell us to vote for the "winning candidate." Advertisers know we tend to feel comfortable doing what others do; we want to be on the winning team. Or ads show a series of people proclaiming "I'm voting for the Senator. I don't know why anyone wouldn't." Again, the audience feels under pressure to conform.

In the marketplace, the bandwagon approach lures buyers. Ads tell us that 22 "nobody doesn't like Sara Lee"[18] (the message is that you must be weird if you don't). They tell us that "most people prefer Brand X two to one over other leading brands"

---

[18] *Sara Lee:* Largest U.S. producer of frozen baked goods.

(to be like the majority, we should buy Brand X). If we don't drink Pepsi, we're left out of "the Pepsi generation." To take part in "America's favorite health kick," the National Dairy Council urges us to drink milk. And Honda motorcycle ads, praising the virtues of being a follower, tell us, "Follow the leader. He's on a Honda."

Why do these propaganda techniques work? Why do so many of us buy the products, viewpoints, and candidates urged on us by propaganda messages? They work because they appeal to our emotions, not to our minds. Often, in fact, they capitalize on our prejudices and biases. For example, if we are convinced that environmentalists are radicals who want to destroy America's record of industrial growth and progress, then we will applaud the candidate who refers to them as "treehuggers." Clear thinking requires hard work: analyzing a claim, researching the facts, examining both sides of an issue, using logic to see the flaws in an argument. Many of us would rather let the propagandists do our thinking for us. 23

Because propaganda is so effective, it is important to detect it and understand how it is used. We may conclude, after close examination, that some propaganda sends a truthful, worthwhile message. Some advertising, for instance, urges us not to drive drunk, to become volunteers, to contribute to charity. Even so, we must be aware that propaganda is being used. Otherwise, we have consented to handing over to others our independence of thought and action. 24

Reading Journal

In your journal, write about one of the following topics.

1 Discuss the use of propaganda in your culture – for example, by the government, political candidates, advertisers, schools, or religious figures.

2 Consider the degree to which you think you are influenced by advertising.

3 Choose a topic of your own related to the reading.

Main Ideas

Answer the following questions, referring to the notes you took when reading the selection. Then share your answers with a partner.

1 List the seven propaganda techniques that are discussed in the article. In your own words, write a sentence for each technique, explaining how it works. Then write a second sentence for each device, explaining why it is successful.

2 In what ways are the seven propaganda techniques discussed in the article alike? Do some function in a similar manner to sway people's opinions?

3 What is the main point McClintock makes in the reading? Summarize her central idea in one or two sentences. Use your own words. Begin with the sentence *In the essay "Propaganda Techniques in Today's Advertising," Ann McClintock argues that . . .*

Reflecting on Content

Answer the following questions with a partner. When possible, support your answers with observations based on your own experiences.

1 Look back at your answers to questions 1 and 2 in the exercise Main Ideas on the previous page. Do you think that some of the propaganda techniques mentioned in the article are more effective than others? Why or why not? Be as specific as possible.

2 How much of a threat does McClintock see in propaganda? Do you agree with her?

3 Create a simile and a metaphor that express some point about propaganda and/ or advertising. Try to think of vivid, original comparisons. (See the discussion of figures of speech on page 145.)

A Writer's Technique: *Figures of Speech*

Review the discussion of figures of speech on page 145.

In her article, McClintock uses several metaphors to convey her ideas. Working with a partner, consider the metaphors in the following sentences. Identify the two things being compared and the main idea that the author expresses. For an example, see below.

> **Example:** *Chevrolet, we are told, is the "heartbeat of America." (par. 8)*
> **Comparison:** *a car company and a person's heartbeat*
> **Main Idea:** *Chevrolet is the vital center of the automobile industry.*

1 . . . the seducers and brainwashers are the advertisers we willingly invite into our homes. (par. 1)

2 Indeed, the vast majority of us are targets in advertisers' propaganda war. (par. 3)

3 Name calling is a propaganda tactic in which negatively charged names are hurled against the opposing side or competitor. (par. 5)

4 . . . General Electric "brings good things to life." (par. 8)

5 Political ads, of course, practically wrap themselves in the flag. (par. 11)

Vocabulary: *Connotations of Words*

To understand figures of speech, or figurative language (see page 145), you need to be aware of the connotations of words. A **connotation** is the implied, or suggested, meaning of a word, as opposed to its literal, dictionary definition, or **denotation**. For example, the denotation of *skeleton* is the rigid framework that supports an organism; the connotations of *skeleton* are *disease, war, death,* and *poison.*

Often words with a similar meaning have very different connotations, or emotional overtones – for instance, *sweat* and *perspire; woman* and *lady.*

Sweat and *perspire* both refer to the production of moisture by the skin. *Perspire*, however, is more neutral than *sweat*, which is a graphic, colloquial term, often implying hard work.

Woman and *lady* both refer to an adult female. *Woman*, however, is more neutral than *lady*, which implies refinement, gentle manners, and cultivated taste. To some people, *lady* is a negative term, connoting, or suggesting, a dainty, conventional, often docile woman.

Look at the following pairs of words (at least one word from each pair is taken from McClintock's article). Decide which word connotes a more negative feeling. Write this word in the blank. If you think the two words are equally negative, write both in the blank. Do this exercise first without using a dictionary.

1   seduce (par. 1)   attract   _____
2   indoctrinate   brainwash (par. 1)   _____
3   sufferer   victim (par. 1)   _____
4   propaganda (par. 1)   persuasion   _____
5   totalitarian (par. 3)   undemocratic   _____
6   foreign (par. 5)   imported (par. 5)   _____
7   praise   boast (par. 8)   _____
8   sentimental   saccharine (par. 16)   _____
9   bias (par. 23)   judgment   _____
10 blemish   flaw (par. 23)   _____

Vocabulary in Context

Locate the following italicized vocabulary items in the reading and see if you can determine their meaning from the context. Then think of an example or situation to illustrate each item, using your personal experience if possible. Do not just define the italicized words and expressions. When you are done, share your answers with a partner.

1 something that might make a TV commercial *alluring,* and why (par. 1)
2 the degree to which you think most people are *immune* to the influence of advertising (par. 1)
3 a time when you *swayed* someone's opinion or when someone *swayed* your opinion (par. 2)
4 the degree to which you think advertising or another form of propaganda is a *menace* to society (par. 3)
5 the use of mass media in a *totalitarian* society (par. 3)
6 a propaganda technique that you think especially *arouses* people's feelings (par. 5)
7 an instance of a politician *capitalizing* on something (pars. 12, 23)

8 a reply that an *adherent* of free speech might make to someone in favor of banning certain types of advertising (par. 15)

9 an example of the *cards being stacked* against someone (par. 18)

10 an example of a *flaw* in an argument (par. 23)

Discussion

Choose one of the following activities to do with a partner or in a small group.

1 Read through the following statements and identify the propaganda technique or techniques used in each. There may be several tactics reflected in some statements.

   a And so, my fellow Americans: ask not what your country can do for you – ask what you can do for your country. My fellow citizens of the world: ask not what America will do for you, but what together we can do for the freedom of man. (John F. Kennedy)

   b All the human culture, all the results of art, science, and technology that we see before us today, are almost exclusively the creative product of the Aryan. This very fact admits of the not unfounded inference that he alone was the founder of all higher humanity, therefore representing the prototype of all we understand by the word "man." (Adolf Hitler)

   c Trident Advantage does something for teeth that milk does for bones. Maintains their strength! How can that be? Well, Trident Advantage has Recaldent, a revolutionary ingredient that replenishes calcium your teeth lose every day. So weakened areas get stronger as you chew. In fact, by chewing Trident Advantage regularly, you can replenish up to 4 times more calcium in your teeth than if you didn't chew at all. Not bad for something that fits in your pocket and doesn't have to be refrigerated. Trident Advantage. The advantage of stronger teeth. (From a magazine advertisement)

   d The way of life that is American, that expounds democracy, is a proud way of life. It is a manner of living so fine, so high in ideals and purpose that it stands over and above all others. The Grabosky Family, makers of Royalist cigars, are proud to be members of the American Family, proud to present a cigar so fine in quality that it stands above all others. Over 50 years of superb cigar-making experience lies behind Royalist . . . a proud name in a proud America. (From a newspaper advertisement titled "Pride in the American Way")

2 Analyze and evaluate several magazine advertisements. Begin with the ads on pages 159 and 160 and then examine others you find yourself. Focus on the strategies used in marketing the products, including the seven propaganda techniques discussed in McClintock's article. Which devices do the advertisers employ to attract people's attention and stimulate their desire to buy the products? Consider the target audience, picture (setting, composition, color), text and slogan, mood, claims and appeals (psychological and emotional), and cultural messages, images, and metaphors. Also discuss the strengths and

weaknesses of the ads. How effective do you find them? Would you suggest any changes to make them more effective?

3 Access the Web site <www.bartleby.com/124>, where you will find the inaugural addresses for all the U.S. presidents. (An inaugural address is the speech that a newly elected president gives to the nation.) With your partner or group, choose one of the speeches and identify as many propaganda techniques as you can. How many of the seven tactics that McClintock discusses can you find? When you are done, share your findings with the rest of the class.

Writing Follow-up

Follow up the discussion activity you chose (item 1, 2, or 3) with the matching writing assignment below.

1 Write two statements similar to the ones in item 1, each using one or more of the propaganda techniques McClintock discusses in her article. Consider using a simile or a metaphor in each to help sway your audience's opinion or behavior. Then write the statements on the board and see if the rest of the class can guess which persuasive devices you are using.

2 Imagine you and several classmates are members of an advertising agency that is marketing a new product. Design an advertisement to appear in a national magazine. Consider the target audience, picture, text and slogan, claims and appeals, cultural messages, and propaganda techniques to use in attracting people's attention and in stimulating their desire to buy the product.

3 Briefly discuss the propaganda techniques you found in the inaugural address. Quote the passages and then identify the propaganda device or devices reflected in each.

MAKING CONNECTIONS

Answer two or three of the following questions relating to the three core readings in this chapter.

1 Many people believe that the Internet is one of the most important technological developments of the last one hundred years. What are Gelernter's and Leonard's views on the revolutionary nature of the Internet? Do the two writers agree with each other?

2 In paragraph 23 of his essay, Gelernter says, "Where technology is concerned, we demolish the past and live in a permanent present." In paragraph 19 of his article, Leonard writes, "E-mail doesn't just collapse distance; it demolishes all boundaries." Are the two authors making a similar point? If so, what is it? If they are making different points, how would you explain the difference between their ideas?

3 Both Gelernter and Leonard provide considerable supporting detail to make their points, including examples, personal experiences, and anecdotes. Reread paragraph 21 in Gelernter's essay and paragraphs 18–19 in Leonard's piece. Through their use of detail, what similar point are the authors making about the nature of technological change?

4 Given what McClintock says in her article about the negative influence of advertising and propaganda, how do you think she would view the potential hazards of the Internet?

5 Reread paragraph 18 of Gelernter's essay, paragraphs 13–14 of Leonard's article, and paragraphs 1 and 23 of McClintock's article. What aspect of human nature and/or technology expressed in each of the readings makes people susceptible to the negative influence of propaganda?

ADDITIONAL READING 1
Students Shall Not Download. Yeah, Sure.

Before You Read

With several classmates or in your journal, discuss the extent to which you agree with the following statements about the Internet.

1 Downloading music or movies from the Internet is like stealing a CD or a DVD from a store.
2 It is all right to download Internet music because the recording industry is charging too much for CDs.
3 People should have to pay a fee to download music from the Internet.
4 It is acceptable for a university to monitor and restrict the amount of material and music that its students download from the Internet.
5 In a school essay, it is not necessary for a student to cite, or document, information found on the Internet.
6 Children are less ethical today than they were when my parents were growing up.

Taking Notes While You Read

As you read the article, note in the margin the attitudes that students express toward downloading music and other material from the Internet. Also indicate the points with which you agree or disagree.

 ## Students Shall Not Download. Yeah, Sure.
Kate Zernike

The article by Kate Zernike focuses on college students' attitudes about the ethics of downloading music from the Internet. The article originally appeared in the New York Times *in the fall of 2003 – a time when the music-recording industry filed a number of lawsuits against U.S. citizens for sharing copyrighted music over the Internet.*

In the rough and tumble[1] of the student union here at Pennsylvania State University, the moral code is purely pragmatic.   1

Thou shalt[2] not smoke – it will kill you.   2
Thou shalt not lift a term paper off the Internet – it will get you kicked out.   3
Thou shalt not use a fake ID – it will get you arrested.   4
And when it comes to downloading music or movies off the Internet, students   5

---

[1] *rough and tumble:* Disorderly action and disregard for rules.
[2] *shalt:* Old English word for "shall" (used in the biblical Ten Commandments).

here compare it with underage drinking: illegal, but not immoral. Like alcohol and parties, the Internet is easily accessible. Why not download, or drink, when "everyone" does it?

This set of commandments has helped make people between the ages of 18 and 29, and college students in particular, the biggest downloaders of Internet music. 6

"It's not something you feel guilty about doing," said Dan Langlitz, 20, a junior here. "You don't get the feeling it's illegal because it's so easy." He held an MP3 player in his hand. "They sell these things; the sites are there. Why is it illegal?" 7

Students say they have had the Internet for as long as they can remember and have grown up thinking of it as theirs for the taking. 8

The array of services available to them on campus has only encouraged that sense. 9

Penn State recently made the student center, known as the Hub, entirely wireless, so students do not even have to dial up to get on the Internet. In comfortable armchairs, they sit clicking on Google searches, their ears attached to iPods,[3] cell phones a hand away. A swipe of a student ID gets them three free newspapers. They do not need cash – only a swipe card, the cost included in their student fees – to buy anything from a caramel caffe latte to tamale pie at an abundance of fast food counters. There is a bank branch and a travel agency, and a daily activities board lists a Nascar simulator[4] as well as rumba lessons. 10

Many courses put all materials – textbook excerpts, articles, syllabuses – online. Residence halls offer fast broadband access – which studies say makes people more likely to download. 11

"It kind of spoils us, in a sense, because you get used to it," said Jill Wilson, 20, a sophomore. 12

The ease of going online has shaped not only attitudes about downloading, but cheating as well, blurring the lines between right and wrong so much that many colleges now require orientation courses that give students specific examples of what plagiarism looks like. Students generally know not to buy a paper off the Internet, but many think it is O.K. to pull a paragraph or two, as long as they change a few words. 13

"Before, when you had to go into the library and at least type it into your paper, you were pretty conscious about what you were doing," said Janis Jacobs, vice-provost for undergraduate education here. "That means we do have to educate students about what is O.K. It's the same whether you're talking about plagiarizing a phrase from a book or article or downloading music – it all seems free to them." 14

Last year and again last week, the university sent out an e-mail message reminding students that downloading copyrighted music was illegal, and pleading with them to "resist the urge" to download. It also warned students that it had begun monitoring how much information students are downloading, and that they could lose their Internet access if their weekly use exceeded a limit administrators described as equivalent to tens of thousands of e-mail messages sent. 15

This year, all students had to take an online tutorial before receiving access to 16

---

[3] *iPod:* Digital music player with extensive storage and downloading capabilities.

[4] *Nascar simulator:* Video device that re-creates the experience of high-speed car racing.

their e-mail accounts, acknowledging that they had read and agreed to university policy prohibiting the downloading of copyrighted material.

At the same time, realizing the difficulties of stopping downloading, Penn State's president, Graham B. Spanier, is hoping to try out a program this spring where the university would pay for the rights to music, and then allow students to download at will. 17

To students, the crackdown seemed like a sudden reversal. 18

"Up until recently, we were not told it was wrong," said Kristin Ebert, 19. "We think if it's available, you can use it. It's another resource." 19

When representatives from the technology services department told students about the bandwidth monitoring, Ms. Ebert said, they outlined the reasonable limits in terms of movies downloaded. "They weren't encouraging it, but they used it as a frame of reference," she said. "They were aware, but they weren't doing anything to correct it." 20

Penn State has taken a harder line than most other campuses. But whether here or at other campuses, students do not seem to be grasping the moral message. 21

According to a study by the Pew Internet and American Life Project last spring, 56 percent of college students download music, compared with about 25 percent of nonstudents, and those students are more likely than downloaders in general – 80 percent to 67 percent – to say they do not care that the music is copyrighted when they download it. (The study came before recent lawsuits by the recording industry against 261 people it says have shared copyrighted music over the Internet. But researchers defend the report's relevancy, saying it came after the industry had shut down Napster[5] and begun a widespread advertising campaign against downloading.) 22

VIEWS ABOUT DOWNLOADING MUSIC

	Agree	Disagree	Not Sure
		(Percentages)	
Downloading and then selling music is piracy and should be prohibited; downloading for personal use is an innocent act and should not be prohibited.	75	14	11
If the price of CDs were a lot lower, there would be a lot less downloading of music off the Internet.	70	21	9
Musicians and the recording companies should get the full financial benefit of their work.	64	17	19
Downloading music off the Internet is no different from buying a used CD or recording music borrowed from a friend.	54	31	15

SOURCE: Harris Poll of 2,306 U.S. adults.

Similarly, studies by the Center for Academic Integrity show a decline in traditional peering-over-someone's-shoulder cheating, but a steady rise in Internet plagiarism from 1999 to 2003. 23

Here, the warnings against plagiarism seem to have sunk in better than those about downloading. But even some of the lessons about plagiarism came as a 24

---

[5] *Napster:* Popular Internet service allowing users to copy songs from each other's hard drives free of charge.

surprise to students who had freely used the Internet in high school.

"When I came in, I didn't expect any of this to be plagiarism," said Maria   25
Sansone, 22, a senior. "The idea you had to cite what you took off the Internet was
new. I think a lot of people don't know where to draw the line."

Elizabeth Kiss, director of the Kenan Institute for Ethics at Duke University, said   26
she suspected that older generations were not more ethical, just less techno-savvy.
"I don't think we've done a very good job of making the argument that it's different
if it's copyrighted," Ms. Kiss said. "If students haven't grown up with that being a
conversation, they're not thinking about it."

Ann Morrissey, 19, confessed that she had not even listened to all the songs she   27
had downloaded. "I have 400 songs, I listen to 20," she said. "I don't know why,"
she added, then laughed self-consciously, and answered herself, "You can, and it's
cool to have them."

She, like others, does not see the harm done, and remains suspicious of the   28
recording industry.

"How are you going to make downloading illegal when you can still smoke legally   29
and give yourself lung cancer?" Ms. Morrissey asked. "There are a lot worse issues
you could focus on."

The university has sent warnings about exceeding bandwidth to a couple of   30
hundred students. But on a campus with 42,000 students, punishment seems
remote to many.

"No one close to home has gotten in trouble," said Andrew Ricken, a junior.   31

A common analogy – downloading music is like stealing a CD – does not sway   32
students. Many argue that they are spending more money on music.

"I never went out and bought CDs; now I go to concerts, because I know what   33
kind of music people play," said Kristen Lipski, 20. "If you can get your music out to
a big group of people to listen to, they'll go to your CD, go to your concert, spend
money on posters. It's really expensive, especially for college students, to buy the
whole CD."

Mr. Langlitz was on his way to a concert downtown by Taking Back Sunday, a   34
band he said he would never have heard without downloading. "A lot of the bands
I know about aren't that well-known," he said. "Before I saw their CDs, I had them
in my computer."

These are the same arguments adults make. But while adults who remember the   35
days of LPs[6] seem willing to pay 99 cents a song, students see any transition from
free as a denial of basic right.

"A dollar a song is just not worth it," said Edwin Shaw, a 20-year-old junior   36
walking across campus with his MP3 player and trying to confirm which night the
Red Hot Chili Peppers were playing on campus.

At best, the new warnings seemed to have some students negotiating new   37
rules.

At a table with friends, John Dixon was debating whether he would be caught   38
if he traded songs only with his roommates on their local area network, off campus.

---

[6] *LPs:* Long-playing records. These vinyl disks, played on turntables (record players), were of the technology that
preceded audiotapes and CDs.

Just to be safe, he is sticking mostly to downloading music from CDs. He is not sharing his files – not because he sees it as illegal, but because he hears that the record industry is going mainly after sharers, not downloaders.

"The risk is higher," Mr. Dixon said.   39

Ms. Wilson, too, is not sharing, though she has continued downloading.   40

"That doesn't make it right," she said. "But it's not that big a deal, right?"   41

After You Read

In your journal, write about one of the following topics.

1 Explain the main point Zernike makes in the article.

2 Do you think that downloading copyrighted music from the Internet without paying for it is an ethical or an unethical practice? Explain.

3 Choose a topic of your own related to the reading.

ADDITIONAL READING 2
Don't Touch That Dial

Before You Read

With several classmates or in your journal, discuss the extent to which you agree with the following statements.

1 There are more advantages than disadvantages to watching TV.

2 TV is inherently dangerous to children, impairing their intellectual and social development.

3 TV usually replaces important activities, such as book reading and family discussions.

4 TV is an active medium that encourages children to think about what they are seeing and hearing.

5 Heavy TV-watching lowers IQ scores and hinders school performance.

6 The government should regulate the amount of sex and violence on TV.

7 TV is the most influential mass medium today.

Taking Notes While You Read

As you read the article, note in the margin common criticisms of watching television. Consider individual and social influences. Also indicate the points with which you agree or disagree.

Don't Touch That Dial

Madeline Drexler

The following article originally appeared in the Boston Globe, *a large daily newspaper, in 1991. Madeline Drexler is a science and medical journalist whose work has appeared in many national publications in the United States.*

Television acts as a narcotic on children – mesmerizing them, stunting their ability   1
to think, and displacing such wholesome activities as book reading and family discussions. Right?

Wrong, says researcher Daniel Anderson, a psychologist at the University of   2
Massachusetts at Amherst. Anderson doesn't have any particular affection for *Garfield and Friends,* MTV clips, or *Gilligan's Island* reruns.[1] But he does believe it's important to distinguish television's impact on children from influences of the family and the wider culture. We tend to blame TV, he says, for problems it doesn't really cause. In the process, we overlook our own roles in shaping children's minds.

One conventional belief about television is that it impairs a child's ability to   3
think and to interpret the world. But Anderson's own research and reviews of the scientific literature discredit this assumption. While watching TV, children do not merely absorb words and images. Instead, they muse upon the meaning of what they see, its plausibility, and its implications for the future – whether they've tuned in to a news report of a natural disaster or an action show. Because television relies on such cinematic techniques as montage and crosscutting,[2] children learn early how to draw inferences about the passage of time, character psychology, and implied events. Even preschoolers comprehend more than just the information supplied on the tube.

Another contention about television is that it displaces reading as a form of   4
entertainment. But according to Anderson, the amount of time spent watching television is not related to reading ability. For one thing, TV doesn't take the place of reading for most children; it takes the place of similar sorts of recreation, such as going to the movies, reading comic books, listening to the radio, and playing sports. Variables such as socioeconomic status and parents' educational background exert a far stronger influence on a child's reading. "Far and away," Anderson says, "the best predictor of reading ability, and of how much a child reads, is how much a parent reads."

Conventional wisdom has it that heavy television-watching lowers IQ scores[3]   5
and hinders school performance. Since the 1960s, SAT scores[4] have dropped, along with state and national assessments of educational achievement. But here, too, Anderson notes that no studies have linked prolonged television exposure

---

[1] Gilligan's Island *reruns*: Repeated episodes of a show, popular in the 1960s, about a group of people stranded on a deserted island. (*Garfield and Friends* is an animated show about a cat, and MTV clips are music videos.)

[2] *crosscutting*: Interweaving parts of two or more separate scenes. (A montage is a rapid sequence of scenes or images.)

[3] *IQ scores*: Scores on a test assessing one's intelligence (IQ stands for "intelligence quotient").

[4] *SAT scores*: Scores on the Scholastic Assessment Test, an admissions test required by most colleges for native English speakers.

in childhood to lower IQ later on. In fact, research suggests that it's the other way around. Early IQ predicts how much TV an older child will watch. "If you're smart young, you'll watch less TV when you're older," Anderson says. Conversely, in the same self-selecting process, people of lower IQ tend to be lifelong television devotees.

When parents watch TV with their young children, explaining new words and 6 ideas to them, the children comprehend far more than they would if they were watching alone. This is due partly to the fact that when kids expect that TV will require thought, they spend more time thinking. What's ironic is that most parents use an educational program as an opportunity to park their kids in front of the set and do something in another room. "Even for parents who are generally wary of television," Anderson says, "*Sesame Street* is considered a show where it's perfectly okay to leave a child alone." The program was actually intended to be viewed by parents and children together, he says.

Because our attitudes inform TV viewing, Anderson applauds the nascent trend 7 of offering high school courses that teach students how to "decode" television. In these classes, students learn to analyze the persuasion techniques of commercials, compare the reality of crime to its dramatic portrayal, inquire into the economics of broadcasting, and understand the mechanics of TV production. Such courses, Anderson contends, teach the kind of critical thinking central to the purpose of education. "Kids can be taught as much about television as about text or computers," he says.

If anything, Anderson's views underscore the fact that television cannot be 8 disparaged in isolation from larger forces. For years researchers have attempted to show that television is inherently dangerous to children, hypnotizing them with its movement and color, cutting their attention span with its fast-paced, disconnected images, curbing intellectual development, and taking the place of loftier pastimes.

By showing that 9 television promotes none of these effects, Anderson intends to shift the discussion to the real issue: content. That, of course, is a thornier discussion. How should our society judge the violence of prime time shows?[5] The sexism of MTV? The materialism of commercials? "I feel television is almost surely having a major social impact on the kids, as opposed to a cognitive impact," Anderson says.

VIOLENCE ON TELEVISION	
% of Programs with Violence	61
Violent Programs	
% that show long-term negative consequences of violence	16
% with perpetrators as bad characters who go unpunished	45
% with perpetrators as attractive characters	40
Violent Scenes	
% with no remorse, criticism, or penalty for violence	71
% with blood and gore	14
% with humor	42
Violent Interactions	
% that show no physical harm or pain to victim	51
% with unrealistically low levels of harm	34
% with lethal violence	54
SOURCE: National Television Violence Study	

In this context, he offers some advice to parents. First, "Parents should think of 10

_____

[5] *prime time shows:* Programs seen during the most popular evening viewing hours.

their kids as actively absorbing everything on television. They are not just passively mesmerized – in one eye and out the other. Some things on TV are probably good for children to watch, like educational TV, and some things are bad."

Second, "If you think your kid is spending lots of time watching television, think about what alternatives there are, from the child's point of view." Does a youngster have too much free time? Are there books, toys, games, or playmates around? "A lot of the time, kids watch TV as a default activity: There's nothing else to do." 11

Finally, "If a child persists in watching too much television, the question is why. It's rare that TV shows are themselves so entertaining." More often than not, the motive is escapism. A teenager may be uncomfortable with his or her peers; a child may want to retreat from a home torn by marital strife; there may be problems at school. 12

For children, as for adults, television can be a source of enlightenment or a descent into mindlessness – depending mostly on the choices of lucre-driven executives.[6] But as viewers, we can't ignore what we ourselves bring to the medium. 13

After You Read

In your journal, write about one of the following topics.

1 Discuss whether you agree or disagree with Anderson that "television is almost surely having a major social impact on the kids, as opposed to a cognitive impact." (par. 9)

2 Explain the meanings of the simile in paragraph 1 and the metaphor in paragraph 13. Which two things are being compared? What is the purpose of the comparisons?

3 Choose a topic of your own related to the reading.

---

[6] *lucre-driven executives:* Executives motivated by making money.

ADDITIONAL READING 3
Conceptual Fruit

Before You Read

With several classmates or in your journal, discuss whether you agree or disagree with the following statement: "The activities that most people are involved in on the Internet have a strong connection to their real lives."

As you read the story, note in the margin the differences you notice between Greta's and her father's reactions to activities on the Internet.

 # Conceptual Fruit
Thaisa Frank

The following short story about the Internet appears in Thaisa Frank's story collection Sleeping in Velvet (1997). *In addition to writing fiction, Frank teaches at the University of San Francisco and practices psychotherapy.*

When he told his family about the site on the Internet where you could create whole streets, his wife and son went on eating their pasta and artichokes. Only his daughter Greta looked up. 1

"I could buy a house on Pomanger Street," he said, "and put as many rooms in it as I wanted. I could fill it with fruit and make my own library." 2

"Sure, Dad," said his son, who was eleven. "You could do that. If you wanted to." His son already knew how to program computers, but wasn't interested. These days he wanted to give away books and devote his life to karate. 3

His wife ate the heart of the artichoke carefully. She cut it into fourths, put salt and pepper on each fourth, and then covered each fourth with hollandaise.[1] His wife was thin and could eat all the hollandaise she wanted. High cholesterol didn't run in her family. 4

"Well?" he said. 5

"The thing is," she answered, "I'm in front of a computer all day and I like to spend evenings in the garden." He understood she wasn't interested. But still. He was about to tell her not to put him down in front of the kids when Greta looked up from her artichoke leaves. She was arranging them in a swirling pattern in her bowl. 6

"You said there were streets. You said there could be fruit." 7

These weren't questions. Greta often repeated whatever she heard. She'd worked hard to tie her shoes by age ten and could read at fifth-grade level, five grades below Joel, even though she was sixteen. She went to a special school where they taught her to collect coupons and save receipts from the supermarket. She still couldn't shop by herself. 8

"I want to see," she said. 9

"I'll show you," he answered. His wife and his son made eyes. *He's at it again.* *He's getting Greta into it, too.* 10

"Come on. I'll show you where you can make up streets and bowls of fruit." His wife cleared the table. His son went to practice the saxophone. 11

Greta sat in his chair, and he sat next to her. Greta could type very slowly. By 12

___

[1] *hollandaise:* Type of creamy sauce.

the time she left her school she might be able to type fast enough to get a word processing job. No one knew for sure.

"There's this guy named Sam who set up this whole library of classics in a house in Boston on Beacon Hill. He lives in Illinois, but he made this incredible place. Watch." He clicked into the program and was about to show Greta the collection of books when he saw her staring into space. "You want something of your own, don't you?" 13

"Yes. Peaches and pears and artichokes." 14

"Do you want them in a house, with bowls in a kitchen? Or maybe in a garden?" He was already typing, creating a street called *Greta's Street,* a house called *Greta's House.* 15

"Why are you writing all that down?" 16

"Because they're yours. They belong to you." 17

Greta looked at the screen. Her blond hair blended with her sweater. Her blue eyes were the only color in her face. She looked beautiful, he thought – carved from a single stone. 18

"I want a bowl in every room," she said. "Peaches in the kitchen and living room and all the bedrooms." 19

"What about artichokes?" 20

Greta picked at her sweater – something she did when she knew she hadn't gotten it right. She'd forgotten about the artichokes, and he was sorry he'd reminded her. "It's okay," he said. "We'll put peaches everywhere. Should the bowls be a color?" 21

"Blue." 22

He asked Greta how many windows she wanted, whether there should be a fireplace, and if there should be curtains. Greta chose eleven windows covered with sheer white curtains like the ones she had in her bedroom. She took a long time thinking about the curtains. He wondered what she was learning in Life Skills.[2] 23

"Okay, now the fruit," he said. "We'll start with the kitchen." He wrote *Greta's Kitchen,* and added, *Walk around. Help yourself to this bowl of fruit.* 24

"But where are the peaches?" 25

"In a minute. Look, this is cool. You click under bowl, and see what happens?" He shielded the screen for a moment and wrote *peaches.* "Try it," he said. "Just click *bowl.*" 26

Greta clicked *bowl.* The word *peaches* appeared. "It's just a word," she said to him. 27

"Well, that's the idea. But you can see a picture of the fruit." 28

"I thought you could make real peaches." 29

"No. You have to go to the store for those." 30

"But these are just words." 31

"Well, yes." 32

"Then why do people like them?" 33

"Because they remind them of what they stand for. Like in your books. Or the coupons you save." 34

A year ago she would have cried. Now she closed her eyes. 35

---

[2] *Life Skills:* Class focusing on practical abilities that will help with daily life, such as cooking and shopping.

"Are you disappointed?" 36

"No. I want fruit in every room." 37

He created other rooms, asking Greta what she wanted: a kitchen, a dining 38
room, a living room, a bedroom, a room for a cat, and one bathroom.

"No, not a bathroom," she decided. "This isn't a real house, so people wouldn't 39
use it."

"You're right," he said. "You don't need a bathroom." 40

He programmed bowls of peaches in every room. "Now," he said to Greta. "You 41
click."

Greta clicked and this time smiled when the word *peaches* appeared. It was a 42
furtive smile – a smile she got when she pretended she understood something that
made no sense.

"There could be other fruit," he said. "There could be apples, pears. There could 43
be flowers."

"Sure," said Greta. "There could be anything." 44

His wife was cutting blackberries in the garden, and Greta was already sliding 45
from the chair to help her. Greta would never have a house of her own. She would
live in a group house with other people like her. He hoped the house would be large
and have sheer white curtains billowing in all the rooms. He hoped it would be an
orchard with fruit to put in real blue bowls: apples, pears, peaches – whatever Greta
wanted.

After You Read

In your journal, write about one of the following topics.

1 What is the main point, or message, that Frank wishes to convey in the
  story? Think especially about the differences between Greta's and her father's
  reactions to activities on the Internet.

2 Discuss the meaning of the metaphor in paragraph 18. What two things are
  being compared? What is the purpose of the comparison?

3 Choose a topic of your own related to the story.

ADDITIONAL READING 4
All Watched Over by Machines of Loving Grace

Before You Read

With several classmates or in your journal, discuss whether you agree or disagree
with the following statement: "Technology more often than not enhances the
ability of people to enjoy their relationships with each other and with nature."

Taking Notes While You Read

As you read the poem, underline the similes and metaphors that poet Richard Brautigan uses to express his ideas.

All Watched Over by Machines of Loving Grace
Richard Brautigan

The following poem by Richard Brautigan (1933–1984), a popular U.S. poet and novelist, deals with computers; it was written at a time when this electronic technology was in its early stages (late 1960s and early 1970s). The poem comes from Brautigan's collection of poetry The Pill Versus the Springhill Mine Disaster *(1968).*

I like to think (and
the sooner the better!)
of a cybernetic[1] meadow
where mammals and computers
live together in mutually   5
programming harmony
like pure water
touching clear sky.

I like to think
(right now, please!)   10
of a cybernetic forest
filled with pines and electronics
where deer stroll peacefully
past computers
as if they were flowers   15
with spinning blossoms.

I like to think
(it has to be!)
of a cybernetic ecology
where we are free of our labors   20
and joined back to nature,
returned to our mammal
brothers and sisters,
and all watched over
by machines of loving grace.   25

---

[1] *cybernetic:* Relating to computers and other electronic communications systems.

After You Read

In your journal, write about one of the following topics.

1 What is the main point, or message, that Brautigan wishes to convey in the poem?

2 Discuss the meaning of one of the similes and one of the metaphors in the poem. Which two things are being compared? What is the purpose of the comparisons?

3 Choose a topic of your own related to the poem.

ADDITIONAL READING 5
Humor: E-mail Mixup

With a partner, read the following joke and cartoon and discuss the issues relating to the mass media and technology.

 ## E-mail Mixup

It is wise to remember how easily this wonderful e-mail technology can be misused, sometimes unintentionally, with serious consequences. Consider the case of the Illinois man who left the snow-filled streets of Chicago for a vacation in Florida. His wife was on a business trip and was planning to meet him there the next day. When he reached his hotel, he decided to send his wife a quick e-mail. Unable to find the scrap of paper on which he had written her e-mail address, he did his best to type it in from memory. Unfortunately, he missed one letter, and his note was directed instead to an elderly preacher's wife, whose husband had passed away only the day before. When the grieving widow checked her e-mail, she took one look at the monitor, let out a piercing scream, and fell to the floor in a dead faint. At the sound, her family rushed into the room and saw this note on the screen:

> Dearest Wife,
>
> Just got checked in. Everything prepared for your arrival tomorrow.
>
> P.S. Sure is hot down here.

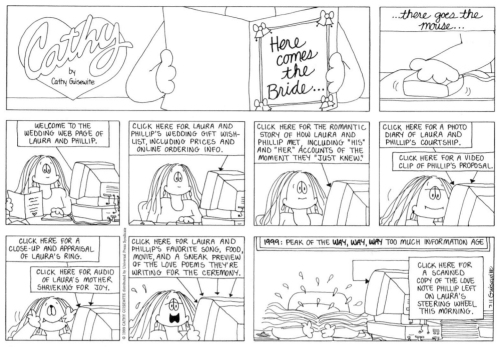

CATHY © (1999) Cathy Guisewite. Reprinted with permission of UNIVERSAL PRESS SYNDICATE. All rights reserved.

ESSAY TOPICS

Write an essay on one of the following topics. Support your points with an appropriate combination of references to the readings in this chapter, library and Internet sources, and personal experiences and observations.

Refer to the section "The Essentials of Writing" on pages 102–132 to help you plan, draft, and revise your essay. Use this special section, too, to assist you in locating, integrating, and documenting your sources.

1 Discuss whether you agree or disagree with the following statement: "The Internet is one of the most important technological innovations in human history."

2 Explore how e-mail and other forms of online communication shape the ways in which people interact with each other.

3 Examine the ways in which a particular technology or form of mass media has been a Faustian bargain – a situation in which something is gained and lost at the same time.

4 Discuss your reaction to the following quotation: "TV is ruining the country. Our society's rot owes more to television than any other single cause." (David Nyhan, U.S. correspondent for the newspaper the *Boston Globe*.)

5 Focus on a particular aspect of one of the following subjects:
   • stereotyping in the mass media (for example, gender, ethnic, or religious)
   • propaganda
   • advertising
   • censorship
   • Internet addiction or privacy rights
   • biotechnology

Gender Roles

A WRITER'S TECHNIQUE
Summarizing and Paraphrasing

In this chapter, you will explore gender roles – the distinct values and
expectations associated with female and with male character, behavior,
and appearance. In addition, you will consider the cultural and biological
factors that shape attitudes toward gender, the consequences of gender
stereotyping, and traditional and changing gender roles.

Questions Raised in Chapter Four

Working with a partner or in a small group, discuss two or three of the following questions.

1 Are gender roles shaped more by biological or by cultural factors?
2 To what extent do social institutions, such as family, school, mass media, and religion, reinforce gender stereotypes?
3 What are the consequences of behaving in a manner that society considers inappropriate for one's sex?
4 Are females or males more restricted by conventional gender roles?
5 Would the world be a better place if there were no distinct gender roles?

Brief Quotations

The following quotations deal with gender issues considered in this chapter. Working with a partner or in a small group, choose two or three quotations and discuss them.

1 *The word* love *has by no means the same sense for both sexes, and this is one of the serious misunderstandings that divide them.* (Simone de Beauvoir, French writer)
2 *The greatest mind must be androgynous.* (Samuel Taylor Coleridge, English poet)
3 *What are little girls made of?*
    Sugar and spice and everything nice,
    and that's what little girls are made of.
  What are little boys made of?
    Snips and snails and puppy dog tails,
    and that's what little boys are made of.
              (English nursery rhyme)
4 *Wives, submit unto your husbands, as unto the Lord. For the husband is the head of the wife, even as Christ is the head of the church.* (Saint Paul, from Ephesians, in the New Testament)
5 *There is more difference within the sexes than between them.* (Ivy Compton-Burnett, English novelist)
6 *Whatever women do, they must do twice as well as men to be thought half as good. Luckily, this is not difficult.* (Charlotte Whitton, Canadian politician)

CORE READING 1
Sex Roles

Journal Writing

Use the **journalist's questions** (*who? what? when? where? why? how?*) to explore one or two nonphysical differences you've noticed between females and males – for example, personality traits, interests, or ways of thinking and behaving. (See asking the journalist's questions, a prewriting strategy, on page 116.) Then share your ideas with several classmates.

Previewing the Topic

Write a list of four or five advantages and disadvantages of being female or male. When you are finished, discuss your ideas in a small group. Write a list, on the board, of all the benefits and drawbacks the group considered.

Agreeing and Disagreeing

To what extent do you agree with the following statements? Fill in each blank with SA (strongly agree), A (agree), U (undecided), D (disagree), or SD (strongly disagree). Then share your responses with several classmates.

_____ 1 Most cultures place equal importance on the appearance of females and of males.

_____ 2 Most parents treat their daughters and sons in the same way.

_____ 3 There are some jobs at which women are better than men.

_____ 4 Feminists do more to hurt women than to help them.

_____ 5 Women are innately better at parenting than males.

_____ 6 The mass media are very important in shaping a person's sense of gender.

_____ 7 The ways females and males learn to behave are the same throughout the world.

_____ 8 Females and males have equal educational and employment opportunities in my culture.

_____ 9 The experiences considered necessary for girls to become women and for boys to become men are very different in my culture.

_____ 10 The world would be a better place if there were no distinct gender roles.

As you read the following selection, note in the margin any differences mentioned between females and males in terms of character, behavior, and social responsibilities. Consider both biological and cultural traits.

Sex Roles
Hamilton McCubbin and Barbara Blum Dahl

The following reading, "Sex Roles," is part of a chapter from the book Marriage and Family: Individuals and Life Cycles *(1985) by Hamilton McCubbin and Barbara Blum Dahl, former professors at the University of Minnesota. In the selection, the authors present the biological, social, and cultural evidence for the formation of gender roles. Because the authors are reporting research to an academic audience, they are careful to cite their sources in the text and to include publication information about the sources at the end of the reading.*

> Man for the field and woman for the hearth:[1]
> Man for the sword and the needle she:
> Man with the head and woman with the heart:
> Man to command and woman to obey: All else confusion.
>
> Alfred, Lord Tennyson[2]

> Many, if not all, of the personality traits which we have called masculine or feminine are as lightly linked to sex as are the clothing, the manners, and the form of headdress that a society at any given period assigns to either sex.
>
> Margaret Mead[3]

> How is it that this world has always belonged to the men?
>
> Simone de Beauvoir[4]

SEX ROLES AND GENDER IDENTITY

A role in a play is a part for an actor; it includes certain scripted actions, ways   1
of walking, talking, expressing feelings, and so forth. A sex role[5] is a part that an individual plays as a social actor – the patterns of feeling and behavior deemed appropriate or inappropriate because of her or his gender. The "script" comes from social expectations about masculine and feminine nature: men should be brave, strong, ambitious, and aggressive, while keeping their feelings under control; women should be gentle, nurturant, passive, dependent, and expressive of their feelings.

---

[1] *hearth:* Home (literally, the stone or cement area in front of a fireplace).

[2] *Alfred, Lord Tennyson* (1809–1892): Well-known English poet.

[3] *Margaret Mead* (1901–1978): Prominent American anthropologist.

[4] *Simone de Beauvoir* (1908–1986): Noted French author and feminist.

[5] *sex role:* Most scholars today use the term *gender role* (not *sex role*) to refer to behaviors and attitudes associated with femininity and masculinity. The word *sex* is commonly used to refer to the biological features that distinguish women from men.

Sex roles are based on social norms – the agreed-upon standards of acceptable   2
behavior within a society. These norms – such as the norms that men should keep
their feelings under control and women should be passive – influence our judgments
not only of others but also of ourselves. Thus, if you are male and prone to tears
during highly emotional moments or female and likely to dominate classroom
discussions and arguments, you may judge yourself harshly because you have
internalized traditional sex-role assumptions. Sex roles, then, are part of our concept
of ourselves, our gender identity.

Sex roles are of great interest to psychologists, sociologists, and other social   3
scientists. Psychologists focus primarily on "inner" personality traits and stereotypes
associated with femininity and masculinity, while sociologists emphasize patterns of
"outer" behavior or interaction in society. For example, a sociologist studying the
paid labor force of the United States would note that most truck drivers are male
while most nurses are female. Family sociologists have studied the inclination of
judges in child custody cases to assume that mothers are innately better at parenting
than fathers.

THE CAUSE OF SEX ROLES: BIOLOGY OR CULTURE?

How do gender differences come about? Do sex roles result from biological   4
differences between the sexes? Or do women and men *learn* to behave differently
because of the effects of culture and society?

We know that women as a group score consistently lower than men as a group on   5
mathematics and science achievement tests. (Notice that we said "as a group"; some
women score extremely high, while some men score extremely low. But women's
average scores are consistently somewhat lower than men's average scores.)

Does this mean that women's brains function differently than men's, that they   6
are not as equipped to do math problems? Does it mean that the male power
structure – which for so long prohibited women from receiving any type of formal
education – is still inhibiting women in the traditionally male preserves of math and
science? Or is it that women lose interest in these subjects because they fear that
achievement in math and science will make them less attractive to men?

In short, are traditional sex roles the result of "nature" (biological differences),   7
"nurture" (culture and socialization), or some combination of both?

GENETICS: THE BIOLOGICAL EVIDENCE

No one disputes that there are biological differences between the sexes. The   8
controversy arises, however, when we try to establish links between these biological
differences and the behavior of men and women. Specifically, does biology limit the
potential achievements of one or both sexes?

Men and women differ in their genetic structure. Women have two "X"   9
chromosomes; men have one "X" and one "Y" chromosome. The complex links
between genes and behavior are now being researched; it is impossible to say at
this time how differences in chromosome structure may affect women's and men's
behavior. We do know that genetic structure determines physical development. The
average male is taller, heavier, and more muscular than the average female. Women
develop breasts and can bear and nurse children; men cannot.

It is not unreasonable to assume that men did the hunting and heavier physical   10 labor in earlier societies because they were better suited to do so, while women raised the children because they could breast-feed them and food was scarce. Perhaps these differing behavioral patterns for women and men in such societies were the result of adaptation; that is, the traits helped them to survive and reproduce at a time when subsistence was a full-time job. But should these differences matter in an industrialized era in which most heavy labor is done by machines and even the fighting of wars relies on sophisticated technology?

11 Researchers have speculated that certain behavioral differences are due to male and female hormones. Both men and women produce the male hormone, androgen, and the female hormone, estrogen, but in differing quantities. The male embryo's "Y" chromosome gives a "command" to release androgen at specific stages of prenatal development. The hormone signals the embryo to develop as a male, with male body shape and male sexual organs. Later on, hormones influence bodily changes during puberty; for example, androgen gives signals to the male's body for the growth of facial and body hair and for the deepening of the voice.

12 Thus, hormones clearly play a role in human physical development. But what effect do they have on emotional development and actual behavior? Again, this question is still being debated and studied. Some research shows that the male hormone testosterone appears to stimulate aggressive behavior in female animals. At the same time, a female hormone, prolactin, seems to stimulate nurturing, motherly activity in male animals (Rose, Gordon, and Bernstein).

13 John Money and his colleagues have conducted studies on those rare individuals known as hermaphrodites who are a mixture of male and female biology. The researchers have looked, for example, at girls who received more androgen at birth than is normal for females. While genetically they were girls with XX chromosomes, they behaved more like our society expects boys to act. That is, they enjoyed rough games, were physically active, and preferred toy trucks to dolls. Money speculates that early exposure to the male hormone influenced the behavior of these girls.

14 Hormones may also have an impact on certain differences in brain functions. Jerre Levy of the University of Chicago has found differences in the way male and female brains are organized. In Levy's view, men's brains work in such a way as to give them superior visual-spatial skills, while women's brains may give them an advantage in verbal skills. Men are therefore better at dealing with abstract concepts; women are more effective in picking up information from the surrounding environment about people, sounds, and so forth. These brain differences may result from the release of certain hormones at critical periods of prenatal development.

15 From the point of view of human evolution, such differences make sense. Men were the hunters and needed good visual skills. In addition, they had to be extremely goal-oriented to succeed in their work. Women lived in groups and took care of children and the sick; thus, sensitivity to others was a crucial skill. As noted earlier, the development of these patterns had an adaptive value in terms of survival and reproduction (Durden-Smith).

16 Still, we must emphasize that the research on hormonal effects remains at an early and primitive stage. The biological differences between the sexes which exist serve only as loose boundaries within which culturally learned differences appear. For example, while prenatal exposure to androgen may have predisposed the girls in

Money's study toward more aggressive, "boyish" behavior, they also needed a social environment that would encourage (or at least allow) such behavior.

Estelle Ramey points out that while men and women vary as groups in their respective levels of male and female hormones, there can also be striking hormonal differences between one man and another or one woman and another. Ramey stresses that these individual differences in levels of testosterone, estrogen, and other hormones are much more significant than any generalized differences between the sexes. 17

Thus, while the biological basis for sex-related distinctions is important, the role that society and culture play is probably more significant. Our biological nature may be like a rough piece of stone from which society, like a sculptor, chisels, sharpens, and defines the shapes of male and female behavior. Research in the next decade should begin to clarify the complex interrelationship of genetic and hormonal differences, environmental influences, and the behavior of women and men. 18

CULTURE: THE ANTHROPOLOGICAL EVIDENCE

How, then, does society shape differences between men and women? Cross-cultural studies, generally conducted by anthropologists, have shown that the typical behavior of males and females in other cultures is quite different from traditional "masculine" and "feminine" behavior in the United States. 19

Margaret Mead, in her pioneering anthropological study, *Sex and Temperament in Three Primitive Societies,* observed three distinct tribes in New Guinea. She found that one of them, the Arapesh, expected both women and men to be warm, cooperative, and nurturing, and generally to exhibit traits that we have traditionally described as "feminine." By contrast, among the Mundugumor tribe, both sexes exhibit traits seen as "masculine" in American society: they were aggressive, competitive, and prone to fighting and controversy. Finally, in the Tchambuli tribe, the character traits seemed the reverse of those expected under our traditional norms. Women were dominant, controlling, and hardworking, while men were emotionally dependent, irresponsible, and extremely concerned about personal appearance. Mead's famous study is often cited by those who argue against the view that biology is the cause of sex differences. If biological distinctions dictate our behavior, they argue, then how can one explain the vast differences in the lives of the Arapesh, the Mundugumor, and the Tchambuli – not to mention the difference between these three cultures and our own? 20

Anthropologists have also noted that a power dynamic is often attached to sex-role distinctions. In early societies, men's role as hunters and warriors gave them more prestige than women. With that prestige came power: men could distribute food for the entire community and determine its social structure. By contrast, women's influence was limited mainly to the domestic sphere. They were not really participants in the public sphere and gained few rights (Rosaldo and Lamphere). 21

In societies where women control their economic well-being, they develop more power. Anthropologist Peggy Sanday has illustrated this pattern through her study of the Afikpo Ibo women of Nigeria. Ibo men had traditionally controlled money and tribal social life because they grew the yam crop – a main source of food with important religious significance. When the tribe increased its contact with European 22

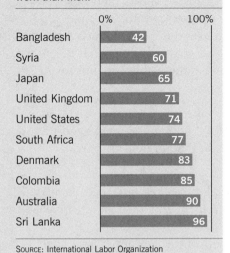

WOMEN'S EARNINGS AS A PERCENTAGE OF MEN'S

In every country in the world, women continue to be paid less for comparable work than men.

Country	0% — 100%
Bangladesh	42
Syria	60
Japan	65
United Kingdom	71
United States	74
South Africa	77
Denmark	83
Colombia	85
Australia	90
Sri Lanka	96

SOURCE: International Labor Organization

cultures, the cassava plant (used for tapioca) was introduced to them.

The Ibo men disdained the new plant, 23 preferring to continue growing the religiously valued yam. However, they permitted women to cultivate the cassava and to keep any profits from its sale. Subsequently, the cassava proved to be extremely lucrative, and the Ibo women became financially independent. With financial independence, the women became less subservient to their husbands and a more powerful force within tribal culture.

SOCIETY: LEARNING EVIDENCE

How do we learn society's standards 24 about appropriate behavior for each sex? Socialization is the general term used to describe the process of learning social roles. Most differences between females and males are learned through family interactions, socialization in schools, and the mass media.

Social learning theory holds that children are rewarded for conforming to their 25 parents' expectations and are punished for behavior that meets with disapproval. Thus, Johnny's parents beam with pride when he shows prowess on the basketball court, but gasp with horror if he displays an interest in becoming a dancer. Johnny learns to act "like a boy" in order to please his parents.

The process of differential treatment of girls and boys begins the minute 26 children are born. Adults describe infant girls as "delicate," "sweet," or "dainty" and hold them more carefully. By contrast, boys are perceived as more active and are described as "bouncing," "sturdy," or "handsome" (Papalia and Olds). As toddlers and preschoolers, children learn that baseball and trucks are for boys while dolls and "dressing up" are for girls.

A study by Judith G. Tudiver demonstrated the differential socialization of 27 preschool-age children. Both mothers and fathers tended to be permissive and supportive with daughters, but did not feel that daughters needed to achieve or perform. However, parents of sons stressed the importance of achievement and independence. Fathers, in particular, were extremely concerned about socializing sons into a rather rigid definition of the masculine role. Tudiver concludes that "a great deal of pressure" is associated with the socialization of sons, which "probably reflects the high value associated with being male in our society" (44).

Children and adolescents are influenced by the role models available in a society. 28 If they see that most doctors, police officers, and U.S. senators are male, while most nurses, secretaries, and early childhood teachers are female, they will begin to draw conclusions about which jobs are for them and which are not. "Real-life" role models affect children's thinking; so, too, do the role models presented in literature (including comics and children's books), film, and television. . . .

FEMINIST CRITIQUE: SEX ROLES AND SOCIAL CONTROL

Jessie Bernard, a feminist sociologist, has suggested that theories about sex roles 29
which emphasize the role of socialization tend to let the power structure off the
hook too easily. In Bernard's view, power and control are the real motives behind
the division of sex roles. Since the male sex role has higher status, men attain power
over women and gain control of many of society's valued rewards.

Bernard argues that socialization theorists make this male-dominated power 30
structure seem respectable and reasonable, and are too complacent about the denial
of equal opportunities to women. She believes that these theorists are saying, in
effect, to women:

> Sorry, girls, too bad you haven't got what it takes ... I know it isn't your
> fault, I know it's just the way you were socialized as a child. You'd be just as
> superior as I am if you had played with trucks instead of dolls. But what can
> I do about it after all (223)?

Bernard and other feminists are critical of socialization research because it fails
to challenge the power structure that keeps women and men in unequal and
prescribed roles.

Barbara Bovee Polk has offered a useful summary of the feminist "power analysis" 31
of sex roles and cultural differences between men and women:

1. Men have power and privilege by virtue of their sex.
2. It is in men's interest to maintain that power and privilege.
3. Men occupy and actively exclude women from positions of economic and
   political power in society.
4. Although most males are oppressed by the system under which we live,
   they are not oppressed, as females are, *because* of their sex.
5. Feminine roles and cultural values are the product of oppression.
   Idealization of them is dysfunctional to change.

Feminists believe that traditional sex roles are used to keep women in their
(disadvantaged) place. In the view of Letty Cottin Pogrebin (54), the messages of
sex role stereotypes can be condensed into two simple propositions: boys are better,
and girls are meant to be mothers.

Works Cited

Bernard, Jessie. *Women, Wives, Mothers: Values and Options.* Chicago: Aldine,
    1975.
Durden-Smith, John. "Male and Female – Why?" *Quest* 80 (1980): 15–19, 93–97,
    99.
Levy, Jerre. In "Male and Female – Why?" *Quest* 80 (1980). John Durden-Smith.
    94.
Margaret Mead. *Sex and Temperament in Three Primitive Societies.* New York:
    Morrow, 1933.
Money, John, and Arnold Ehrhardt. *Man and Woman, Boy and Girl.* Baltimore:
    Johns Hopkins UP, 1972.

Papalia, Dora, and Sherry Olds. *Human Development.* New York: McGraw-Hill, 1979.

Pogrebin, Letty Cottin. *Growing Up Free: Raising Your Child in the '80's.* New York: McGraw-Hill, 1980.

Polk, Barbara Bovee. "Male Power and the Women's Movement." *Journal of Applied Behavioral Science* 10 (1974): 415–431.

Ramey, Estelle. "Sex Hormones and Executive Ability." *Annals of the New York Academy of Sciences* 208 (1973): 237–245.

Rosaldo, Mary, and Lori Lamphere. *Woman, Culture and Society.* Stanford: Stanford UP, 1974.

Rose, Robert, Terry Gordon, and Ian Bernstein. "Plasma Testosterone Levels in the Male Rhesus: Influences of Sexual and Social Stimuli." *Science* 178 (1972): 638–643.

Sanday, Peggy. "Toward a Theory of the Status of Women." *Anthropologist* 75 (1973): 1682–1700.

Tudiver, Judith G. "Parents and the Sex-Role Development of the Pre-School Child." *Sex Roles: Origins Influences and Implications for Women.* Ed. Stark Adamo. Montreal: Eden's Press Women's Publications, 1980.

Reading Journal

In your journal, write about one of the following topics.

1 Consider whether biology or culture is more important in shaping gender roles.

2 Describe how your life would be different if you woke up tomorrow and discovered that you were the opposite sex.

3 Choose a topic of your own related to the reading.

Main Ideas

Answer the following questions, referring to the notes you took when reading the essay. Then share your answers with a partner.

1 What distinction do the authors make, in paragraphs 1–2, between "sex roles" and "gender identity"?

2 In paragraph 12, the authors write, "Thus, hormones clearly play a role in human physical development. But what effect do they have on emotional development and actual behavior?" How do the authors answer this question in the rest of the section titled "Genetics: The Biological Evidence"? Summarize their conclusions in one or two sentences.

3 What is the main subject that the authors discuss in the reading? Summarize their central topic in one or two sentences. Begin with the sentence *In their chapter "Sex Roles," Hamilton McCubbin and Barbara Blum Dahl focus on . . .*

Reflecting on Content

Answer the following questions with a partner. When possible, support your answers with observations based on your own experiences.

1 How persuasive do you find the biological evidence that the authors present for the formation of gender roles? Be as specific as possible.

2 Do you think that biological, anthropological, or social factors are most important in determining gender roles? Why?

3 What is your opinion of the feminist power analysis of sex roles summarized in paragraph 30? Do you agree with the main points? Explain.

A Writer's Technique: *Summarizing and Paraphrasing*

Summarizing

A **summary** is a brief restatement, in your own words, of the main points in a reading. Summaries are a common writing assignment used for various purposes.

- *To demonstrate that you fully understand what you have read.* Summarizing a reading focuses your attention on the content, purpose, and organization of a selection as you separate the main ideas from the supporting details.
- *To integrate source material into an essay or research paper.* Summarizing sources is a common way of presenting the ideas that you will explore in a paper.
- *To study for examinations.* Summarizing is a good study tool for tests because it helps you to understand and remember the most important information in textbooks and lectures.

1 Write a one-sentence summary of the following paragraphs. Express the main idea in your own words.

> Example: *Thus, hormones clearly play a role in human physical development. But what effect do they have on emotional development and actual behavior? Again, this question is still being debated and studied. Some research shows that the male hormone testosterone appears to stimulate aggressive behavior in female animals. At the same time, a female hormone, prolactin, seems to stimulate nurturing, motherly activity in male animals. (par. 12)*
>
> Summary: *Hormones are shown to influence physical development, but their link to emotions and behavior is less certain.*

a. Paragraph 3

b. Paragraph 16

c. Paragraph 21

d. Paragraph 27

Paraphrasing

Writing a **paraphrase** of a passage is similar to writing a summary of it: both involve restating someone else's ideas in your own words. However, a summary is a condensed, or shortened, version of the original; whereas a paraphrase is a complete restatement. It retains all of the writer's ideas and key supporting details and is therefore about the same length as the original. Similar to summarizing, paraphrasing can help you understand the content and purpose of a passage, incorporate sources into an essay or research paper, and study for examinations.

2 Write a one-sentence paraphrase of the following sentences from the reading. Look for synonyms of words and phrases in the original and consider changing the sentence structure and the word order.

> Example: *While the biological basis for sex-related distinctions is important, the role that society and culture play is probably more significant. (par. 18)*

> Paraphrase: *The physical origin of gender differences is essential, but culture and society may have an even greater impact.*

a. Researchers have speculated that certain behavioral differences are due to male and female hormones. (par. 11)

b. Our biological nature may be like a rough piece of stone from which society, like a sculptor, chisels, sharpens, and defines the shapes of male and female behavior. (par. 18)

c. Anthropologists have also noted that a power dynamic is often attached to sex-role distinctions. (par. 21)

d. Thus, Johnny's parents beam with pride when he shows prowess on the basketball court, but gasp with horror if he displays an interest in becoming a dancer. (par. 25)

Vocabulary: *Affixes and Word Roots*

Review the discussion of prefixes, suffixes, and roots (page 15).

If you are reading a passage and come across an unfamiliar word whose meaning you can't figure out from the context, don't immediately reach for your dictionary. Often by looking at the **affixes** (prefixes and suffixes) and **word roots** (many of which come from Greek and Latin), you can get a good sense of the meaning of the words. Learning how to analyze key components of words can help you understand what you are reading and expand your vocabulary.

The following words are made up of smaller parts: a prefix and a root; a root and a suffix; or a prefix, a root, and a suffix. Analyze the parts that make up the words. Then explain the meaning of the word and use it correctly in a sentence. You may use a dictionary to help you. When you are done, share your answers with a partner.

Example: interaction *(par. 3)*

Word analysis: *Made up of a prefix, a root, and a suffix:* inter- + act + -ion: Inter- *(from Latin) means "between" or "among";* act *(from Latin) means "do" or "thing done";* -ion *makes the verb* interact *a noun.*

Meaning: *communication between two or more people*

Sentence: *When groups who are unfamiliar with each other's culture work together, the* interaction *can be highly productive.*

1 inclination (par. 3)

2 prohibit (par. 6)

3 prenatal (par. 11)

4 androgen (par. 13)

5 sensitivity (par. 15)

6 anthropologists (par. 19)

7 complacent (par. 30)

8 dysfunctional (par. 31)

Vocabulary in Context

Locate the following italicized vocabulary items in the reading and see if you can determine their meaning from the context. Then think of an example or situation to illustrate each item, using your personal experience if possible. Do not just define the italicized words and expressions. When you are done, share your answers with a partner.

1 the question of whether women or men are more *prone to* stress (par. 2)

2 something that you think *inhibits* females' and/or males' emotional growth (par. 6)

3 one or two reasons that men seem to be more *predisposed toward* violent behavior than women (par. 16)

4 the possibility of *vast* emotional and behavioral differences between females and males (par. 20)

5 a reason that some people might *disdain* feminists, macho men, or homosexuals – and whether you think their disdain is justified (par. 23)

6 a way to *cultivate* an understanding among teenagers of the negative effects of gender-role stereotyping (par. 23)

7 the degree to which *lucrative* professions are open to women in your culture (par. 23)

8 an example of parents behaving in a *permissive* manner toward their children (par. 27)

9 an example of someone being *let off the hook* because of his or her sex (par. 29)

10 the degree to which you think your culture is *complacent* about achieving equal opportunities for women and men (par. 30)

Discussion

Choose one of the following activities to do with a partner or in a small group.

1 Make a chart similar to the one on the right. Fill in the columns with traits and behaviors considered typical of females or males in your culture. Think about positive and negative images of the ways in which females and males are said to think, feel, look, act, and communicate. After you have filled in both columns with at least six items, discuss your reactions. Consider the degree to which the descriptions reflect stereotypes or reality.

Females	Males

2 Analyze gender images in several magazine advertisements. Start with the ads on pages 220 and 224 and then examine others you find. Consider the following questions.

　a. Which types of products are geared toward females and which types toward males?

　b. What traits, activities, and values are associated with each gender?

　c. What social messages are conveyed about female and about male roles?

　d. Do the advertisements reflect any type of gender stereotyping? Explain.

After you have finished your analysis, share your findings and conclusions with the rest of the class.

3 Do a library or Internet search of material relating to the cultural versus the biological origins of gender roles. Photocopy or print out the most interesting information you find and discuss it with your partner or group. Then share your findings and conclusions with the rest of the class. You might look for material contradicting Margaret Mead's findings in her study *Sex and Temperament in Three Primitive Societies*, discussed in paragraph 20 of "Sex Roles." One Web site questioning Mead's conclusions is at <www.heretical.org/sexsci-w/cdeterm.html>.

Writing Follow-up

Follow up the discussion activity you chose (item 1, 2, or 3) with the matching writing assignment below.

1 Write a paragraph discussing the traditional images of females or males in your culture. Then write a second paragraph explaining the ways in which these images have been changing, if at all, over the last few decades.

2 With a partner or by yourself, write several paragraphs discussing female and/or male images in various advertisements and the conclusions you reached about gender roles, expectations, and stereotyping.

3 Write a one-paragraph summary of the library or Internet material you found about cultural and/or biological influences on gender roles.

CORE READING 2
Boys Will Be Boys

Journal Writing

In your journal, write for ten to fifteen minutes about whether you think females or males are more restricted by traditional gender roles. Then share your ideas with several classmates.

Previewing the Topic

Write a list of the positive and negative consequences of females and males conforming to traditional gender roles. Consider personal and social effects. When you are finished, discuss your ideas in a small group. Then list on the board all of the consequences the group considered.

Agreeing and Disagreeing

To what extent do you agree with the following statements? Fill in each blank with SA (strongly agree), A (agree), U (undecided), D (disagree), or SD (strongly disagree). Then share your responses with several classmates.

_____ 1 Gender roles have changed a lot in my culture over the last thirty years.

_____ 2 Females are more restricted by traditional gender roles than are males.

_____ 3 The macho ideal for boys and men is very strong in my culture.

_____ 4 Biology is more important than culture in shaping gender roles.

_____ 5 Homosexuals are not discriminated against in my culture.

_____ 6 Boys tend to be more emotionally expressive than girls.

_____ 7 I have felt some pressure to conform to traditional gender roles.

_____ 8 Girls and boys mature physically and emotionally at very different rates.

_____ 9 Because of their innate aggressiveness, males commit more violent crimes than females do.

_____ 10 Parents should not allow their children to play with toy guns.

Taking Notes While You Read

> As you read the article, note in the margin traditional masculine roles and their effects on boys. Also indicate the points with which you agree or disagree.

Boys Will Be Boys
Barbara Kantrowitz and Claudia Kalb

In the following article, U.S. journalists Barbara Kantrowitz and Claudia Kalb explore differences in the emotional and social development of boys and girls. The authors focus on the challenges that boys face in conforming to traditional masculine roles. The article originally appeared in Newsweek *magazine in 1998.*

It was a classic Mars-Venus encounter.[1] Only in this case, the woman was from Harvard and the man – well, boy – was a 4-year-old at a suburban Boston nursery school. Graduate student Judy Chu was in his classroom last fall to gather observations for her doctoral dissertation on human development. His greeting was startling: he held up his finger and pretended to shoot her. "I felt bad," Chu recalls. "I felt as if he didn't like me." Months later and much more boy-savvy, Chu has a different interpretation: the gunplay wasn't hostile – it was just a way for him to say hello. "They don't mean it to have harsh consequences. It's a way for them to connect." 1

Researchers like Chu are discovering new meaning in lots of things boys have done for ages. In fact, they're dissecting just about every aspect of the developing male psyche and creating a hot new field of inquiry – the study of boys. They're also producing a slew of new books with titles like *Real Boys: Rescuing Our Sons from the Myths of Boyhood* and *Raising Cain:*[2] *Protecting the Emotional Life of Boys* that will hit the stores in the next few months. 2

What some researchers are finding is that boys and girls really are from two different planets. But since the two sexes have to live together here on Earth, they should be raised with special consideration for their distinct needs. Boys and girls have different "crisis points," experts say, stages in their emotional and social development where things can go very wrong. Until recently, girls got all the attention. But boys need help, too. They're much more likely than girls to have discipline problems at school and to be diagnosed with attention deficit disorder[3] (ADD). Boys far outnumber girls in special-education classes. They're also more likely to commit violent crimes and end up in jail. Consider the headlines: Jonesboro, Arkansas; Paducah, Kentucky; Pearl, Mississippi. In all these school shootings, the perpetrators were young adolescent boys. 3

Even normal boy behavior has come to be considered pathological in the wake of the feminist movement. An abundance of physical energy and the urge to conquer – these are normal male characteristics, and in an earlier age they were good things, even essential to survival. "If Huck Finn or Tom Sawyer[4] were alive today," says Michael Gurian, author of *The Wonder of Boys*, "we'd say they had ADD or a conduct disorder." He says one of the new insights we're gaining about boys is a 4

---

[1] *Mars-Venus encounter:* Reference to John Gray's best-selling book *Men Are from Mars, Women Are from Venus* (1992), which explores conflicts between women and men based on differences in gender roles.

[2] *Raising Cain:* Play on the biblical name Cain (son of Adam and Eve who killed his brother, Abel) and on the idiom *to raise Cain*, meaning "to behave in a noisy, disorderly way."

[3] *attention deficit disorder:* A learning disorder characterized by hyperactivity and short attention span (or easy distractability).

[4] *Huck Finn or Tom Sawyer:* Adventurous boy characters in two novels by the well-known U.S. author Mark Twain (1835–1910).

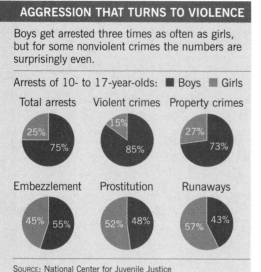

AGGRESSION THAT TURNS TO VIOLENCE

Boys get arrested three times as often as girls, but for some nonviolent crimes the numbers are surprisingly even.

Arrests of 10- to 17-year-olds: ■ Boys ■ Girls

Total arrests
25%
75%

Violent crimes
15%
85%

Property crimes
27%
73%

Embezzlement
45% 55%

Prostitution
52% 48%

Runaways
57% 43%

SOURCE: National Center for Juvenile Justice

very old one: boys will be boys. "They are who they are," says Gurian, "and we need to love them for who they are. Let's not try to rewire them."

Indirectly, boys are benefiting from the research done on girls, especially the landmark work done by Harvard University professor Carol Gilligan. Her 1982 book, *In a Different Voice: Psychological Theory and Women's Development,* inspired Taking Our Daughters to Work Day, along with best-selling spinoffs like Mary Pipher's *Reviving Ophelia.*[5] The traditional, unisex way of looking at child development was profoundly flawed. Gilligan says: "It was like having a one-dimensional perspective on a two-dimensional scene." At Harvard, where she chairs the gender-studies department, Gilligan is now supervising work on males, including Chu's project. Other researchers are studying mental illness and violence in boys.

While girls' horizons have been expanding, boys' have narrowed, confined to rigid ideas of acceptable male behavior no matter how hard their parents tried to avoid stereotypes. The macho ideal still rules. "We gave boys dolls and they used them as guns," says Gurian. "For 15 years, all we heard was that [gender differences] were all about socialization. Parents who raised their kids through that period said in the end, "That's not true. Boys and girls can be awfully different." I think we're awakening to the biological realities and sociological realities."

But what exactly is the essential nature of boys? Even as infants, boys and girls behave differently. A recent study at Children's Hospital in Boston found that boy babies are more emotionally expressive; girls are more reflective. (That means boy babies tend to cry when they're unhappy; girl babies suck their thumbs.) This could indicate that girls are innately more able to control their emotions. Boys have higher levels of testosterone and lower levels of the neurotransmitter serotonin, which inhibits aggression and impulsivity. That may help explain why more males than females carry through with suicide, become alcoholics, and are diagnosed with ADD.

The developmental research on the impact of these physiological differences is still in the embryonic stage, but psychologists are drawing some interesting comparisons between boys and girls. For girls, the first crisis point often comes in early adolescence. Until then, Gilligan and others found, girls have enormous capacity for establishing relationships and interpreting emotions. But in their early teens, girls clamp down, squash their emotions, blunt their insight. Their self-esteem plummets. The first crisis for boys comes much earlier, researchers now say.

---

[5] *Reviving Ophelia:* Play on the name Ophelia, a female character in William Shakespeare's play *Hamlet* (1601), who loses her mind and kills herself after being rejected by Prince Hamlet.

"There's an outbreak of symptoms at age 5, 6, 7, just like you see in girls at 11, 12, 13," says Gilligan. Problems at this age include bed-wetting and separation anxiety. "They don't have the language or experience" to articulate it fully, she says, "but the feelings are no less intense." That's why Gilligan's student Chu is studying preschoolers. For girls at this age, Chu says, hugging a parent goodbye "is almost a non-issue." But little boys, who display a great deal of tenderness, soon begin to bury it with "big boy" behavior to avoid being called sissies. "When their parents drop them off, they want to be close and want to be held, but not in front of other people," says Chu. "Even as early as 4, they're already aware of those masculine stereotypes and are negotiating their way around them."

It is a phenomenon that parents, especially mothers, know well. One morning 9 last month, Lori Dube, a 37-year-old mother of three from Evanston, Illinois, visited her oldest son, Abe, almost 5, at his nursery school, where he was having lunch with his friends. She kissed him, prompting another boy to ask scornfully: "Do you know what your mom just did? She kissed you!" Dube acknowledges, with some sadness, that she'll have to be more sensitive to Abe's new reactions to future public displays of affection. "Even if he loves it, he's getting these messages that it's not good."

There's a struggle – a desire and need for warmth on the one hand and a 10 pull toward independence on the other. Boys like Abe are going through what psychologists long ago declared an integral part of growing up: individualization and disconnection from parents, especially mothers. But now some researchers think that process is too abrupt. When boys repress normal feelings like love because of social pressure, says William Pollack, head of the Center for Men at Boston's McLean Hospital and author of the forthcoming *Real Boys*, "they've lost contact with the genuine nature of who they are and what they feel. Boys are in silent crisis. The only time we notice it is when they pull the trigger."

No one is saying that acting like Rambo[6] in nursery school leads directly to 11 tragedies like Jonesboro.[7] But researchers do think that boys who are forced to shut down positive emotions are left with only one socially acceptable outlet: anger. The cultural ideals boys are exposed to in movies and on TV still emphasize traditional masculine roles – warrior, rogue, adventurer – with heavy doses of violence. For every Mr. Mom,[8] there are a dozen Terminators.[9] "The feminist movement has done a great job of convincing people that a woman can be nurturing and a mother and a tough trial lawyer at the same time," says Dan Kindlon, an assistant professor of psychiatry at Harvard Medical School. "But we haven't done that as much with men. We're afraid that if they're too soft, that's all they can be."

And the demands placed on boys in the early years of elementary school can 12 increase their overall stress levels. Scientists have known for years that boys and girls develop physically and intellectually at very different rates. Boys' fine motor skills – the ability to hold a pencil, for example – are usually considered behind girls.

---

6 *Rambo*: Male character in a series of U.S. action films who behaves in an aggressive, macho manner.

7 *Jonesboro*: City in Arkansas with a middle school that was the site of a mass shooting in 1998 by two boys, age 11 and 13, resulting in the death of many classmates.

8 *Mr. Mom*: Main male character of the 1983 film *Mr. Mom*, a father who stays at home and takes care of the kids while his wife goes to work.

9 *Terminator*: Main male character in a series of U.S. action films who behaves in a violent, aggressive manner.

THE WONDER (AND WORRY) YEARS

There may be no such thing as *child* development anymore. Instead, researchers are now studying each gender's development separately and discovering that boys and girls face very different sorts of challenges. Here is a rough guide to the major phases in their development.

Age	Boys	Girls
0–3 years	At birth, boys have brains that are 5% larger than girls' (size doesn't affect intelligence) and proportionately larger bodies – disparities that increase with age.	Girls are born with a higher proportion of nerve cells to process information. More brain regions are involved in language production and recognition.
4–6 years	The start of school is a tough time, as boys must curb aggressive impulses. They lag behind girls in reading skills, and hyperactivity may be a problem.	Girls are well suited to school. They are calm, get along with others, pick up on social cues, and reading and writing come easily to them.
7–10 years	While good at gross motor skills, boys trail girls in finer control. Many of the best students but also nearly all of the poorest ones are boys.	Very good years for girls. On average, they outperform boys at school, excelling in verbal skills while holding their own in math.
11–13 years	A mixed bag. Dropout rates begin to climb, but good students start pulling ahead of girls in math skills and catching up in verbal ones.	The start of puberty and girls' most vulnerable time. Many experience depression; as many as 15% may try to kill themselves.
14–16 years	Entering adolescence, boys hit another rough patch. Indulging in drugs, alcohol, and aggressive behavior is a common form of rebellion.	Eating disorders are a major concern. Although anorexia can manifest itself as early as 8, it typically afflicts girls starting at 11 or 12; bulimia at 15.

They often learn to read later. At the same time, they're much more active – not the best combination for academic advancement. "Boys feel like school is a game rigged against them," says Michael Thompson, coauthor with Kindlon of *Raising Cain*. "The things at which they excel – gross motor skills, visual and spatial skills, their exuberance – do not find as good a reception at school" as the things girls excel at. Boys (and girls) are also in academic programs at much younger ages than they used to be, increasing the chances that males will be forced to sit still before they are ready. The result, for many boys, is frustration, says Thompson: "By fourth grade, they're saying the teachers like girls better."

A second crisis point for boys occurs around the same time their sisters are 13 stumbling, in early adolescence. By then, say Thompson and Kindlon, boys go one step further in their drive to be "real guys." They partake in the "culture of cruelty," enforcing male stereotypes on one another. "Anything tender, anything compassionate or too artistic is labeled gay," says Thompson. "The homophobia[10] of boys in the 11, 12, 13 range is a stronger force than gravity."

Boys who refuse to fit the mold suffer. Glo Wellman of the California Parenting 14 Institute in Santa Rosa has three sons, 22, 19, and 12. One of her boys, she says, is a non-typical boy: he's very sensitive and caring and creative and artistic." Not surprisingly, he had the most difficulty growing up, she says. "We've got a long way to go to help boys . . . to have a sense that they can be anything they want to be."

---

[10] *homophobia:* Fear and hatred of homosexuals and discrimination against them.

In later adolescence, the once affectionate toddler has been replaced by a sulky 15 stranger who often acts as though torture would be preferable to a brief exchange of words with Mom or Dad. Parents have to try even harder to keep in touch. Boys want and need attention, but often just don't know how to ask for it. In a recent national poll, teenagers named their parents as their No. 1 heroes. Researchers say a strong parental bond is the most important protection against everything from smoking to suicide.

For *San Francisco Chronicle* columnist Adair Lara, that message sank in when she 16 was traveling to New York a few years ago with her son, then 15. She sat next to a woman who told her that until recently she would have had to change seats because she would not have been able to bear the pain of seeing a teenage son and mother together. The woman's son was 17 when his girlfriend dumped him: he went into the garage and killed himself. "This story made me aware that with a boy especially, you have to keep talking because they don't come and talk to you," she says. Lara's son is now 17; she also has a 19-year-old daughter. "My daughter stalked me. She followed me from room to room. She was yelling, but she was in touch. Boys don't do that. They leave the room and you don't know what they are feeling." Her son is now 6 feet 3. "He's a man. There are barriers. You have to reach through that and remember to ruffle his hair."

With the high rate of divorce, many boys are growing up without any adult men 17 in their lives at all. Don Elium, coauthor of the best-selling 1992 book *Raising a Son*, says that with troubled boys, there's often a common theme: distant, uninvolved fathers, and mothers who have taken on more responsibility to fill the gap. That was the case with Raymundo Infante Jr., a 16-year-old high school junior who lives with his mother, Mildred, 38, a hospital administrative assistant in Chicago, and his sister, Vanessa, 19. His parents divorced when he was a baby and he had little contact with his father until a year ago. The hurt built up – in sixth grade, Raymundo was so depressed that he told a classmate he wanted to kill himself. The classmate told a teacher, who told a counselor, and Raymundo saw a psychiatrist for a year. "I felt that I just wasn't good enough, or he just didn't want me," Raymundo says. Last year Raymundo finally confronted his dad, who works two jobs – in an office and on a construction crew – and accused him of caring more about work than his son. Now the two spend time together on weekends or go shopping, but there is still a huge gap of lost years.

Black boys are especially vulnerable, since they are more likely than whites to 18 grow up in homes without their fathers. They're often on their own much sooner than whites. Black leaders are looking for alternatives. In Atlanta, the Rev.[11] Tim McDonald's First Iconium Baptist Church just chartered a Boy Scout troop.[12] "Gangs are so prevalent because guys want to belong to something," says McDonald. "We've got to give them something positive to belong to." Black educators, like Chicagoan Jawanza Kunjufu, think mentoring programs will overcome the bias against academic success as "too white." Some cities are also experimenting with all-boy classrooms in predominantly black schools.

---

[11] *Rev.*: Reverend (title used for a minister).

[12] *Boy Scout troop*: Local group of Boy Scouts – a national organization promoting character development and good citizenship in boys 11–17 years old.

Researchers hope that in the next few years, they'll come up with strategies 19
that will help boys the way the work of Gilligan and others helped girls. In the
meantime, experts say, there are some guidelines. Parents can channel their sons'
energy into constructive activities, like team sports. They should also look for
"teachable moments" to encourage qualities such as empathy. When Diane Fisher,
a Cincinnati-area psychologist, hears her 8- and 10-year-old boys talking about
"finishing somebody," she knows she has mistakenly rented a violent videogame.
She pulls the plug and tells them: "In our house, killing people is not entertainment,
even if it's just pretend."

Parents can also teach by example. New Yorkers Dana and Frank Minaya say 20
they've never disciplined their 16-year-old son Walter in anger. They insist on
resolving all disputes calmly and reasonably, without yelling. If there is a problem,
they call an official family meeting "and we never leave without a big hug," says
Frank. Walter tries to be open with his parents. "I don't want to miss out on any
advice," he says.

Most of all, wise parents of boys should go with the flow. Cindy Lang, 36, a full- 21
time mother in Woodside, California, is continually amazed by the relentless energy
of her sons, Roger Lloyd, 12, and Chris, 9. "You accept the fact that they're going to
involve themselves in risky behavior, like skateboarding down a flight of stairs." Just
last week, she got a phone call from school telling her that Roger Lloyd was in the
emergency room because he'd fallen backward while playing basketball, and school
officials thought he might have a concussion. He's fine now, but she's prepared for
the next emergency: "I have a cell phone so I can be on alert." Boys will be boys.
And we have to let them.

Reading Journal

In your journal, write about one of the following topics.

1 Describe a time when you experienced a conflict concerning the roles society
   expected you to play as a female or as a male. Did you find yourself pulled in
   different directions – by cultural expectations, on the one hand, and by your
   own expectations and desires, on the other?

2 Write a one-paragraph summary of the article "Boys Will Be Boys."

3 Choose a topic of your own related to the reading.

Main Ideas

Answer the following questions, referring to the notes you took when reading the
article. Then share your answers with a partner.

1 In paragraph 6, the authors maintain that "while girls' horizons have been
   expanding, boys' have narrowed, confined to rigid ideas of acceptable male
   behavior." How do the authors account for this difference?

2 When authors write something, they have a reason for doing – for example, to inform, persuade, and entertain (see Chapter 2, page 64). Why, in your opinion, did the authors of "Boys Will Be Boys" choose their particular subject? What is their central purpose in writing the article? Who is the principal audience the writers are addressing?

3 What is the main point the authors make in the article? Summarize their central topic in one or two sentences. Use your own words. Begin with the sentence *In their article "Boys Will Be Boys," Kantrowitz and Kalb state . . .*

Reflecting on Content

Answer the following questions with a partner. When possible, support your answers with observations based on your own experiences.

1 What point are the authors making with their title "Boys Will Be Boys"? Write down two other titles that would also be appropriate for the article.

2 Do you agree with the authors that girls have more freedom to challenge traditional gender roles than boys? Give one or two examples.

3 In the chart "The Wonder (and Worry) Years" (page 204), look at the behaviors characteristic of girls and of boys at various ages. What biological, cultural, and/or social factors might account for the differences between the sexes? Focus on two behaviors.

A Writer's Technique: *Summarizing and Paraphrasing*

Summarizing

Review the discussion of summarizing on page 196.

1 Write a one-sentence summary of the following paragraphs. Express the main idea in your own words. Refer to the example on page 196.
   a. Paragraph 4
   b. Paragraph 10
   c. Paragraph 11
   d. Paragraph 16

Paraphrasing

Review the discussion of paraphrasing on page 197.

2 Paraphrase the following sentences from the article by restating the ideas in your own words. Look for synonyms of words and phrases in the original and consider changing the sentence structure and the word order. Refer to the example of paraphrasing on page 197.
   a. Even normal boy behavior has come to be considered pathological in the wake of the feminist movement. (par. 4)
   b. The traditional, unisex way of looking at child development was profoundly flawed. (par. 5)

c. While girls' horizons have been expanding, boys' have narrowed, confined to rigid ideas of acceptable male behavior. (par. 6)

d. The developmental research on the impact of these physiological differences is still in the embryonic stage. (par. 8)

e. In later adolescence, the once affectionate toddler has been replaced by a sulky stranger who often acts as though torture would be preferable to a brief exchange of words with Mom or Dad. (par. 15)

Vocabulary: *Related Sets of Words*

One way to build your vocabulary is to learn related sets of vocabulary, such as different ways of walking: *stroll, limp, saunter, stride;* or different emotions: *anger, fear, dread, sadness.*

Here is a large set of adjectives that express different human personality traits.

adventurous	jealous
aggressive	obstinate
ambitious	self-reliant
compassionate	sensitive
competitive	sentimental
decisive	sophisticated
frivolous	submissive
intuitive	

Make a chart similar to the one on the right. Then place each word into either the column headed FEMALE TRAITS or the one labeled MALE TRAITS, depending on which gender is most commonly associated with the trait. If you think a trait applies equally to the two genders, put the word in both columns. You don't necessarily have to agree with the associations; fill in the columns according to what you think most people would say.

Female Traits	Male Traits

Then share your lists of personality traits with several classmates. Discuss whether you feel that a particular trait reflects stereotyping or reality.

Vocabulary in Context

Locate the following italicized vocabulary items in the reading and see if you can determine their meaning from the context. Then think of an example or situation to illustrate each item, using your personal experience if possible. Do not just define the italicized words and expressions. When you are done, share your answers with a partner.

1 a time when you *gained insight* into some aspect of gender roles (par. 4)

2 an example of a *flawed* argument relating to gender (par. 5)

3 one or two ways in which females and males are often thought to be *innately* different (par. 7)

4 an example of one person speaking *scornfully* about another because of his or her sex (par. 9)

5 an experience that is seen as an *integral* part of becoming a woman or a man in your culture (par. 10)

6 something that women or men are traditionally said to *excel* at and whether you think this characterization is a gender stereotype (par. 12)

7 whether *homophobia* is prevalent in your culture (par. 13)

8 the degree to which you think that women are more emotionally *vulnerable* than men (par. 18)

9 whether you think that *empathy* is a traditional male quality (par. 19)

10 something you may have *missed out on* in life because of your gender (par. 20)

Discussion

Choose one of the following activities to do with a partner or in a small group.

1 Make a chart similar to the one on the right. Fill in each column with at least four behaviors that would be seen as inappropriate for females or males in your culture. When you are finished, write a list on the board of all the inappropriate behaviors the group named, share your reactions, and identify and discuss any gender stereotypes and double standards.

Inappropriate Female Behavior	Inappropriate Male Behavior

2 Go to a children's clothing shop or toy store and observe the types of items being sold and the manner in which they are marketed. Focus on the products, colors, activities, traits, images, and gender stereotypes associated with girls and with boys. Then share your observations and conclusions with your partner or group.

3 Access the National Public Radio Web site <www.npr.org>. Click on *Archives* and search for the radio commentary "Gender Roles Around the House," in which Joseph Phillips discusses his wife's and his own gender roles. (Remember to include the quotation marks when you search.) After you listen to the commentary, work with a partner or a group and write a list of the traditional female and male roles that Phillips identifies. Then discuss his main points and your reactions to them.

Writing Follow-up

Follow up the discussion activity you chose (item 1, 2, or 3) with the matching writing assignment below.

1 Write one or two paragraphs comparing inappropriate behaviors for females and for males. Focus on differences in gender roles and expectations.

2 Summarize your findings in the children's clothing shop or toy store and discuss your conclusions about differences in gender roles and expectations. Also consider any gender stereotypes or double standards you noticed.

3 Write a one-paragraph summary of the radio commentary "Gender Roles Around the House."

CORE READING 3
Sex, Sighs, and Conversation: Why Men and Women Can't Communicate

Journal Writing

In your journal, write for ten to fifteen minutes about one or two differences you've noticed in the way women and men speak – for example, differences in styles of talking, in words used, and in subjects discussed. Then share your ideas with several classmates.

Previewing the Topic

In a small group, discuss your personal speaking patterns in different classes. When, how, and why do you speak in class? How comfortable do you feel talking in a large group? Do you enjoy debating ideas? As you discuss your speaking habits, consider whether females and males tend to communicate in class in different ways. Then share your ideas with the other groups.

Agreeing and Disagreeing

To what extent do you agree with the following statements? Fill in each blank with SA (strongly agree), A (agree), U (undecided), D (disagree), or SD (strongly disagree). Then share your responses with several classmates.

_____ 1 Women usually communicate very differently from the way men do.

_____ 2 Men are more likely than women to ask for directions if they're lost.

_____ 3 Girls tend to share secrets more with their good friends than boys do.

_____ 4 Women are usually more talkative than men.

_____ 5 Men are generally more competitive than women.

_____ 6 Men tend to talk more about their personal problems than women do.

_____ 7 Women are usually more independent than men.

_____ 8 Women generally offer more advice to their friends than males do.

_____ 9 Female friendships are usually stronger than male ones.

_____ 10 Men tend to talk to other men differently than they do to women.

Taking Notes While You Read

> As you read the article, note in the margin different ways females and males use language to convey information, ideas, and feelings. Also indicate the points with which you agree or disagree.

 ## Sex, Sighs, and Conversation: Why Men and Women Can't Communicate
Deborah Tannen

Deborah Tannen, a well-known professor of linguistics at Georgetown University, has written several popular books on gender differences in language use, including You Just Don't Understand: Women and Men in Conversation *and* That's Not What I Meant!: How Conversational Style Makes or Breaks Relationships. *The following article first appeared in the* Boston Globe, *a large daily newspaper, in 1990.*

A man and a woman were seated in a car that had been circling the same area for 1 a half hour. The woman was saying, "Why don't we just *ask* someone?" The man was saying, not for the first time, "I'm sure it's around here somewhere. I'll just try this street."

Why are so many men reluctant to ask directions? Why aren't women? And why 2 can't women understand why men don't want to ask? The explanation, for this and for countless minor and major frustrations that women and men encounter when they talk to each other, lies in the different ways that they use language – differences that begin with how girls and boys use language as children, growing up in different worlds.

Anthropologists, sociologists, and psychologists have found that little girls play in small groups or in pairs; they have a best friend, with whom they spend a lot of time talking. It's the telling of secrets that makes them best friends. They learn to use language to negotiate intimacy – to make connections and feel close to each other. 3

Boys, on the other hand, tend to play competitive games in larger groups, which are hierarchical. High-status boys give orders, and low-status boys are pushed around. So boys learn to use language to preserve independence and negotiate their status, trying to hold center stage, challenge and resist challenges, display knowledge and verbal skill. 4

These divergent assumptions about the purpose of language persist into adulthood, where they lie in wait behind cross-gender conversations, ready to leap out and cause puzzlement or grief. In the case of asking for directions, the same interchange is experienced differently by women and men. From a woman's perspective, you ask for help, you get it, and you get to where you're going. A fleeting connection is made with a stranger, which is fundamentally pleasant. But a man is aware that by admitting ignorance and asking for information, he positions himself one-down to someone else. Far from pleasant, this is humiliating. So it makes sense for him to preserve his independence and self-esteem at the cost of a little extra travel time. 5

Here is another scene from the drama of the differences in men's and women's ways of talking. A woman and a man return home from work. She tells everything that happened during the day: what she did, whom she met, what they said, what that made her think. Then she turns to him and asks, "How was your day?" He says, "Same old rat race." She feels locked out: "You don't tell me anything." He protests, "Nothing happened at work." They have different assumptions about what's "anything" to tell. To her, telling life's daily events and impressions means she's not alone in the world. Such talk is the essence of intimacy – evidence that she and her partner are best friends. Since he never spent time talking in this way with his friends, best or otherwise, he doesn't expect it, doesn't know how to do it, and doesn't miss it when it isn't there. 6

Another source of mutual frustration is the difference in women's and men's assumptions about "troubles talk." She begins to talk about a problem; he offers a solution; she dismisses it, with pique. He feels frustrated: "She complains, but she doesn't want to do anything to solve her problems." Indeed, what she wants to do about it is talk. She is frustrated because his solution cuts short the discussion and implies she shouldn't be wasting time talking about it. 7

The female search for connection and the male concern with hierarchy is evident here, too. When a woman tells another woman about a problem, her friend typically explores the problem ("And then what did he say?" "What do you think you might do?"); expresses understanding ("I know how you feel"); or offers a similar experience ("It's like the time I . . ."). All these responses express support and bring them closer. But offering a solution positions the problem-solver as one-up. This asymmetry is distancing, just the opposite of what she was after in bringing up the discussion. 8

A similar mismatch of expectations occurs when a woman complains about her boss, and a man tries to be helpful by explaining the boss's point of view. 9

She perceives this as an attack, and a lack of loyalty to her. One man told me, incredulously, "My girlfriend just wants to talk about her point of view." He feels that offering opposing views is obviously a more constructive conversational contribution. But conversations among women are usually characterized by mutual support and exploration. Alternative views may be introduced, but they are phrased as suggestions and questions, not as direct challenges. This is one of the many ways that men value oppositional stances, whereas women value harmonious ones.

A woman was hurt when she heard her husband telling the guests at a dinner party about an incident involving his boss that he hadn't told her. She felt this proved that he hadn't been honest when he'd said nothing happened at work. But he didn't think of this experience as a story to tell until he needed to come up with material to put himself forward at the dinner party. 10

Thus, it isn't that women always talk more, while men are taciturn and succinct. Women talk more at home, since talk, for them, is a way of creating intimacy. Since men regard talk as a means to negotiate status, they often see no need to talk at home. But they talk more in "public" situations with people they know less well. At a meeting, when questions are solicited from the floor, it is almost always a man who speaks first. When the phones are opened on a radio talk show, the vast majority of calls are from men, who are more likely to speak at length, giving introductions to their questions (if they have any) and addressing multiple topics. 11

Generalizing about groups of people makes many of us nervous. We like to think of ourselves as unique individuals, not representatives of stereotypes. But it is more dangerous to ignore patterns than to articulate them. 12

If women and men have different ways of talking (and my research, and that of others, shows that they do), then expecting us to be the same leads to disappointment and mutual accusation. Unaware of conversational style differences, we fall back on mutual blame: "You go on and on about nothing." "You don't listen to me." 13

Realizing that a partner's behavior is not his or her individual failing, but a normal expression of gender, lifts this burden of blame and disappointment. Surprisingly, years together can make the mutual frustration worse, rather than better. After 57 years of marriage, my parents are still grappling with the different styles I have described. When my mother read my book,[1] she said, "You mean it isn't just Daddy? I always thought he was the only one." 14

Understanding gender differences in ways of talking is the first step toward changing. Not knowing that people of the other gender have different ways of talking, and different assumptions about the place of talk in a relationship, people assume they are doing things right and their partners are doing things wrong. Then no one is motivated to change; if your partner is accusing you of wrong behavior, changing would be tantamount to admitting fault. But when they think of the differences as cross-cultural, people find that they and their partners are willing, even eager, to make small adjustments that will please their partners and improve the relationship. 15

---

[1] *my book: You Just Don't Understand: Women and Men in Conversation* (1990).

Reading Journal

In your journal, write about one of the following topics.

1 Discuss a point with which you agree or disagree in Tannen's article.
2 Describe how your friendships with females differ from those with males.
3 Choose a topic of your own related to the reading.

Main Ideas

Answer the following questions, referring to the notes you took when reading the essay. Then share your answers with a partner.

1 According to Tannen, what are the major differences in the ways females and males use language?
2 What does Tannen mean, in paragraph 12, when she says, "it is more dangerous to ignore patterns than to articulate them"?
3 What is the main point Tannen makes in the article? Summarize her central idea in one or two sentences. Use your own words. Begin with the sentence *In her article "Sex, Sighs, and Conversation," Deborah Tannen maintains that* . . .

Reflecting on Content

Answer the following questions with a partner. When possible, support your answers with observations based on your own experiences.

1 How do the gender differences in language use that Tannen discusses reflect traditional female and male roles and expectations? Give at least two examples.
2 What is the primary audience for which the article was written? How does the nature of the audience help shape the content of the piece?
3 In the last paragraph, Tannen refers to gender differences as "cross-cultural." What does she mean by this? How accurate do you think her characterization is?

A Writer's Technique: *Summarizing and Paraphrasing*

Summarizing

When you write a summary of an entire article or other selection, your goal is to give the reader an accurate sense of the content and emphasis of the original. A summary of a complete reading is usually one paragraph in length and should be:

- *Concise.* Include only one statement of the thesis (main idea), review the main points, and provide, if necessary, several major supporting details.
- *Accurate.* Include all of the main ideas, express them clearly, and reflect the writer's emphasis.
- *Objective.* Include only the writer's ideas, not your own opinions, interpretations, and judgments.

When you write a summary, it is important not just to copy statements from the original reading and put them together. Rather, you should restate the main ideas in your own words and synthesize the material – combine information and group ideas in a way that shows the relationships among them. This might not necessarily be the same order of material as in the original.

1 Using your own words, write a one-paragraph summary of Tannen's article. Start with the sentence *In her article "Sex, Sighs, and Conversation: Why Men and Women Can't Communicate," Deborah Tannen focuses on . . .* Be sure that your paragraph is concise, accurate, and objective. When you are finished, share your summary with a partner.

Before you begin, look at this sample summary of the second core reading on pages 201–206 "Boys Will Be Boys" by Barbara Kantrowitz and Claudia Kalb.

> *In their article "Boys Will Be Boys," Barbara Kantrowitz and Claudia Kalb focus on recent developmental research relating to boys and on the implications for parents in terms of raising their sons. Over the last few decades, the study of child development has centered on girls. Recently, however, researchers have directed their attention to boys, especially to their unique stages of emotional and social development and the crisis points where serious problems can arise. Although the tendency has been to view the aggressiveness of boys as unhealthy, it is now being seen more and more as a natural male trait that needs to be understood and not changed. Boys and girls are clearly different and should be raised with their distinct needs in mind. Although girls, as a result of the feminist movement, have become freer in terms of gender roles, boys have been increasingly limited by traditional masculine stereotypes. This macho image leads boys to repress positive feelings, such as love and compassion, and causes a range of emotional and social problems, including stress, depression, alcoholism, and violent crime. Boys need help in breaking out of restrictive male roles, and parents are essential in the process. Mothers and fathers need to find as many opportunities as possible to communicate with their sons, to teach them empathy, and to channel their innate energy into positive activities.*

Paraphrasing

Review the discussion of paraphrasing on page 197.

2 Paraphrase the main ideas of the following sentences. Use your own words. Look for synonyms of words and phrases in the original and consider changing the sentence structure and word order. Refer to the example of paraphrasing on page 197.

   a. These divergent assumptions about the purpose of language persist into adulthood, where they lie in wait behind cross-gender conversations, ready to leap out and cause puzzlement or grief. (par. 5)

   b. Offering a solution positions the problem-solver as one-up. This asymmetry is distancing, just the opposite of what she was after in bringing up the discussion. (par. 8)

c. This is one of the many ways that men value oppositional stances, whereas women value harmonious ones. (par. 9)

d. Realizing that a partner's behavior is not his or her individual failing, but a normal expression of gender, lifts this burden of blame and disappointment. (par. 14)

Vocabulary: *Connotations of Words*

Review the discussion of connotations and denotations (pages 166–167).

Studying the denotations (literal definitions) of words and their connotations (suggested meanings or associations) is an important aspect of vocabulary development.

Look at the chart below and do the following with a partner.

- Complete the chart with the equivalent male or female term.
- Discuss the denotation and connotations of each term.
- Discuss whether one item in each pair has more positive or more negative connotations than the other.

Female	Male		Female	Male
lady			nurse	
	widower			landlord
Miss			bride	
	master			chairman
spinster			maid	
	sissy			wizard
housewife			stewardess	
	host			businessman

Vocabulary in Context

Locate the following italicized vocabulary items in the reading and see if you can determine their meaning from the context. Then think of an example or situation to illustrate each item, using your personal experience if possible. Do not just define the italicized words and expressions. When you are done, share your answers with a partner.

1 an example of someone using language to *negotiate* intimacy or status (par. 3)

2 a reason females are not encouraged as much as males to *hold center stage* (par. 4)

3 one or two reasons someone might *resist* traditional gender roles (par. 4)

4 an example of a woman or a man feeling *incredulous* about some aspect of traditional or changing gender roles (par. 9)

5 a *constructive* way to combat sexist attitudes (par. 9)

6 one or two reasons conversations among women tend to reflect more *mutual* support than those among men (par. 9)

7 an example of an *oppositional* stance reflected in the use of language (par. 9)

8 whether *harmonious* behavior is a typical male value in your culture (par. 9)

9 the degree to which you think that males are naturally more *taciturn* than females (par. 11)

10 whether you think it is important for males to create *intimacy* in their relationships with others (par. 11)

Discussion

Choose one of the following activities to do with a partner or in a small group.

1 Discuss the gender differences in language use and the problems caused by these differences, as described in Tannen's article. Do you agree with her? Why or why not? Base your responses on your own experiences and observations, and discuss the degree to which changes are taking place today. Then share your ideas with the rest of the class.

2 Observe a class at an educational institution – preschool, elementary, secondary, or postsecondary. Focus on the nature of the student-to-student and student-to-teacher interaction. What conclusions can you draw about gender roles, expectations, and language use? Share your observations and conclusions with the rest of the class.

3 Access Tannen's home page <www.georgetown.edu/faculty/tannend> and locate the section titled "Interviews with Deborah Tannen." Read or listen to one of the online interviews with her. Then write a list of the main points she makes about gender and language and discuss them with your partner or group.

Writing Follow-up

Follow up the discussion activity you chose (item 1, 2, or 3) with the matching writing assignment below.

1 With a partner or by yourself, write a one-page summary of your discussion of Tannen's article.

2 Summarize your classroom observations and discuss your conclusions about gender differences in roles, expectations, and language use.

3 Write a paragraph summarizing the main points that Tannen makes in the online interview.

MAKING CONNECTIONS

Answer two or three of the following questions relating to the three core readings in this chapter.

1 Reread paragraph 18 in "Sex Roles" and paragraphs 4 and 6 in "Boys Will Be Boys." Do you think that Michael Gurian, mentioned in the second article, would agree with the conclusion of the authors of the first article about the biological origins of gender roles?

2 How might one of the types of evidence presented in "Sex Roles" – biological, anthropological, or social – help explain a major difference in gender roles and expectations that Tannen discusses in "Sex, Sighs, and Conversation"? Speculate on the origin of at least one gender difference.

3 Reread the feminist "power analysis" of gender roles and cultural differences between women and men in paragraph 31 of "Sex Roles." Then reread paragraphs 10–13 of "Boys Will Be Boys," in which William Pollack, Dan Kindlon, and Michael Thompson discuss traditional male roles. Would these men disagree with any aspect of the power analysis of gender roles in the first article? Why or why not?

4 Reread paragraphs 1, 15, and 16 in "Boys Will Be Boys." How would Tannen, the author of the third core reading, explain the linguistic behaviors of the boys mentioned in these paragraphs?

5 The authors of "Boys Will Be Boys" (Kantrowitz and Kalb) and of "Sex, Sighs, and Conversation" (Tannen) discuss differences in gender roles and expectations. Do you think Kantrowitz and Kalb are suggesting that boys need to change in some way? Is Tannen recommending that females and males change their speech habits?

ADDITIONAL READING 1
Women Have What It Takes

Before You Read

With several classmates, or in your journal, discuss the female gender roles in the advertisement on page 220. What values, expectations, traits, and activities do you see in the ad?

Taking Notes While You Read

As you read the essay, note in the margin the reasons the author thinks women should be allowed to serve in military combat units. Also indicate the points with which you agree or disagree.

Women Have What It Takes
Carol Barkalow

The following essay by Carol Barkalow originally appeared in Newsweek *magazine in 1991, shortly after the end of the Persian Gulf War. Barkalow, a graduate of the U.S. military academy at West Point, served as a colonel in a noncombat army unit in Kuwait during the Gulf War. Although women in the U.S. military are currently allowed to serve in some combat units on the ground and to fly combat missions, they are prohibited from fighting in front-line ground units. Following Barkalow's essay is a letter to the editor that presents an opposing point of view.*

1   I realized I wanted a military career when I was 16, the summer between my junior and senior years of high school. I had been very active in athletics. I enjoyed the discipline, the comradeship, the physicalness of sports, helping teammates. I also wanted to serve my country. For me, the answer was the Army. My guidance counselor told me that West Point[1] was starting to accept women. I was in the first class.

2   As plebes,[2] we were required to greet the upperclassmen "Good morning, sir." Too often we'd hear back, "Mornin', bitch."[3] I was naive, I guess. I thought my classmates wanted the same thing I wanted. I thought they would just accept me for that. By the time we graduated, the men's attitudes had begun to mellow somewhat. The women's attitudes had changed, too. If we weren't feminists when we went in, we were when we came out. I went back for my 10-year reunion in October 1990. There was a big difference. My male classmates had changed tremendously. They recognized us as peers. I realized they had been going through their own growth a decade ago, the hell of being a cadet. The reunion was the best time I ever had at West Point.

---

[1] *West Point:* Military academy, located north of New York City.

[2] *plebe:* First-year student at a military or navel academy.

[3] *bitch:* rude and insulting reference to a woman. (A bitch is a female dog.)

But some of those old attitudes still linger when the question of women in combat arises. It's a generational issue for the most part. Most of the senior leadership had little opportunity to work with women as peers. Many see us as a mother, a wife, a daughter – especially a daughter. They always say they wouldn't want to see their daughters in combat. What I ask them in return is, Would you really want to see your *son* in combat? And isn't it the daughter's choice? One lesson our society learned in the Persian Gulf[4] is that it is no more tragic to lose a mother, a sister, a daughter than it is to lose a father, a brother or a son – and no less so.

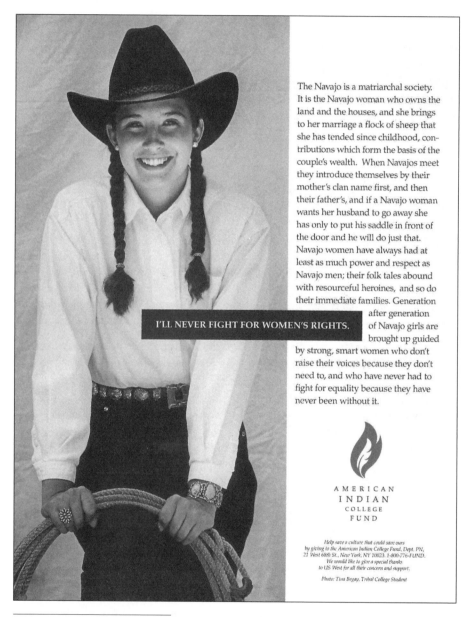

I'LL NEVER FIGHT FOR WOMEN'S RIGHTS.

The Navajo is a matriarchal society. It is the Navajo woman who owns the land and the houses, and she brings to her marriage a flock of sheep that she has tended since childhood, contributions which form the basis of the couple's wealth. When Navajos meet they introduce themselves by their mother's clan name first, and then their father's, and if a Navajo woman wants her husband to go away she has only to put his saddle in front of the door and he will do just that. Navajo women have always had at least as much power and respect as Navajo men; their folk tales abound with resourceful heroines, and so do their immediate families. Generation after generation of Navajo girls are brought up guided by strong, smart women who don't raise their voices because they don't need to, and who have never had to fight for equality because they have never been without it.

AMERICAN
INDIAN
COLLEGE
FUND

Help save a culture that could save ours by giving to the American Indian College Fund, Dept. PN, 21 West 68th St., New York, NY 10023. 1-800-776-FUND. We would like to give a special thanks to US West for all their concern and support.

Photo: Tina Begay, Tribal College Student

---

[4] *Persian Gulf:* Part of the Arabian Sea. (The reference is to the Persian Gulf War, between Iraq – which invaded Kuwait in 1990 – and a military coalition consisting of the United States, Saudi Arabia, Kuwait, and many other nations. In 1991, the allied troops defeated the Iraqi military, forcing it to leave Kuwait.)

I volunteered to go to the Gulf. I was attached to the 24th Infantry Division, the unit that spearheaded the end-around attack.[5] Our support outfit was in just as much danger as the combat element. The Iraqi weapons had just as much capability of hitting us as the men in front. The difference was that we didn't have the capability to defend ourselves like the combat troops. 4

One question that is always raised is whether women have what it takes to kill an enemy face to face – whether we can handle that particular brand of stress. After my book[6] came out last year, a Vietnam vet[7] named Bill Hanake came to see me. He had a leg and a foot blown off in Vietnam. I think Bill's experience is an eloquent answer to the naysayers who think women don't have what it takes for combat. Both times his unit was overrun in 'Nam, he said, it was the Viet Cong *women* who were the more disciplined, the tougher, who were the most willing to make sure their enemy wasn't going to come back at 'em. 5

Then there's the argument that men will be overprotective of women. When men are overprotective of men, we give them awards for valor. In May, our country awarded an Air Force pilot its second highest medal for leading a nine-hour rescue mission for a fallen flier. That wasn't looked upon as overprotective. Would it have been so if the downed flier had been a woman? 6

Some believe females would interfere with male bonding. In Saudi,[8] I saw a new type of relationship forming between men and women, one that has traditionally been described among men. It was a nurturing relationship based upon respect, based on sharing the same hardships. The big worry before Vietnam was that blacks couldn't bond with whites. When the bullets started flying, that went away pretty fast. The same type of relationships developed in the Gulf between men and women soldiers. 7

Do I believe women should be allowed to serve in the infantry? Yes, if qualified. The training and physical-strength standards should be uniform. We have standards that we must keep. Our military readiness should never suffer. But I saw a number of physically strong men very scared in Saudi Arabia. It's not just a matter of physical strength. It's mental and emotional strength as well. I think God knew what he was doing when he allowed women to bear the children and gave us the ability to handle that mental and emotional stress. 8

Pregnancy? The military doesn't have a good handle on the question. When the military looks at pregnancy, it sees it as nonavailability. We had more injuries and nonavailability among men than women in Saudi. Too often, the women are the only ones held responsible for pregnancy, not the men who helped get them that way. 9

No normal person wants to go into combat. Soldiers are the last people who want to. But we've volunteered. We understand our commitment. Everybody raises a hand, male and female, and swears to support and defend the same Constitution. 10

---

[5] *spearheaded the end-around attack:* Led a surprise attack from the side and the rear.

[6] *my book: In the Man's House* (1990), about Barkalow's experience at the U.S. Military Academy at West Point.

[7] *Vietnam vet:* Veteran of the Vietnam War (1954–1975). This war between South Vietnam, aided by the United States, and Communist guerrillas (Viet Cong), aided by North Vietnam, ended in a Communist victory.

[8] *Saudi:* Saudi Arabia. During the Persian Gulf War, a number of U.S. troops were stationed there.

Women are competent, capable and committed. We are an integral part of the best-trained military force in the world. The services should have the flexibility to assign the best-qualified person to the job, regardless of gender. That's the bottom line.

An Opposing View

The following letter to the editor of the Wall Street Journal, *published in 1997, presents an opposing view.*

To the Editor:

There is an overarching reason why women should never be in combat units. 1 A bond develops among infantrymen which organizational scholars identify as cohesion. It is defined as the willingness to subordinate self-interest to the needs and well-being of the group.

Women destroy cohesion for three reasons. The first arises from differential 2 standards. Suboptimal performance is not an option when in harm's way. Those who cannot contribute equally have no place. Next, there are sexual tensions that cannot be resolved. I do not mean to address the issues of rape or harassment as they are codified but rather the consensual liaisons that occur. Are the unit members focused on mission or love interest? How are these conflicting goals reconciled when the first incoming round impacts? How do the have-nots react – those yearning for companionship but excluded from it? Finally, there is the issue of physical inferiority. Egalitarianism is a bankrupt concept. If not, may I have forty million a year to play for the Bulls like Michael Jordan? The reality is that he is a gifted athlete; I am not. The very essence of "differently gifted" carries the implicit message that we all have limitations. Explicitly, there are some things that we cannot do.

The argument has been framed by feminists in terms of career opportunities for 3 women. Why, they ask, should women be barred from advancement solely because of gender? The central issue is not career advancement for women but the combat readiness of a warrior class. That objective is sufficiently important that it must have primacy over misguided humanism.

Bill Norton

After You Read

In your journal, write about one of the following topics.

1 Write a one-paragraph summary of "Women Have What It Takes."
2 Consider the extent to which you agree with Barkalow's main point or with Norton's central point in his letter to the editor.
3 Choose a topic of your own related to Barkalow's essay or Norton's letter to the editor.

ADDITIONAL READING 2
The Androgynous Male

Before You Read

With several classmates, or in your journal, discuss the male gender roles in the advertisement on page 224. What images, values, expectations, and stereotypes do you see in the ad?

While You Read

As you read the essay, note in the margin what the author considers the disadvantages of traditional males roles and the advantages of androgyny (a society with no specific gender roles). Also indicate the points with which you agree or disagree.

The Androgynous Male
Noel Perrin

The following essay by Noel Perrin originally appeared in the New York Times *in 1984. A professor of English at Dartmouth College, Perrin has written a number of books for adults and for children.*

The summer I was 16, I took a train from New York to Steamboat Springs, Colorado, where I was going to be assistant horse wrangler[1] at a camp. The trip took three days, and since I was much too shy to talk to strangers, I had quite a lot of time for reading. I read all of *Gone with the Wind.*[2] I read all the interesting articles in a couple of magazines I had, and then I went back and read all the dull stuff. I also took all the quizzes, a thing of which magazines were even fuller of then than now. 1

The one that held my undivided attention was called "How Masculine/Feminine Are You?" It consisted of a large number of inkblots. The reader was supposed to decide which of four objects each blot most resembled. The choices might be a cloud, a steam engine, a caterpillar, and a sofa. 2

When I finished the test, I was shocked to find that I was barely masculine at all. On a scale of 1 to 10, I was about 1.2. Me, the horse wrangler? (And not just wrangler, either. That summer, I had to skin a couple of horses that died – the camp owner wanted the hides.) 3

The results of that test were so terrifying to me that for the first time in my life I did a piece of original analysis. Having unlimited time on the train, I looked at the "masculine" answers over and over, trying to find what it was that distinguished real men from people like me – and eventually I discovered two very simple patterns. It 4

---

[1] *horse wrangler:* Person who takes care of horses trained for riding.

[2] *Gone with the Wind:* Popular novel about the American Civil War (1861–1865), written in 1936 by the U.S. author Margaret Mitchell. It was later made into a very popular movie.

was "masculine" to think the blots looked like manmade objects, and "feminine" to think they looked like natural objects. It was masculine to think they looked like things capable of causing harm, and feminine to think of innocent things.

Even at 16, I had the sense to see that the compilers of the test were using rather limited criteria – maleness and femaleness are both more complicated than *that* – and I breathed a huge sigh of relief. I wasn't necessarily a wimp, after all.

5

That the test did reveal something other than the superficiality of its makers I realized only many years later. What it revealed was that there is a large class of men and women both, to which I belong, who are essentially androgynous. That doesn't mean we're gay, or low in appropriate hormones, or uncomfortable performing the jobs traditionally assigned our sexes. (A few years after that summer, I was leading troops in combat and, unfashionable as it now is to admit this, having a very good time. War is exciting. What a pity the 20th century went and spoiled it with high-tech weapons.)

What it does mean to be spiritually androgynous is a kind of freedom. Men who are all-male, or he-men, or 100 percent red-blooded Americans, have a little biological set that causes them to be attracted to physical power, and probably also to dominance. Maybe even to watching football. I don't say this to criticize them. Completely masculine men are quite often wonderful people: good husbands, good (though sometimes overwhelming) fathers, good members of society. Furthermore, they are often so unselfconsciously at ease in the world that other men seek to imitate them. They just aren't as free as us androgynes. They pretty nearly have to be what they are; we have a range of choice open.

The sad part is that many of us never discover that. Men who are not 100 percent red-blooded Americans – say, those who are only 75 percent red-blooded – often fail to notice their freedom. They are too busy trying to copy the he-men ever to realize that men, like women, come in a wide variety of acceptable types. Why this frantic imitation? My answer is mere speculation, but not casual. I have speculated on this for a long time.

Partly they're just envious of the he-man's unconscious ease. Mostly they're terrified of finding that there may be something wrong with them deep down, some weakness at the heart. To avoid discovering that, they spend their lives acting out the role that the he-man naturally lives. Sad.

One thing that men owe to the women's movement is that this kind of failure is less common than it used to be. In releasing themselves from the single ideal of the dependent woman, women have more or less accidentally released a lot of men from the single ideal of the dominant male. The one mistake the feminists have made, I think, is in supposing that *all* men need this release, or that the world would be a better place if all men achieved it. It wouldn't. It would just be duller.

So far I have been pretty vague about just what the freedom of the androgynous man is. Obviously it varies with the case. In the case I know best, my own, I can be quite specific. It has freed me most as a parent. I am, among other things, a fairly good natural mother. I like the nurturing role. It makes me feel good to see a child eat – and it turns me to mush to see a 4-year-old holding a glass with both hands, in order to drink. I even enjoyed sewing patches on the knees of my daughter Amy's Dr. Dentons[3] when she was at the crawling stage. All that pleasure I would have lost if I had made myself stick to the notion of the paternal role that I started with.

Or take a smaller and rather ridiculous example. I feel free to kiss cats. Until recently it never occurred to me that I would want to, though my daughters have been doing it all their lives. But my elder daughter is now 22, and in London. Of

[3] *Dr. Dentons:* Popular brand of pajamas for young children.

course, I get to look after her cat while she is gone. He's a big, handsome farm cat named Petrushka, very unsentimental, though used from kittenhood to being kissed on the top of the head by Elizabeth. I've gotten very fond of him (he's the adventurous kind of cat who likes to climb hills with you), and one night I simply felt like kissing him on top of the head, and did. Why did no one tell me sooner how silky cat fur is?

Then there's my relationship to cars. I am completely unembarrassed by my 13 inability to diagnose even minor problems in whatever object I happen to be driving and don't have to make some insider's remark to mechanics to try to establish that I, too, am a "Man with His Machine."

The same ease extends to household maintenance. I do it, of course. Service 14 people are expensive. But for the last decade my house has functioned better than it used to because I've had the aid of a volume called "Home Repairs Any Woman Can Do," which is pitched just right for people at my technical level. As a youth, I'd as soon have touched such a book as I would have become a transvestite. Even though common sense says there is really nothing sexual whatsoever about fixing sinks.

Or take public emotion. All my life I have easily been moved by certain kinds 15 of voices. The actress Siobhan McKenna's, to take a notable case. Give her an emotional scene in a play, and within ten words my eyes are full of tears. In boyhood, my great dread was that someone might notice. I struggled manfully, you might say, to suppress this weakness. Now, of course, I don't see it as a weakness at all, but as a kind of fulfillment. I even suspect that the true he-men feel the same way, or one kind of them does, at least, and it's only the poor imitators who have to struggle to repress themselves.

Let me come back to the inkblots, with their assumption that masculine equates 16 with machinery and science, and feminine with art and nature. I have no idea whether the right pronoun for God is He, She, or It. But this I'm pretty sure of. If God could somehow be induced to take that test, God would not come out macho,[4] and not feminismo,[5] either, but right in the middle. Fellow androgynes, it's a nice thought.

After You Read

In your journal, write about one of the following topics.

1 Write a one-paragraph summary of "The Androgynous Male."

2 Explain whether you agree or disagree with Perrin's views.

3 Choose a topic of your own related to the reading.

---

[4] *macho*: Characterized by an exaggerated sense of masculine power and strength (from the Spanish word for "male").

[5] *feminismo*: Spanish word for "feminism" – a belief that women should have the same rights and opportunities as men. (In this context, *feminismo* contrasts with *macho* and refers to an exaggerated stress on the interests and qualities of females.)

ADDITIONAL READING 3
The Princess and the Admiral

Before You Read

Look at the bar graph on the right. With several classmates or in your journal, discuss whether you agree with the following statement: "The world would be a better place if there were more female leaders of countries."

TOTAL FEMALE HEADS OF STATE DURING THE TWENTIETH CENTURY	
Europe	16
Asia	11
West Indies and Bermuda	7
Africa	3
South America	3
Central America	3

Taking Notes While You Read

As you read the story, note in the margin the differences between the Princess and the Admiral, including styles of leadership, military strategies, ways of interacting and speaking with people, and reactions.

The Princess and the Admiral
Charlotte Pomerantz

The following narrative is a type of fable – a short story, often using animals as characters, that teaches a moral truth or a lesson. The story is based on the invasion of Vietnam in the thirteenth century by the imperial navy of Kublai Khan – the Mongol emperor and founder of the Yüan dynasty in China. Written in 1975 by Charlotte Pomerantz, a U.S. author of over thirty children's books and plays, "The Princess and the Admiral" won a literary award for "its contribution to the dignity and equality of all."

A very long time ago, there was a small patch of dry land called the Tiny Kingdom. 1
Most of its people were poor farmers or fisherfolk. Their bodies were lean and brown and strong from working long hours in the sun. They built the thatched mud huts in which they lived. They wove the simple earth-colored clothing they wore. And everyone, even the children, helped to plow the fields, harvest the rice, and catch the fish that they ate.

The land of the Tiny Kingdom was as poor as its people. The soil had neither 2
gold nor silver, which was why no country, in the memory of the oldest man or woman, had ever made war against them. The people were good-humored about the poverty of the land. It had given them a hundred years of peace.

The ruler of the Tiny Kingdom was Mat Mat, a dark-eyed young princess, as 3
lean and brown as her people. One night, almost a thousand years ago, the Princess
looked out the window of her royal bedchamber at the fishing boats in the harbor
below, then up at the pale sliver of a moon.

Tonight the young Princess was too excited to sleep. For this month marked 4
the anniversary of One Hundred Years of Peace in the Tiny Kingdom. It would be
celebrated, as were all great events, with a Carnival and Fireworks Display. Tomorrow
morning, at the Council of Three Advisers, the Princess would choose the date.

There would be all kinds of firecrackers – flares, petards,[1] and pinwheels that 5
burst into flowers and waterfalls and fishes. Birds and butterflies would flit among
trees of green fire. Then, at midnight, one – no, three – fantastic red dragons would
slither and writhe across the night sky.

The next morning, the Princess was the first to arrive at the Council Chamber. 6
The three advisers followed. First, the Elder, a man of ninety years. Then, the Younger,
a man of eighty years. And finally, In-Between, who was exactly eighty-five.

The advisers were strangely silent and stone-faced. 7

The Elder broke the silence. "Excuse me, Your Highness, but there can be no 8
peace celebration."

"Why not?" demanded the Princess. 9

"There are rumors of invasion," said the Younger. 10

"It looks like war," said In-Between. 11

The Princess stared at them, unbelieving. "But we have no enemies." 12

"I fear we do," said the Elder. "We have just had a report from our fishing boats 13
that a large fleet of warships is at this very moment sailing toward our kingdom."

"How terrible!" said the Princess. "How many ships are coming?" 14

"Our fishing boats report twenty ships of war," said In-Between, "including the 15
flagship of the Admiral."

"How large are the ships?" 16

"I would judge each to be about five times the size of the Royal Swan Boat," said 17
the Elder.

"More like four times the size of the largest fishing boat," said the Younger . 18

"Mmm," said In-Between. "I'd say the truth lies somewhere in the middle." 19

"Never mind," said the Princess impatiently. "How long will it be before the 20
enemy fleet reaches the harbor of the Tiny Kingdom?"

"Two days, more or less," the advisers replied. 21

The Princess settled herself on her throne. "Let us review our capabilities," she 22
said, "and make some contingency plans."

The Elder spoke first. "We have no ships of war." 23

"We have no men or women under arms," said the Younger . 24

"We do have an inexhaustible supply of firecrackers," said In-Between. "Totally 25
useless in the present emergency."

The Princess stepped down from her throne, walked to the window, and looked 26
at the harbor below. "No forts, no soldiers, no weapons, no sinews of war,"[2] she

---

[1] *petard:* Type of firework that makes a very loud noise.

[2] *sinews of war:* Traditional sources of power and strength.

CHAPTER FOUR Gender Roles

mused. "Clearly, we shall have to rely on . . . other things." She walked briskly back to the throne. "Call in the Court Astrologer," she said.

The advisers shrugged. "With all due respect," said the Younger, "astrology is no 27 substitute for weapons."

"We shall see," said the Princess. 28

An ancient and withered old woman tottered into the Council Chamber. 29 "Your Highness wants me?" she asked. "I haven't been consulted since your great-grandmother swallowed a chicken neck."

"I seek information about the position of the sun and the moon," said the 30 Princess.

"With pleasure," said the old woman. "When the moon is in her first or third 31 quarter, it's as if she were a stranger to the sun. But when she is a new moon or a full moon, there is a special, rather remarkable, attraction. We feel it on earth, in plants and oceans. I often feel it in my bones."

"And what of the moon tonight?" 32

"Tonight it is a new moon that hangs her fragile lantern over your Tiny Kingdom." 33

"Interesting," said the Princess. 34

She beckoned her three advisers to come close. "Our course is clear," she said. 35 "As clear as the lantern moon." The four of them huddled together while the Princess whispered her plan.

"And so," she concluded, "the first order of business is to send out a dozen of our 36 fishing boats to tease the enemy. Their ships will chase ours, and if all goes well, the enemy ships should get here at the right time."

The next day, upon orders of Princess Mat Mat, hundreds of farmers, fisherfolk, 37 and children gathered in a nearby forest to cut down the tallest trees. The strongest men and women sawed through the trunks. The less strong sharpened both ends of the fallen trees, and the children stripped off the branches.

Then everyone helped to haul the tree poles to the riverbed. When the tide had 38 gone down enough for them to drag the poles into the water, they hammered them – dozens and dozens of them – into the muddy bottom of the riverbed.

The Princess watched from the window of her royal bedchamber. When she had 39 counted 253 poles jutting out of the water like a crazy, staggered picket fence, she gave orders for the people to return to their huts.

The next morning, when the Princess and her advisers stood on the Royal 40 Balcony, not a single pole was visible.

"I thought the tide would be higher," said the Elder. 41

"I thought it would be lower," said the Younger. 42

"Your Highness," said In-Between, "I think you guessed just right." 43

"It was no guess," said the Princess. "Not after I talked to the Court Astrologer. 44 We know the tides are caused by the attraction of the sun and the moon. Therefore, when I learned that these two celestial bodies are especially close at this time, I knew that the tides would be exceptionally high. High enough to cover the tree poles." She smiled. "The moon is a faithful ally."

Just then, the first ships of the enemy fleet were sighted approaching the mouth 45 of the riverbed. They were in full chase of the twelve fishing boats that had been sent out to tease them.

The enemy fleet sailed up the middle of the river. As they faced the village, fifty 46 more fishing boats appeared from all directions and surrounded them.

Aboard the enemy flagship, the Admiral gave the command: *"Furl sails and drop* 47 *anchor! Get ready to fight!"*

From the Royal Balcony the Princess looked down at the enemy ships and 48 clapped her hands. "He did it! The Admiral did just what I hoped he would do!" she exclaimed, trying hard not to jump up and down.

On the river, the Admiral peered uneasily at all the fishing boats. "It looks as if 49 they are going to climb aboard."

As he spoke, the fisherfolk began to hurl cooking pots, soup ladles, coconuts, 50 mangoes, melons, chickens – whatever they had been able to lay hold of – at the enemy fleet. One tall fisherman, in his enthusiasm, took a whole pail of eels and threw it aboard the Admiral's flagship. Then the little fishing boats turned around and quickly sailed past the harbor, leaving the Admiral and his warships in full command of the river.

The Admiral chortled. "Did they really think they could conquer our mighty 51 armada with coconuts?"

"It would seem they are a rather primitive people, sir," said the Helmsman. 52

The Admiral surveyed the village and the castle. "No trouble here," he said 53 smugly. "The fishing boats have disappeared behind a bend in the river. Not a living soul on the streets, except for a few scrawny chickens and goats. It's clear the natives are terrified." He looked down at the water. "The tide is going out, but there's still plenty of depth here in the middle of the river. We'll wait for low tide to make sure we can dock."

Settling comfortably into his deck chair, he said, "Tomorrow, first thing, we'll 54 surround the palace, destroy the arsenal, seize the jewels, and behead the Princess."

"Princess?" said the Helmsman. "What makes you think it's a Princess?" 55

The Admiral snickered. "Only a girl would be silly enough to fight a great 56 naval battle with fruits and vegetables." He spotted an eel at his feet and kicked it scornfully. "Even fish! Ridiculous!"

An hour later, a tremendous shout came from below deck. *"Shipping water!"* 57

"What's that supposed to mean?" barked the Admiral. "It means there's a leak," 58 said the Helmsman. From all over the fleet came the cry *"Shipping water! We're shipping water!"*

The Admiral dashed down to the hold. There an extraordinary sight greeted his 59 eyes. What appeared to be the top of a tree was poking through the bottom of the ship! Even as the Admiral watched, the tree top was slowly coming upward. Then another tree . . . and another . . . and another. By Neptune,[3] more than a dozen were coming through the bottom! And where the hull had splintered around the tree trunks, the water was seeping in, slowly but steadily.

"Start bailing and saw off those crazy trees," bawled the Admiral. 60

"Beg pardon, sir," said the Helmsman, "but if you get rid of the trees, the water 61 will rush through. The trees are like corks. Take away the corks, and we'll all drown in the onrushing waters."

---

[3] *By Neptune*: Exclamation of surprise meaning "by God!" (Neptune was the Roman god of the sea.)

"Never mind," said the Admiral testily. "Send a message to the fleet. *'All ships to continue bailing. All ships' captains to report to my cabin for a Council of War.'*" 62

Some two hours later, when the captains were all assembled aboard the Admiral's flagship, the Helmsman stuck his head in the cabin door. "Sorry to interrupt, sir, but the water is draining out of the ships." 63

"Naturally, you blockhead," said the Admiral. "The men are bailing." 64

"No, no," said the Helmsman. "It's happening all by itself ." 65

"Ye[4] gods and little fishes!" gasped the Admiral. 66

He strode out on deck, stumbled on a coconut, then stopped and stared goggle-eyed at the astounding spectacle. All around, his whole fleet was stuck up on tree poles! 67

Suddenly everything became clear to the Admiral. He had been trapped. These devilish fisherfolk had used the tide against him. They had put in poles at low tide. He had come in with his ships at high tide. Then, when the tide went out, he was left stuck up on the poles. 68

Now he could hear a muted roar of laughter from the farmers, fisherfolk, and children who crowded the riverbank and docks. 69

From around the bend, the little fishing boats reappeared and surrounded the fleet. At their head was a golden Swan Boat, flying a flag of truce under the royal standard. It sailed up alongside the Admiral's flagship. 70

"Ahoy,"[5] said a fisherman. "Ready to surrender?" 71

The Admiral looked down and shook his fist. "Never! You just wait till we come ashore." 72

The tall fisherman grinned. "If you're thinking of sending your men swimming or wading to shore, think again. Because any man found in the water will be whacked on the head with an oar." 73

"Who the devil are you?" thundered the Admiral. 74

"I'm a fisherman. In fact, I'm the best fisherman around. Because I sacrificed a whole pail of eels for the glory of the Tiny Kingdom, the Princess has bestowed on me the honor of taking you to shore to negotiate the terms of peace." 75

"Never!" said the Admiral. "I'll go down with my ship." 76

"Your ship isn't going to go down," said the fisherman. "It will stay stuck up there on the tree poles until the ebb and flow of the tide breaks the fleet to smithereens." 77

The Admiral sighed, climbed down, and settled gloomily into the stern of the Royal Swan Boat. The tall fisherman rowed him to shore. 78

After the Admiral had changed into dry socks, he was summoned to the Council Chamber to face Princess Mat Mat and her three advisers. 79

"What humiliation!" cried the Admiral. "To be defeated by a woman!" He glanced at the young princess. "Not even a woman. A slip of a girl." He drooped miserably. "What's the difference? I shall be beheaded." 80

"Certainly we will behead you," said the Elder. 81

"I would cut off his feet," said the Younger. 82

---

[4] *Ye:* Old word for "you" (usually plural).

[5] *Ahoy:* Word used to greet people on a passing ship.

"In my opinion," said In-Between, "justice lies somewhere in the middle." 83

The Princess clucked her tongue in disapproval. "No," she said. "Revenge is not 84
our way. We do not believe that those who have wronged us should be punished or
humiliated beyond what is necessary."

"You are not going to behead me?" said the Admiral. 85

"Ugh," said the Princess. "How distasteful." 86

The Admiral was completely fogbound. "Your Highness, what *are* you going to 87
do?"

"Simple," said the Princess. "I shall supply you with two guides to take you and 88
your men through the harsh mountainous terrain that leads back to your country
and your Emperor. I shall also provide you with a two-week supply of food and
water, as well as five water buffalo to help carry your provisions." The Princess was
thoughtful. "We would appreciate your returning the water buffalo."

The Admiral knelt down before the Princess and kissed her hand. "Be assured, 89
your animals shall be returned." His voice trembled with gratitude and relief. "Your
Highness, I shall never forget you, nor the kind and gentle ways of your kingdom."
Tears filled his eyes, rolled down his cheeks and onto his medals. "If there is anything
I can ever do for you . . ."

"As a matter of fact, there is," said the Princess coolly. "I would ask you not to 90
make unkind remarks about women and girls – especially princesses."

That evening, from the Royal Balcony, Princess Mat Mat and her three advisers 91
watched the long winding caravan of enemy soldiers and sailors. At the front,
leading his men, the Admiral, bedecked with medals and sniffling from a head cold,
sat astride the fattest water buffalo. All along the road winding into the mountains,
the farmers, fisherfolk, and children waved goodbye to them.

"It is good," said the Princess to her advisers. "We won the battle, and since the 92
Admiral is returning home with his men, he will not lose too much face with his
Emperor." She sighed wistfully. "How close we came to celebrating One Hundred
Years of Peace."

"Dear Princess," said the Elder, "what happened this morning could hardly be 93
called a battle. The only casualty was a sailor who got bonged on the head with a
mango. Surely we can forget one small incident in a hundred years of peace."

"For the first time," said the Younger, "the three of us are in agreement about the 94
number of firecrackers, flares, torches, Bengal lights,[6] petards, Roman candles,[7] and
pinwheels for the celebration. One thousand."

The Princess was jubilant. 95

Thus it came to pass that within the week, the Tiny Kingdom celebrated One 96
Hundred Years of Peace – well, almost – with the biggest Carnival and Fireworks
Display in its history. Not one, not three, but *twelve* fantastic red dragons slithered
and writhed across the night sky.

And of all the happy farmers, fisherfolk, and children in the Tiny Kingdom, not 97
one was happier than Princess Mat Mat.

---

[6] *Bengal light:* Type of bright blue firework formerly used for illumination and for signaling other ships.

[7] *Roman candle:* Type of firework consisting of a tube from which balls of fire are ejected.

After You Read

In your journal, write about one of the following topics.

1 Write a one-paragraph plot summary of "The Princess and the Admiral." Then write an additional paragraph in which you identify the main point or message of the story.

2 Examine the differences between the Princess and the Admiral (styles of leadership, military strategies, ways of interacting and speaking with people, reactions) and the degree to which these differences reflect gender roles and expectations. Refer to the notes you took while reading the story.

3 Choose a topic of your own related to the story.

ADDITIONAL READING 4
The Greater God

Before You Read

With a classmate or in your journal, discuss the ways in which a person's relationship with his or her mother might typically differ from that with his or her father. Do these differences reflect gender roles and expectations?

Taking Notes While You Read

> As you read the poem, note in the margin the traditional female roles you see. Consider expectations, values, emotions, and behaviors.

 # The Greater God
Rakesh Ratti

The following poem was written by Rakesh Ratti, a psychologist and writer who was born in 1959 in Punjab, India, and immigrated, at the age of nine, with his family to California. "The Greater God" appears in a collection of essays and poems by various writers titled Boyhood, Growing Up Male *(1998).*

She the lesser god,
a shadow of the greater,
She the fearful,
more powerless than I.
She with sandhur[1] in her hair,   5

---
[1] *sandhur:* Bright reddish-orange compound used as a hair dye.

a crimson chain of subservience,
passed from father to husband,
a servant in all houses.
She of the slavish devotion,
of the tongue forever bitten   10
and words left unsaid.
She of the camphor² and coconuts.
She of the soft voice,
that I once saw as insanely yielding,
of the kind eyes   15
I once saw as timorous.
She who once towered above me
yet looked me in the eye.
She of the divas³ and bhajans.⁴
She, the central thread   20
that held the tapestry together.
She who absorbed all pain and sorrow
yet radiated light and nourishment
in every direction.
She of the rituals of mystery   25
that became for me a way of life.
She whose threats
I often laughed at,
for through the fissures
between her words   30
flowed the love she embodied.
She who was nothing was all.
She the lesser
was to me
the greater god.   35

After You Read

In your journal, write about one of the following topics.

1 Identify the female roles or expectations reflected in the poem.

2 A childhood memory you have of your mother or father.

3 Choose a topic of your own related to the poem.

---

² *camphor:* Type of tree whose wood and bark are used to produce a pleasant-smelling substance with medicinal properties.

³ *diva:* Principal female singer in an opera (from the Latin word for "goddess").

⁴ *bhajan:* Person with divine qualities (part of Hinduism, the dominant religion of India).

ADDITIONAL READING 5
Humor: The Gender of Computers

With a partner, read the following joke and cartoon and discuss gender roles and stereotypes.

 ## The Gender of Computers

A scientist had previously been a sailor. He was very aware that ships were addressed   1
as "she" and "her." He often wondered what gender computers should be addressed
as. To answer that question, he set up two groups of computer experts.

The first group was composed of women and the second of men. Each group   2
was asked to recommend whether computers should be referred to in the feminine
gender or the masculine gender. They were asked to give four reasons for their
recommendations.

The group of women reported that computers should be referred to in the   3
masculine gender because:

1. In order to get their attention you have to turn them on.
2. They have a lot of data but are still clueless.
3. They are supposed to help you solve problems, but half the time they are
   the problem themselves.
4. As soon as you commit to one, you realize that if you had waited a little
   longer, you could have had a better model.

The group of men, on the other hand, concluded that computers should be   4
referred to in the feminine gender because:

1. No one but the Creator understands their internal logic.
2. The native language they use to communicate with other computers is
   incomprehensible to everyone else.
3. Even your smallest mistakes are stored in long-term memory for later
   retrieval.
4. As soon as you make a commitment to one, you find yourself spending half
   your paycheck on accessories for it.

CATHY © (1997) Cathy Guisewite. Reprinted by permission of
UNIVERSAL PRESS SYNDICATE. All rights reserved.

ESSAY TOPICS

Write an essay on one of the following topics. Support your points with an appropriate combination of references to the readings in this chapter, library and Internet sources, and personal experiences and observations.

Refer to the section "The Essentials of Writing" on pages 102–132 to help you plan, draft, and revise your essay. Use this special section, too, to assist you in locating, integrating, and documenting your sources.

1 Discuss whether you think biological or social and cultural factors are more important in shaping gender roles.

2 Examine the degree to which traditional gender roles and expectations have changed in your culture over the last thirty years.

3 Consider whether females or males are more restricted by conventional gender roles.

4 Focus on the ways in which you have been influenced, positively and negatively, by traditional gender roles and expectations.

5 Explore one of the following topics in terms of gender roles and stereotypes:
   - rites of passage for girls or for boys
   - women or homosexuals in the military
   - the sports or toy industry
   - anorexia and other eating disorders
   - the body-image trade (diets, exercise fads, cosmetics, fragrance, fashion)
   - a particular product of the mass media – for example, a TV program, film, magazine advertisement, music video, or children's picture book

Work

A WRITER'S TECHNIQUE
Tone

In this chapter, you will explore attitudes toward work and examine the reasons some individuals find their jobs enjoyable and rewarding and others do not. In addition, you will consider concepts of success – both professional and personal – the qualities of an ideal job, and the notion of the American Dream.

Questions Raised in Chapter Five

In a small group, discuss two or three of the following questions.

1 What skills and traits are necessary to be a scientist? A business executive? A journalist?

2 Do most of the people you know see a strong connection between their work and their private lives?

3 What jobs or professions are valued most in your culture?

4 What different sources of stress do people commonly encounter at work?

5 What are your career goals, and how do you hope to achieve them?

Brief Quotations

The following quotations deal with job-related issues considered in this chapter. Working with a partner or in a small group, choose two or three quotations and discuss them.

1 *Every calling is great when greatly pursued.* (Studs Terkel, U.S. author and radio commentator)

2 *There is perhaps only one human being in a thousand who is passionately interested in his job for the job's sake.* (Dorothy Sayers, British author)

3 *Men, for the sake of getting a living, forget to live.* (Margaret Fuller, U.S. writer and early feminist)

4 *The work ethic holds that labor is good in itself; that a man or woman at work not only makes a contribution to his fellow man, but becomes a better person by virtue of the act of working.* (Richard Nixon, U.S. president)

5 *Whereas labor produces miracles for the rich, for the worker it produces destitution. Labor produces palaces, but for the worker hovels.* (Karl Marx, German political philosopher and socialist)

6 *Everyone who is prosperous or successful must have dreamed of something. It is not because he is a good worker that he is prosperous, but because he dreamed.* (Lost Star, of the Native American Maricopa tribe)

CORE READING 1
The New American Dreamers

Journal Writing

In your journal, write for ten or fifteen minutes about how you imagine your life in the future. What would you like to be doing in your professional or personal life ten years from now? Then, with several classmates, share your vision of your future.

Previewing the Topic

Write a list of the ideas that come to mind when you think of success. Consider your personal and professional life, as well as financial and other forms of success. When you are finished, share your ideas in a small group and then create a list of your points on the board. Are your group's concepts of success similar to those of the rest of the class?

Agreeing and Disagreeing

To what extent do you agree with the following statements? Fill in each blank with SA (strongly agree), A (agree), U (undecided), D (disagree), or SD (strongly disagree). Then share your responses with several classmates.

_____ 1 I think that women and men have equal job opportunities in my country.

_____ 2 People have the ability to determine their future professional and personal lives.

_____ 3 To get a good job in my country, you need a college education.

_____ 4 You cannot be successful without having a job that pays well.

_____ 5 With hard work and determination, most people can achieve the American Dream.

_____ 6 A person's job opportunities are largely determined by the social class into which he or she is born.

_____ 7 It is easier for women than for men to balance their careers and family life.

_____ 8 In my country, there are many opportunities for technical and vocational training.

_____ 9 No one job has any more value than another.

_____ 10 Most people are concerned about "keeping up with the Joneses," that is, following the latest fashions and having as many material possessions as their neighbors do.

The New American Dreamers
Ruth Sidel

Ruth Sidel is a professor of sociology at Hunter College of the City University of New York. She has written a number of books focusing on women's roles in society, including On Her Own: Growing Up in the Shadow of the American Dream *(1990), from which the following selection is taken. In the reading, Sidel discusses the hopes and dreams that young women in the United States have for their personal and professional lives.*

She is the prototype of today's young woman – confident, outgoing, knowledgeable,   1
involved. She is active in her school, church, or community. She may have a wide
circle of friends or simply a few close ones, but she is committed to them and to
their friendship. She is sophisticated about the central issues facing young people
today – planning for the future, intimacy, sex, drugs, and alcohol – and discusses
them seriously, thoughtfully, and forthrightly. She wants to take control of her life
and is trying to figure out how to get from where she is to where she wants to go.
Above all, she is convinced that if she plans carefully, works hard, and makes the
right decisions, she will be a success in her chosen field; have the material goods she
desires; in time, marry if she wishes; and, in all probability, have children. She plans,
as the expression goes, to "have it all."

She lives in and around the major cities of the United States, in the towns of   2
New England, in the smaller cities of the South and Midwest, and along the West
Coast. She comes from an upper-middle-class family, from the middle class, from
the working class, and even sometimes from the poor. What is clear is that she has
heard the message that women today should be the heroines of their own lives. She
looks toward the future, seeing herself as the central character, planning her career,
her apartment, her own success story. These young women do not see themselves as
playing supporting roles in someone else's life script; it is their own journeys they are
planning. They see their lives in terms of *their* aspirations, *their* hopes, *their* dreams.

Beth Conant is a sixteen-year-old high school junior who lives with her mother   3
and stepfather in an affluent New England college town. She has five brothers, four
older and one several years younger. Her mother is a librarian, and her stepfather
is a stockbroker. A junior at a top-notch public high school, she hopes to study
drama in college, possibly at Yale, "like Meryl Streep." She would like to live and
act in England for a time, possibly doing Shakespeare. She hopes to be living in
New York by the age of twenty-five, in her own apartment or condo, starting on her
acting career while working at another job by which she supports herself. She wants

to have "a great life," be "really independent," and have "everything that's mine – crazy furniture, everything my own style."

By the time she's thirty ("that's so boring"), she feels, she will need to be sensible, 4 because soon she will be "tied down." She hopes that by then her career will be "starting to go forth" and that she will be getting good roles. By thirty-five she'll have a child ("probably be married beforehand"), be working in New York and have a house in the country. How will she manage all this? Her husband will share responsibilities. She's not going to be a "supermom." They'll both do child care. He won't do it as a favor; it will be their joint responsibility. Moreover, if she doesn't have the time to give to a child, she won't have one. If necessary, she'll work for a while, then have children, and after that "make one movie a year."

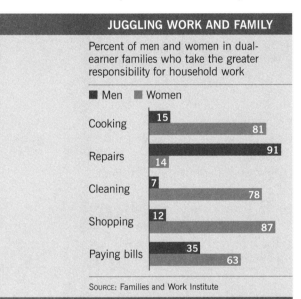

JUGGLING WORK AND FAMILY

Percent of men and women in dual-earner families who take the greater responsibility for household work

■ Men ■ Women

	Men	Women
Cooking	15	81
Repairs	14	91
Cleaning	7	78
Shopping	12	87
Paying bills	35	63

SOURCE: Families and Work Institute

Amy Morrison is a petite, black, fifteen-year-old high school sophomore who lives in Ohio. Her mother works part-time, and her father works for a local art museum. She plans to go to medical school and hopes to become a surgeon. She doesn't want to marry until she has a good, secure job but indicates that she might be living with someone. She's not sure about having children but says emphatically that she wants to be successful, to make money, to have cars. In fact, originally she wanted to become a doctor "primarily for the money," but now she claims other factors are drawing her to medicine.

Jacqueline Gonzalez is a quiet, self-possessed, nineteen-year-old Mexican-American woman who is a sophomore at a community college in southern California. She describes her father as a "self-employed contractor" and her mother as a "housewife." Jacqueline, the second-youngest of six children, is the first in her family to go to college. Among her four brothers and one sister, only her sister has finished high school. Jacqueline's goal is to go to law school and then to go into private practice. While she sees herself as eventually married with "one or two children," work, professional achievement, and an upper-middle-class lifestyle are central to her plans for her future.

If in the past, and to a considerable extent still today, women have hoped to 7 find their identity through marriage, have sought to find "validation of . . . [their] uniqueness and importance by being singled out among all other women by a man," the New American Dreamers are setting out on a very different quest for self-realization. They are, in their plans for the future, separating identity from intimacy, saying that they must first figure out who they are and that then, and only then, will they form a partnership with a man. Among the young women I interviewed, the New American Dreamers stand apart in their intention to make their own way in the world and determine their own destiny prior to forming a significant and lasting intimate relationship.

Young women today do not need to come from upper-middle-class homes such as Beth's or middle-class homes such as Amy's or working-class homes such as Jacqueline's to dream of "the good life." Even young women with several strikes against them see material success as a key prize at the end of the rainbow. Some seem to feel that success is out there for the taking. Generally, the most prestigious, best-paying careers are mentioned; few women of any class mention traditional women's professions such as teaching or nursing. A sixteen-year-old unmarried Arizona mother of a four-and-a-half-month-old baby looks forward to a "professional career either in a bank or with a computer company," a "house that belongs to me," a "nice car," and the ability to buy her son "good clothes." She sees herself in the future as dating but not married. "There is not so much stress on marriage these days," she says.

Yet another young woman, a seventeen-year-old black unmarried mother of an infant, hopes to be a "professional model," have "lots of cash," be "rich," maybe have another child. When asked if a man will be part of the picture, she responds, "I don't know."

An eighteen-year-old Hispanic unmarried mother hopes to "be my own boss" in a large company, have a "beautiful home," send her daughter to "the best schools." She wants, in her words, to "do it, make it, have money."

These young women are bright, thoughtful, personable. And they are quintessentially American: they believe that with enough hard work they will "make it" in American society. No matter what class they come from, their fantasies are of upward mobility, a comfortable life filled with personal choice and material possessions. The upper-middle-class women fantasize a life even more upper-middle-class; middle-class and working-class women look toward a life of high status in which they have virtually everything they want; and some young women who come from families with significant financial deprivation and numerous other problems dream of a life straight out of "Dallas," "Dynasty," or "L.A. Law."[1] According to one young woman, some of her friends are so determined to be successful that they are "fearful that there will be a nuclear war and that they will die before they have a chance to live their lives. If there is a nuclear war," she explained, "they won't live long enough to be successful."

Young women are our latest true believers.[2] They have bought into the image of a bright future. Many of them see themselves as professional women, dressed in handsome clothes, carrying a briefcase to work, and coming home to a comfortable house or condo, possibly to a loving, caring husband and a couple of well-behaved children. How widespread is the dream? How realistic is it? What is the function of this latest American dream? What about those young women who cling to a more traditional dream? What about those who feel their dreams must be deferred? What about those with no dream at all? And what about those who "share the fantasy," as the Chanel No. 5 perfume advertisement used to say, but have little or no chance of achieving it?

8

9

10

11

12

---

[1] "Dallas," "Dynasty," "L.A Law": Popular TV shows in the 1980s and 1990s portraying "the good life" (wealth and success).

[2] true believers: People who are fully committed to an idea or a way of life, or are zealous promoters of a particular cause.

Perhaps the most poignant example of the impossible dream is Simone Baker, a   13
dynamic, bright, eighteen-year-old black woman from Louisiana. Simone's mother
is a seamstress who has been off and on welfare over the years, and her father is a
drug addict. Simone herself has been addicted to drugs of one kind or another since
she was five. She has been in and out of drug-abuse facilities, and although she
attended school for many years and was passed from grade to grade, she can barely
read and write. When I met her in a drug rehabilitation center, she was struggling
to become drug-free so that she could join the Job Corps,[3] finish high school, and
obtain some vocational training. Her dream of the future is so extraordinary, given
her background, that she seems to epitomize the Horatio Alger[4] myth of another
era. When asked what she would like her life to be like in the future, Simone replies
instantly, her eyes shining: "I want to be a model. I want to have a Jacuzzi. I want to
have a *big*, BIG house and a BIG family – three girls and two boys."

"And what about the man?" I ask her.   14

"He'll be a lawyer. He'll be responsible, hardworking, and sensitive to my feelings.   15
Everything will be fifty-fifty. And he'll take the little boys out to play football and I'll
have the girls inside cooking. That would be a dream come true!"

Simone's dream is an incredible mixture of the old and the new – a Dick-and-   16
Jane reader[5] updated. And she's even mouthing the supreme hope of so many
women in this age of the therapeutic solution to personal problems that she'll find a
man who is "sensitive" to her "feelings." She has lived a life far from the traditional
middle class and yet has the quintessential image of the good life as it has been
formulated in the last quarter of the twentieth century. But for Simone, it is virtually
an impossible dream. One wishes that that were not so; listening to her, watching
her excitement and hope at the mere thought of such a life, one gets caught up and
wants desperately for it all to happen. The image is clear: the white house in the
suburbs with the brass knocker on the front door, the leaves on the lawn in the fall,
the boy's playing football with this incredibly wonderful husband/father, and Simone
sometimes the successful model, other times at home, cooking with her daughters.
But we know how very unlikely it is that this particular dream will come true. And
yet, maybe . . .

A key message the New American Dreamers are both receiving and sending is   17
one of optimism – the sense that they can do whatever they want with their lives.
Many Americans, of course – not just young people or young women – have a
fundamentally optimistic attitude toward the future. Historically, Americans have
believed that progress is likely, even inevitable, and that they have the ability to
control their own destinies. . . . In looking toward the future, young men clearly
dream of "the good life," of upward mobility and their share of material possessions.
While young women historically have had far less control over their lives than men,
for the past twenty-five years they have been urged to take greater control, both in

---

[3] *Job Corps:* Federally supported program of employment training for disadvantaged youths.

[4] *Horatio Alger* (1834–1899): American writer of more than 100 novels for boys, portraying characters who rise
from poverty to success through hard work and self-reliance (the rags-to-riches myth).

[5] *Dick-and-Jane reader:* Popular elementary school textbook in the 1950s and 1960s that depicted a white middle-
class family with traditional values (the mother stays at home and the father goes to work).

the workplace and in their private lives, and they have clearly taken the message very much to heart.

Angela Dawson, a sixteen-year-old high-school junior from southern California, 18 sums up the views of the New American Dreamers: "It's your life. You have to live it yourself. You must decide what you want in high school, plan your college education, and from there you can basically get what you want. If you work hard enough, you will get there. You must be in control of your life, and then somehow it will all work out."

Reading Journal

In your journal, write about one of the following topics.

1 Consider whether you agree with Angela Dawson's statement about the ability of people to control their lives. (par. 18)
2 Discuss your personal definition of success in your private or professional life.
3 Choose a topic of your own related to the reading.

Main Ideas

Answer the following questions, referring to the notes you took when reading the essay. Then share your answers with a partner.

1 What does Sidel mean by the phrase "the New American Dreamers"?
2 What are the major aspects of the American Dream that Sidel discusses in the reading?
3 What is the main point Sidel makes in the reading? Summarize her central idea in one or two sentences. Use your own words. Begin with the sentence *In her essay "The New American Dreamers," Ruth Sidel maintains that . . .*

Reflecting on Content

Answer the following questions with a partner. When possible, support your answers with observations based on your own experiences.

1 Do you think the title "The New American Dreamers" is an effective one for this reading? Why or why not? After you have answered this question, write down two titles of your own that you think would be appropriate for the selection.
2 How realistic does Sidel believe the New American Dream is? What are the chances that most young women and men will achieve it?
3 How similar are your personal and professional hopes and dreams to those of the young women interviewed in the reading? Do you share their sense of optimism?

A Writer's Technique: *Tone*

When people speak, their tone of voice can reveal a lot about their attitude toward a subject. Similarly, when people write, their "voice" can express a wide range of tones, or feelings, such as anger, amusement, surprise, sorrow, and excitement.

The **tone** of a piece of writing is the author's attitude toward the subject, as reflected in the choice of words and details. A writer's tone depends on his or her audience, subject matter, and purpose. Learning to recognize the tone of a piece of writing is essential to understanding and evaluating the ideas the author is conveying.

The adjectives below, which are given with their meanings, are commonly used to describe the tone of a piece of writing.

objective	factual; not identifying or expressing the author's feelings and interpretations
subjective	reflecting the author's personal feelings and judgments
sarcastic	saying one thing but meaning the opposite
ambivalent	uncertain or indecisive
enthusiastic	showing a great deal of interest and excitement
pessimistic	gloomy or cynical
longing	yearning or desirous, especially for something unattainable
anxious	uneasy or worried
determined	resolved; set on doing something even if it's difficult or risky
aggressive	forceful or assertive
self-evident	obvious; not requiring proof or explanation

Look at the following sentences; each expresses one of the tones, or attitudes, listed above.

- I've had a great time living in the United States. My visit has been one of the best experiences of my life. (*Tone:* enthusiastic)
- I came to the United States because of all the educational opportunities. After studying in an intensive ESL program for one year, I'm now in my first semester at a liberal arts college. (*Tone:* objective)
- I don't really know if I want to stay in the United States another year. There are certain things I like here, but I miss my family and friends back home. (*Tone:* ambivalent)
- Living in the United States has been a very valuable experience for me. When I return home, I can now tell my friends that I know the difference between a hot dog and a hamburger. (*Tone:* sarcastic)

Read through the following passages from "The New American Dreamers," each expressing a particular tone, or attitude. Next to each item, write the adjective, from the list above, that best describes the overall tone of the passage. Then share your answers with a partner.

1 If in the past, and to a considerable extent still today, women have hoped to find their identity through marriage, have sought to find "validation of . . . [their] uniqueness and importance by being singled out among all other women by a man," the New American Dreamers are setting out on a very different quest for self-realization. (par. 7)

2 According to one young woman, some of her friends are so determined to be successful that they are "fearful that there will be a nuclear war and that they will die before they have a chance to live their lives. If there is a nuclear war," she explained, "they won't live long enough to be successful." (par. 11)

3 When asked what she would like her life to be like in the future, Simone replies instantly, her eyes shining: "I want to be a model. I want to have a Jacuzzi. I want to have a *big*, BIG house and a BIG family – three girls and two boys." (par. 13)

4 But for Simone, it is virtually an impossible dream. One wishes that that were not so; listening to her, watching her excitement and hope at the mere thought of such a life, one gets caught up and wants desperately for it all to happen. . . . But we know how very unlikely it is that this particular dream will come true. And yet, maybe . . . (par. 16)

5 "It's your life. You have to live it yourself. You must decide what you want in high school, plan your college education, and from there you can basically get what you want. If you work hard enough, you will get there. You must be in control of your life, and then somehow it will all work out." (par. 18)

Vocabulary: *Synonyms*

Synonyms are words or idioms that have the same or nearly the same meaning – for example, *pleasant* and *agreeable, put off* and *postpone*. Studying synonyms is a good way to develop your vocabulary and your ability to figure out the meaning of unknown words from their context – that is, from the other words in the sentence and paragraph.

Look at the sentences on the next page from "The New American Dreamers."

- Guess the meaning of each italicized vocabulary item from the context.
- In the set of items beneath the sentence, cross out the item that is *not* a synonym.
- Write a sentence using the vocabulary item in such a way that its meaning is clear.

   Example: *A junior at a **top-notch** public high school, she hopes to study drama in college, possibly at Yale. (par. 3)*

          a. first-rate   b. exemplary   c. med~~io~~cre   d. superior

   Sentence: *Renée did a **top-notch** job on her final research paper and received an A.*

1 She is the *prototype* of today's young woman – confident, outgoing, knowledgeable, involved. (par. 1)
    a. standard   **b.** model   **c.** archetype   **d.** antithesis

2 She is sophisticated about the central issues facing young people today . . . and discusses them seriously, thoughtfully, and *forthrightly*. (par. 1)
    a. frankly   **b.** accurately   **c.** candidly   **d.** explicitly

3 She's not sure about having children but says *emphatically* that she wants to be successful. (par. 5)
    a. intricately   **b.** unhesitatingly   **c.** directly   **d.** unambiguously

4 Jacqueline Gonzalez is a quiet, *self-possessed*, nineteen-year-old Mexican-American woman. (par. 6)
    a. composed   **b.** self-absorbed   **c.** controlled   **d.** collected

5 What about those young women who *cling to* a more traditional dream? (par. 12)
    a. hold on to   **b.** adhere to   **c.** respond to   **d.** stick to

6 What about those who feel their dreams must be *deferred*? (par. 12)
    a. abandoned   **b.** suspended   **c.** postponed   **d.** delayed

7 Perhaps the most *poignant* example of the impossible dream is Simone Baker. . . . (par. 13)
    a. striking   **b.** penetrating   **c.** pervasive   **d.** touching

8 She has lived a life far from the traditional middle class and yet has the *quintessential* image of the good life as it has been formulated in the last quarter of the twentieth century. (par. 16)
    a. typical   **b.** mundane   **c.** perfect   **d.** representative

Vocabulary in Context

Locate the following italicized vocabulary items in the reading and see if you can determine their meaning from the context. Then think of an example or situation to illustrate each item, using your personal experience if possible. Do not just define the italicized words and expressions. When you are done, share your answers with a partner.

1 an occupation in which it would be helpful for an employee to have an *outgoing* personality (par. 1)

2 something you are *committed to*, and why (par. 1)

3 a major *aspiration* in your personal or professional life (par. 2)

4 several *prestigious* careers in your culture (par. 8)

5 one or two possible results of severe financial *deprivation* (par. 11)

6 someone you know who has a *dynamic* personality (par. 13)

7 a person you are familiar with who *epitomizes* success (par. 13)

8 the degree to which people in your culture have historically believed that progress is *inevitable* (par. 17)

9 whether you would *take to heart* your parents' advice about your future if it differed from what you believed (par. 17)

10 the manner in which you would *sum up* your personal or career goals (par. 18)

Discussion

Choose one of the following activities to do with a partner or in a small group.

1 Discuss your career goals, considering several of the following questions.

   a. Have you already decided on a career? If so, how did you make your decision?

   b. Do you feel any pressure to pursue a particular career?

   c. How do you plan to achieve your career goals?

   d. What difficulties do you anticipate in realizing your dreams?

2 In a library or on the Internet, research the American Dream from the perspective of two individuals – one who is native to a particular country and one who is an immigrant. Look for oral histories in which people discuss whether they feel they have achieved their dreams. When you have completed your research, share your findings with the rest of the class.

3 The Myers-Briggs inventory is a well-known questionnaire designed to identify various personality types. It is often used to help people decide which career they would like to pursue. Access the Web site <www.humanmetrics.com>. Take the Jung typology test (based on the Myers-Briggs inventory), calculate your score, identify your personality type, and read the description of this type. Then access the Web site <www.LearningChoices.com/career-personality.htm> to see which careers you might find most enjoyable. Finally, share your results with your partner or group and discuss how accurate you think they are.

Writing Follow-up

Follow up the discussion activity you chose (item 1, 2, or 3) with the matching writing assignment below.

1 Good writers are able to create different *tones,* or moods. Practice this skill, on your own or with a classmate, by writing two paragraphs, each describing the same career in a different tone. For instance, you might change the tone from positive to negative, confident to uncertain, or serious to humorous. Consider changing the details of the paragraph, the style, or both. When you have finished, read your paragraphs to several classmates and see if they can guess the tones you are trying to create.

2 Write two or three paragraphs summarizing your findings about the American Dream. Describe the attitudes and experiences of the individuals you researched, including the degree to which they feel they have achieved, or can achieve, their dreams.

3 Write two paragraphs discussing the results of the Jung typology test that you completed online. In the first paragraph, discuss whether you think the inventory accurately identified your personality type. In the second paragraph, explain whether you think you would be well suited to any of the careers listed on the LearningChoices.com Web site.

CORE READING 2
Someone Is Stealing Your Life

Journal Writing

In your journal, spend ten to fifteen minutes discussing whether you agree with the following statement: "Unskilled workers around the world are always exploited by those in power." When you are finished, share your ideas with several classmates.

Previewing the Topic

With several classmates, write a list of the reasons, in your view, many people dislike their jobs. Consider as many aspects of the work environment as you can. Then share your ideas with the rest of the class and create a list on the board of the major reasons for job dissatisfaction.

Agreeing and Disagreeing

To what extent do you agree with the following statements? Fill in each blank with SA (strongly agree), A (agree), U (undecided), D (disagree), or SD (strongly disagree). Then share your responses with several classmates.

_____ 1 Most people are not very satisfied with their jobs.

_____ 2 Most children today will lead a less affluent lifestyle when they become adults than their parents do now.

_____ 3 The majority of people lack a sense of freedom and control in their jobs.

_____ 4 Workers today are less exploited by their employers than workers were fifty years ago.

_____ 5 Most employees in my country receive a reasonable amount of vacation each year.

_____ 6 A high standard of living in one country is always based on the exploitation of workers in other nations.

_____ 7 It is immoral for business executives to earn far more then their employees.

_____ 8 Free health insurance should be the right of working people in all countries.

_____ 9 Most retired people in my culture have enough money on which to live.

_____ 10 Most people who start a business of their own eventually succeed.

Taking Notes While You Read

As you read the article, note in the margin the reasons, according to the author, most workers in the United States dislike their jobs. Also indicate the points with which you agree or disagree.

 ## Someone Is Stealing Your Life
Michael Ventura

Michael Ventura is a U.S. newspaper columnist and novelist who has held a variety of jobs. The following article, "Someone Is Stealing Your Life," originally appeared in the newspaper L.A. Weekly _in 1990 and was reprinted the following year in_ Utne Reader – _a monthly magazine that includes articles with alternative and often socially critical points of view. This selection generated considerable controversy among the editorial staff of_ Utne Reader, _some finding it "misleading and shortsighted" and others "a moving and accurate description of most Americans' experience in the workplace."_

Most American adults wake around 6 or 7 in the morning. Get to work at 8 or 9. Knock off around 5. Home again, 6-ish. Fifty weeks a year. For about 45 years.   1

Most are glad to have the work, but don't really choose it. They may dream,   2 they may study and even train for work they intensely want; but sooner or later, for most, that doesn't pan out. Then they take what they can and make do. Most have families to support, so they need their jobs more than their jobs admit to needing them. They're employees. And, as employees, most have no say whatsoever about much of anything on the job. The purpose and standards of the product or service, the short- and long-term goals of the company, are considered quite literally "none of their business" – though these issues drastically influence every aspect of their lives. No matter that they've given years to the day-to-day survival of the business; employees (even when they're called "managers") mostly take orders. Or else. It seems an odd way to structure a free society: Most people have little or no authority over what they do five days a week for 45 years. Doesn't sound much like "life, liberty, and the pursuit of happiness."[1] Sounds like a nation of drones.

It used to be that one's compensation for being an American drone was the   3 freedom to live in one's own little house, in one's own quirky way, in a clean and safe community in which your children had the chance to be happier, richer drones than you. But working stiffs[2] can't afford houses now, fewer communities are clean, none

---

[1] _life, liberty, and the pursuit of happiness:_ Natural rights guaranteed in the U.S. Declaration of Independence (1776).

[2] _working stiffs:_ Ordinary, hardworking people.

are safe, and your kids' prospects are worse. (This condition *may* be because for five days a week, for 45 years, you had no say – while other people have been making decisions that haven't been good for you.) I'm not sure whose happiness we've been pursuing lately, but one thing is clear: It's not the happiness of those who've done our society's work.

On the other hand – or so they say – you're free, and if you don't like your job you can pursue happiness by starting a business of your very own, by becoming an "independent" entrepreneur. But you're only as independent as your credit rating. And to compete in the business community, you'll find yourself having to treat others – *your* employees – as much like slaves as you can get away with. Pay them as little as they'll tolerate and give them no say in anything, because that's what's most efficient and profitable. Money is the absolute standard. Freedom, and the dignity and well-being of one's fellow creatures, simply don't figure in the basic formula. 4

This may seem a fairly harsh way to state the rules America now lives by. But if I sound radical, it's not from doing a lot of reading in some cozy university, then dashing off to dispense opinion as a prima donna of the alternative press.[3] I learned about drones by droning. From ages 18 to 29 (minus a few distracted months at college when I was 24) I worked the sort of jobs that I expected to have all 5

ANNUAL VACATION TIME	
Country	Minimum Paid Vacation Days by Law
Sweden, Austria, Denmark, France, Spain	25
United Kingdom, Switzerland, Ireland, Hungary, Czech Republic, Italy, Greece	20
Australia	No national law 20 (average)
Chile, Venezuela, Saudi Arabia, South Africa	15
China	No national law 15 (average)
Argentina, Israel	14
Turkey	12
Japan, South Korea	10
United States	No national law 10 (average)
Singapore, Taiwan	7
Mexico	6

Source: International Labor Law Committee

my life: typesetter for two years, tape transcriber[4] for three, proofreader (a grossly incompetent one) for a few weeks, messenger for a few months, and secretary (yes, secretary) for a year and a half. Then I stopped working steadily and the jobs got funkier: hospital orderly, vacuum-cleaner salesman, Jack-in-the-Box counterperson,[5] waiter, nail hammerer, cement mixer, toilet scrubber, driver.

It was during the years of office work that I caught on: I got two weeks' paid vacation per year. A year has 52 weeks. Even a comparatively unskilled, uneducated worker like me, who couldn't (still can't) do fractions or long division – even I had enough math to figure that two goes into 52 . . . how many times? Twenty-six. Meaning it would take me 26 years on the job to accumulate one year for myself. And I could only have that in 26 pieces, so it wouldn't even feel like a 6

---

[3] *prima donna of the alternative press:* Prominent journalist in the nontraditional news media. (The term *prima donna,* the principal female singer in an opera company, can also refer to a temperamental, conceited person.)

[4] *tape transcriber:* Someone who types copies of material recorded on cassette tape.

[5] *Jack-in-the-Box counterperson:* Employee taking food orders at the Jack-in-the-Box fast food restaurant.

year. In other words, no time was truly mine. My boss merely allowed me an illusion of freedom, a little space in which to catch my breath, in between the 50 weeks that I lived that *he* owned. My employer uses 26 years of my life for every year I get to keep. And what do I get in return for this enormous thing I am giving? What do I get in return for my *life*?

A paycheck that's as skimpy as they can get away with. If I'm lucky, some health 7 insurance. (If I'm *really* lucky, the employer's definition of "health" will include my teeth and my eyes – maybe even my mind.) And, in a truly enlightened workplace, just enough pension or "profit sharing"[6] to keep me sweet but not enough to make life different. And that's it.

Compare that to what my employer gets: If the company is successful, he (it's 8 usually a he) gets a standard of living beyond my wildest dreams, including what I would consider fantastic protection for his family, and a world of access that I can only pitifully mimic by changing channels on my TV. His standard of living wouldn't be possible without the labor of people like me – but my employer doesn't think that's a very significant fact. He certainly doesn't think that this fact entitles me to any say about the business. Not to mention a significant share in ownership. Oh no. The business is his to do with as he pleases, and he owns my work. Period.

I don't mean that bosses don't work. Most work hard, and have the satisfaction 9 of knowing that what they do is *theirs*. Great. The problem is: What I do is theirs too. Yet if my companion workers and I didn't do what we do – then nobody would be anybody's. So how come what we do is hardly ours? How come he can get rich while we're lucky to break even? How come he can do anything he wants with the company without consulting us, yet we do the bulk of the work and take the brunt of the consequences?

The only answer provided is that the employer came up with the money to start 10 the enterprise in the first place; hence, he and his money people decide everything and get all the benefits.

Excuse me, but that seems a little unbalanced. It doesn't take into account 11 that nothing happens unless work is done. Shouldn't it follow that, work being so important, the doers of that work deserve a more just formula for measuring who gets what? There's no doubt that the people who risked or raised the money to form a company, or bail it out of trouble, deserve a fair return on their investment – but is it fair that they get *everything*? It takes more than investment and management to make a company live. It takes the labor, skill, and talent of the people who do the company's work. Isn't *that* an investment? Doesn't it deserve a fair return, a voice, a share of the power?

I know this sounds awfully simplistic, but no school ever taught me anything 12 about the ways of economics and power (perhaps because they didn't want me to know), so I had to figure it out slowly, based on what I saw around me every day. And I saw:

That it didn't matter how long I worked or what a good job I did. I could get 13 incremental raises, perhaps even medical benefits and a few bonuses, but I would not be allowed power over my own life – no power over the fundamental decisions

---

[6] *profit sharing:* System in which employees receive part of the profits of a business enterprise.

my company makes, decisions on which my *life* depends. My future is in the hands of people whose names I often don't know and whom I never meet. Their investment is the only factor taken seriously. They feed on my work, on my life, but reserve for themselves all power, prerogative, and profit.

Slowly, very slowly, I came to a conclusion that for me was fundamental: My   14
employers are stealing my life.

They. Are. Stealing. My. Life.   15

If the people who do the work don't own some part of the product and don't   16
have any power over what happens to *their* enterprise – they are being robbed. *You*
are being robbed. And don't think for a minute that those who are robbing you don't
know they are robbing you. They know how much they get from you and how little
they give back. They are thieves. They are stealing your life.

The assembly-line worker isn't responsible for the decimation of the American   17
auto industry,[7] for instance. Those responsible are those who've been hurt least,
executives and stockholders who, according to the *Los Angeles Times*, make 50 to
500 times what the assembly-line worker makes, but who've done a miserable job
of managing. Yet it's the workers who suffer most. Layoffs, plant closings, and such
are no doubt necessary – like the bumper stickers say, shit happens[8] – but it is not
necessary that workers have no power in the fundamental management decisions
involved.

---

[7] *decimation of the American auto industry:* Drastic reduction in U.S. car production in the 1980s because of a
severe economic recession and intense competition from foreign car manufacturers.

[8] *shit happens:* Negative things naturally occur.

As a worker, I am not an "operating cost." I am how the job gets done. I *am* the 18
job. I am the company. Without me and my companion workers, there's nothing. I'm
willing to take my lumps in a world in which little is certain, but I deserve a say. Not
just some cosmetic "input," but significant power in good times or bad. A place at
the table where decisions are made. Nothing less is fair. So nothing less is moral.

And if you, as owners or management or government, deny me this – then you 19
are choosing not to be moral, and you are committing a crime against me. Do you
expect me not to struggle?

Do you expect us to be forever passive while you get rich by stealing our lives? 20

Reading Journal

In your journal, write about one of the following topics.

1 Discuss a point that the author makes with which you agree or disagree.

2 Describe a job you had that you liked or disliked.

3 Choose a topic of your own related to the reading.

Main Ideas

Answer the following questions, referring to the notes you took when reading the
article. Then share your answers with a partner.

1 In paragraph 6, Ventura speaks of "an illusion of freedom" that U.S. workers
   have in their jobs. What does he mean by this phrase?

2 In which ways does Ventura think most Americans lack power in the workplace?

3 What is the main point Ventura makes in the article? Summarize his central
   idea in one or two sentences. Use your own words. Begin with the sentence *In
   his article "Someone Is Stealing Your Life," Michael Ventura argues that . . .*

Reflecting on Content

Answer the following questions with a partner. When possible, support your
answers with observations based on your own experiences.

1 What do you consider Ventura's purpose in writing the article? What does he
   hope to accomplish? (See the discussion on page 64 of the three main purposes
   of writing: to inform, persuade, and entertain.)

2 Do you agree with Ventura that "money is the absolute standard" in the
   workplace and that "freedom, and the well-being of one's fellow creatures,
   simply don't figure in the basic formula" (par. 4)? Why or why not?

3 What do you think of Ventura's statement, in paragraph 14, that employers
   are intentionally "stealing" their employees' lives? Is this a valid analogy or
   comparison? By denying workers "power," are business owners and company
   management being immoral and "committing a crime" (par. 19)? Explain your
   response.

A Writer's Technique: *Tone*

Review the discussion of tone on page 246.

Some pieces of writing are **subjective**; that is, they reflect the author's personal feelings and interpretations. Others are more **objective**, stressing facts rather than personal feelings and judgments. Depending on your topic, audience, and purpose, your tone will be objective, subjective, or a combination of the two.

Read through the following passages from "Someone Is Stealing Your Life." Each expresses a particular tone, or attitude. Next to each item, write the adjective, from the list on page 246 that best describes the overall tone of the passage. If you think a passage is *objective* (emphasizing facts rather than personal reactions), write this word to indicate the central tone. Then share your answers with a partner.

1 Most American adults wake around 6 or 7 in the morning. Get to work at 8 or 9. Knock off around 5. Home again, 6-ish. Fifty weeks a year. For about 45 years. (par. 1)

2 It used to be that one's compensation for being an American drone was the freedom to live in one's own little house, in one's own quirky way, in a clean and safe community in which your children had the chance to be happier, richer drones than you. (par. 3)

3 It takes more than investment and management to make a company live. It takes the labor, skill, and talent of the people who do the company's work. Isn't *that* an investment? Doesn't it deserve a fair return, a voice, a share of the power? (par. 11)

4 And if you, as owners or management or government, deny me this [power] – then you are choosing not to be moral, and you are committing a crime against me. Do you expect me not to struggle? Do you expect us to be forever passive while you get rich by stealing our lives? (pars. 19–20)

Vocabulary: *Collocations*

The study of **collocations** is a useful way to develop your vocabulary. Collocations are two or more words that often occur together. These word combinations can appear in a number of patterns, for example:

adjective + noun:	heavy smoker, slim chance, public enemy
verb + noun:	conduct research, set a record, break the law
verb + adverb:	travel widely, document fully, sleep soundly

For each of the word combinations below that appear in the article "Someone Is Stealing Your Life," do the following:

- Form collocations by matching each word in the left-hand column with an appropriate vocabulary item in the right-hand column. (Sometimes more than one collocation is possible.)
- Find the word combinations in the reading and compare your answers.
- Write a sentence of your own for each collocation, in such a way that its meaning is clear.

1	significant	a. a family (par. 2)
2	take	b. goals (par. 2)
3	commit	c. happiness (par. 3)
4	long-term	d. standard (par. 4)
5	medical	e. formula (par. 4)
6	support	f. fact (par. 8)
7	absolute	g. money (par. 11)
8	pursue	h. benefits (par. 13)
9	basic	i. seriously (par. 13)
10	raise	j. a crime (par. 19)

Vocabulary in Context

Locate the following italicized vocabulary items in the reading and see if you can determine their meaning from the context. Then think of an example or situation to illustrate each item, using your personal experience if possible. Do not just define the italicized words and expressions. When you are done, share your answers with a partner.

1 whether you think most employees *have a say* in important management decisions (par. 2)

2 a way to discourage people from becoming *drones* in the workplace (par. 2)

3 your *prospects* of achieving contentment and success in your future career (par. 3)

4 a *harsh* work environment for most people (par. 5)

5 the manner in which an employer might deal with an *incompetent* worker (par. 5)

6 the number of years it would take most people in your culture to *accumulate* one year of vacation (par. 6)

7 one or two characteristics of an *enlightened* workplace (par. 7)

8 whether you agree with Michael Ventura that most workers are lucky to *break even* in their jobs (par. 9)

9 the meaning of Ventura's statement "I'm willing to *take my lumps* in a world in which little is certain, but I deserve a say" (par. 18)

10 an example of a *cosmetic* change in a company's attempts to improve its work environment (par. 18)

Discussion

Choose one of the following activities to do with a partner or in a small group.

1 Make a chart similar to the one on the right. Fill in the first column with at least five characteristics of the U.S. workplace that Ventura criticizes. Fill in the second column with your reactions to his criticisms.

Ventura's Criticisms	My Reactions

2 Write a list of the most important features that you would look for in a job. Consider the type of work, the work environment, and any other aspects of your ideal employment. Then share your ideas with several classmates and write your collective wish list on the board. Finally, group all the desired qualities into major categories.

3 Go through the employment ads in a local newspaper – usually found in the "Classified" or "Help Wanted" section – and discuss the positions that you find interesting. You can look in an actual newspaper or an online version. What aspects of the jobs appeal to you, and why?

Writing Follow-up

Follow up the discussion activity you chose (item 1, 2, or 3) with the matching writing assignment below.

1 Imagine you and several classmates are employees who are upset about one or more aspects of work life that you listed above. Write a short letter of two or three paragraphs to the manager, expressing your concerns and arguing the necessity of improving the work environment. Provide some specific recommendations. Write in a *tone* that will help you achieve your purpose.

2 Write two or three paragraphs discussing what you would look for in a job. Consider the type of work, the work environment, and any other qualities of your ideal job.

3 Imagine you are applying for one of the positions advertised in a local newspaper. You already have a résumé. Write a cover letter explaining why you are interested in the job and what your qualifications are. Remember that you will probably be one of many applicants for the position. What makes you a special candidate?

CORE READING 3
Our Schedules, Our Selves

Journal Writing

Choose one of the following prewriting strategies: **brainstorming, freewriting, clustering,** or the **journalist's questions** (see pages 113–116). In your journal, use one of these strategies to respond to the following statement: "Most people have such hectic daily schedules that they don't have time to enjoy life fully." Then share your ideas with several classmates.

Previewing the Topic

Many people believe that, over the last few decades, life has become increasing hurried and stressful. Write a list of the ways that you think this has been true. Consider the nature of people's fast-paced lives today and various reasons for it. When you are finished, discuss your ideas in a small group. Then create a list of all the reasons identified on the board.

Agreeing and Disagreeing

To what extent do you agree with the following statements? Fill in each blank with SA (strongly agree), A (agree), U (undecided), D (disagree), or SD (strongly disagree). Then share your responses with several classmates.

_____ 1 People have more human contact today than they did forty years ago.

_____ 2 In my culture, it is common for both parents to work outside the home.

_____ 3 Single-parent households are becoming more and more common in my culture.

_____ 4 Most working people have enough annual vacation time.

_____ 5 Technological advances, such as cell phones and e-mail, have given people more time for themselves.

_____ 6 People's lives today are less hectic and stressful than they were a half century ago.

_____ 7 The number of hours in the average person's work week should be reduced.

_____ 8 Children today have more opportunities and lead a more interesting life than they did when I was growing up.

_____ 9 Most people I know have too many obligations and scheduled activities in their daily lives.

_____ 10 In nonindustrial societies, people usually have more time to enjoy life than in industrial ones.

Taking Notes While You Read

As you read the essay, note in the margin the reasons the author cites for people's increasingly hectic lifestyles and the results of this fast pace. Also indicate the points with which you agree or disagree.

Our Schedules, Our Selves
Jay Walljasper

Jay Walljasper is the editor of Utne Reader – *a monthly magazine that reprints articles with an alternative and often socially critical viewpoint. The following selection, "Our Schedules, Our Selves," from a 2003 issue of* Utne Reader, *is one of several articles in the magazine dealing with ways to reexamine time and increase one's enjoyment of daily life. The title of the collection of articles is "How to Stop Time: Rip Up Your Schedule and Take Back Your Life."*

DAMN! You're 20 minutes – no, more like half an hour – late for your breakfast meeting, which you were hoping to scoot out of early to make an 8:30 seminar across town. And, somewhere in there, there's that conference call. Now, at the last minute, you have to be at a 9:40 meeting. No way you can miss it. Let's see, the afternoon is totally booked, but you can probably push back your 10:15 appointment and work through lunch. That would do it. Whew! The day has barely begun and already you are counting the hours until evening, when you can finally go home and happily, gloriously, triumphantly, do nothing. You'll skip yoga class, blow off the neighborhood meeting, ignore the piles of laundry and just relax. Yes! . . . No! Tonight's the night of the concert. You promised Nathan and Mona weeks ago that you would go. *DAMN!*

Welcome to the daily grind circa¹ 2003 – a grueling 24-7² competition against the clock that leaves even the winners wondering what happened to their lives. Determined and sternly focused, we march through each day obeying the orders of our calendars. The idle moment, the reflective pause, serendipity of any sort have no place in our plans. Stopping to talk to someone or slowing down to appreciate a sunny afternoon will only make you late for your next round of activities. From the minute we rise in the morning, most of us have our day charted out. The only surprise is if we actually get everything done that we had planned before collapsing into bed at night.

On the job, in school, at home, increasing numbers of North Americans are virtual slaves to their schedules. Some of what fills our days are onerous obligations, some are wonderful opportunities, and most fall in between, but taken together they add up to too much. Too much to do, too many places to be, too many things happening too fast, all mapped out for us in precise quarter-hour allotments on our Palm Pilots or day planners. We are not leading our lives, but merely following a dizzying timetable of duties, commitments, demands, and options. How did this

---
¹ *circa:* Latin for *about* or *approximately.*
² *24-7:* Informal way of saying, "Twenty-four hours a day, seven days a week."

1

2

3

happen? Where's the luxurious leisure that decades of technological progress was supposed to bestow upon us?

The acceleration of the globalized economy, and the accompanying decline 4 of people having any kind of a say over wages and working conditions, is a chief culprit. Folks at the bottom of the socio-economic ladder feel the pain most sharply. Holding down two or three jobs, struggling to pay the bills, working weekends, no vacation time, little social safety net, they often feel out of control about everything happening to them. But even successful professionals, people who seem fully in charge of their destinies, feel the pinch. Doctors, for example, working impossibly crowded schedules under the command of HMOs,[3] feel overwhelmed. Many of them are now seeking union representation, traditionally the recourse of low-pay workers.

The onslaught of new technology, which promised to set us free, has instead 5 ratcheted up the rhythms of everyday life. Cell phones, e-mail, and laptop computers instill expectations of instantaneous action. While such direct communication can loosen our schedules in certain instances (it's easier to shift around an engagement on short notice), overall they fuel the trend that every minute must be accounted for. It's almost impossible to put duties behind you now, when the boss or committee chair can call you at a rap show or sushi restaurant, and documents can be e-mailed to you on vacation in Banff[4] or Thailand. If you are never out of the loop, then are you ever not working?

Our own human desire for more choices and new experiences also plays a role. 6 Just like hungry diners gathering around a bountiful smorgasbord, it's hard not to pile too many activities on our plates. An expanding choice of cultural offerings over recent decades and the liberating sense that each of us can fully play a number of different social roles (worker, citizen, lover, parent, artist, etc.) has opened up enriching and exciting opportunities. Spanish lessons? Yes. Join a volleyball team? Why not. Cello and gymnastics classes for the kids? Absolutely. Tickets to a blues festival, food and wine expo, and political fundraiser? Sure. And we can't forget to make time for school events, therapy sessions, protest rallies, religious services, and dinner with friends.

Yes, these can all add to our lives. But with only 24 hours allotted to us each 7 day, something is lost too. You don't just run into a friend anymore and decide to get coffee. You can't happily savor an experience, because your mind races toward the next one on the calendar. In a busy life, nothing happens if you don't plan it, often weeks in advance. Our "free" hours become just as programmed as the workday. What begins as an idea for fun frequently turns into an obligation obstacle course. Visit that new barbecue restaurant. *Done!* Go to tango lessons. *Done!* Fly to Montreal for a long weekend. *Done!*

We've booked ourselves so full of prescheduled activities there's no time left 8 for those magic, spontaneous moments that make us feel most alive. We seldom stop to think of all the experiences we are eliminating from our lives when we load

---

[3] *HMOs:* Health maintenance organizations (organizations that provide health care to voluntarily enrolled individuals and families).

[4] *Banff:* Town in southwestern Canada.

The table below indicates the average number of hours people work per week in various countries (excluding lunchtime).

Country	Weekly Hours Worked
South Korea	47.1
Japan	40.0
Greece	36.9
Mexico	35.8
Australia	35.3
United States	35.0
Britain	32.9
Italy	30.9
France	29.5

SOURCE: Galileo Group

up our appointment book. Reserving tickets for a basketball game months away could mean you miss out on the first balmy evening of spring. Five P.M. skating lessons for your children fit so conveniently into your schedule that you never realize it's the time all the other kids in the neighborhood gather on the sidewalk to play.

9 A few years back, radical Brazilian educator Paulo Freire was attending a conference of Midwestern political activists and heard over and over about how overwhelmed people felt about the duties they face each day. Finally, he stood up and, in slow, heavily accented English, declared, "We are bigger than our schedules." The audience roared with applause.

10 Yes, we are bigger than our schedules. So how do we make sure our lives are not overpowered by an endless roster of responsibilities? Especially in an age where demanding jobs, two-worker households or single-parent families make the joyous details of everyday life – cooking supper from scratch or organizing a block party[5] – seem like an impossible dream? There is no set of easy answers, despite what the marketers of new convenience products would have us believe. But that doesn't mean we can't make real steps to take back our lives.

11 Part of the answer is political. So long as Americans work longer hours than any other people on Earth, we are going to feel hemmed in by our schedules. Expanded vacation time for everyone, including part-time and minimum wage workers, is one obvious and overdue solution. Shortening the work week, something the labor movement and progressive politicians successfully accomplished in the early decades of the 20th century, is another logical objective. There's nothing preordained about 40 hours on the job; Italy, France, and other European nations have already cut back working hours. An opportunity for employees outside academia to take a sabbatical every decade or so is another idea whose time has come. And how about more vacation and paid holidays? Let's start with Martin Luther King's[6] birthday, Susan B. Anthony's[7] birthday, and your own! Any effort to give people more clout in their workplaces – from strengthened unions to employee ownership – could help us gain much-needed flexibility in our jobs and our lives.

12 On another front, how you think about time can make a big difference in how you feel about your life, as other articles in this cover section[8] illustrate. Note how some of your most memorable moments occurred when something in your schedule fell through. The canceled lunch that allows you to spend an hour strolling around town. Friday night plans scrapped for a bowl of popcorn in front of the fireplace.

---

[5] *block party:* Party with people from one's neighborhood, often outdoors.

[6] *Martin Luther King, Jr.* (1929–1968): U.S. civil rights leader. A national holiday honoring King has existed since 1986, but it was not celebrated by all fifty states until 1999.

[7] *Susan B. Anthony* (1820–1906): Leader of U.S. women's right-to-vote movement.

[8] *cover section:* Special section in a magazine with various articles on a certain subject.

Don't be shy about shucking your schedule whenever you can get away with it. And with some experimentation, you may find that you can get away with it a lot more than you imagined.

Setting aside some time on your calendar for life to just unfold in its own surprising way can also nurture your soul. Carve out some nonscheduled hours (or days) once in a while and treat them as a firm commitment. And resist the temptation to turn every impulse or opportunity into another appointment. It's neither impolite nor inefficient to simply say, "Let me get back to you on that tomorrow" or "Let's check in that morning to see if it's still a good time." You cannot know how crammed that day may turn out to be, or how uninspired you might feel about another engagement, or how much you'll want to be rollerblading or playing chess or doing something else at that precise time.

In our industrialized, fast-paced society, we too often view time as just another mechanical instrument to be programmed. But time possesses its own ever-shifting shape and rhythms, and defies our best efforts to corral it within the tidy lines of our Palm Pilots or datebooks. Stephan Rechtschaffen, author of *Time Shifting*, suggests you think back on a scary auto collision (or near miss), or spectacular night of lovemaking. Time seemed almost to stand still. You can remember everything in vivid detail. Compare that to an overcrammed week that you recall now only as a rapid-fire blur. Keeping in mind that our days expand and contract according to their own patterns is perhaps the best way to help keep time on your side.

Reading Journal

In your journal, write about one of the following topics.

1 Consider whether you agree or disagree with Walljasper that people are increasingly becoming slaves to their schedules.

2 Discuss the degree to which your own life is controlled by obligations and scheduled activities.

3 Choose a topic of your own related to the reading.

Main Ideas

Answer the following questions, referring to the notes you took when reading the article. Then share your answers with a partner.

1 According to Walljasper, what are the major factors contributing to people's increasingly hectic lifestyles?

2 What are the results of the fast-paced life that Walljasper mentions? What kinds of activities and experiences do people miss out on? Give at least two examples.

3 What is the main point Walljasper makes in the essay? Summarize his central idea in one or two sentences. Use your own words. Begin with the sentence *In his essay "Our Schedules, Our Selves," Jay Walljasper argues that . . .*

Reflecting on Content

Answer the following questions with a partner. When possible, support your answers with observations based on your own experiences.

1 Some have argued that cell phones, e-mail, laptop computers, and other recent technologies liberate people, making their lives more efficient and providing more leisure and quality time. Others, such as Walljasper, maintain that new technology more often enslaves people, escalating the pace of life and creating more work and obligations (par. 5). Which of these points of view do you find more persuasive, and why?

2 In paragraphs 11–14, Walljasper provides several suggestions for helping people free themselves from their hectic lifestyles. Which one of his recommendations do you think would be especially helpful in allowing people to take back their lives?

3 In paragraph 14, Walljasper says, "In our industrialized, fast-paced society, we too often view time as just another mechanical instrument to be programmed." Do you think this is the prevalent concept of time in your culture? Why or why not?

A Writer's Technique: *Tone*

With a partner, review the discussion of tone on page 246.

Then read through the following passages from "Our Schedules, Our Selves" and discuss the predominant tone of each one. Next to each passage, write one or two adjectives that best describe the author's attitude or feeling. If you think a passage is objective (stressing facts rather than personal feelings, opinions, or judgments), indicate this as the central tone.

1 You're 20 minutes – no, more like half an hour – late for your breakfast meeting, which you were hoping to scoot out of early to make an 8:30 seminar across town. And, somewhere in there, there's that conference call. Now, at the last minute, you have to be at a 9:40 meeting. No way you can miss it. Let's see, the afternoon is totally booked, but you can probably push back your 10:15 appointment and work through lunch. That would do it. Whew! (par. 1)

2 The day has barely begun and already you are counting the hours until evening, when you can finally go home and happily, gloriously, triumphantly, do nothing. You'll skip yoga class, blow off the neighborhood meeting, ignore the piles of laundry and just relax. Yes! . . . No! Tonight's the night of the concert. You promised Nathan and Mona weeks ago that you would go. *DAMN!* (par. 1)

3 Folks at the bottom of the socio-economic ladder feel the pain most sharply. Holding down two or three jobs, struggling to pay the bills, working weekends, no vacation time, little social safety net, they often feel out of control about everything happening to them. But even successful professionals, people who seem fully in charge of their destinies, feel the pinch. (par. 4)

4 An expanding choice of cultural offerings over recent decades and the liberating sense that each of us can fully play a number of different social roles . . . has opened up enriching and exciting opportunities. Spanish lessons? Yes. Join a volleyball team? Why not. Cello and gymnastics classes for the kids? Absolutely. Tickets to a blues festival, food and wine expo, and political fundraiser? Sure. (par. 6)

Vocabulary: *Phrasal Verbs*

A phrasal verb is a combination of a verb and a preposition or a verb and an adverb that creates a new vocabulary item. Review the discussion of phrasal verbs on page 146.

Fill in the following blanks with the appropriate preposition(s) and adverb(s). Then write the meaning of the phrasal verb and a sentence of your own, using it correctly.

> **Example:** *You don't just* run ___*into*___ *a friend anymore and decide to get coffee. (par. 7)*
>
> **Meaning:** *To meet someone by chance or to experience something unexpectedly (especially something unpleasant)*
>
> **Sentence:** *I* ran into *some financial problems last year and had to borrow a lot of money from my parents.*

1 You'll skip yoga class, *blow* _____ the neighborhood meeting, ignore the piles of laundry and just relax. (par. 1)

2 Some of what fills our days are onerous obligations, some are wonderful opportunities, and most fall in between, but taken together they *add* _____ _____ too much. (par. 3)

3 *Holding* _____ two or three jobs, struggling to pay the bills, working weekends, no vacation time, little social safety net, they often feel out of control. (par. 4)

4 Reserving tickets for a basketball game months away could mean you *miss* _____ _____ the first balmy evening of spring. (par. 8)

5 There's nothing preordained about 40 hours on the job; Italy, France, and other European nations have already *cut* _____ working hours. (par. 11)

6 Note how some of your most memorable moments occurred when something in your schedule *fell* _____. (par. 12)

7 Don't be shy about shucking your schedule whenever you can *get* _____ _____ it. And with some experimentation, you may find that you can *get* _____ _____ it a lot more than you imagined. (par. 12)

8 *Setting* _____ some time on your calendar for life to just unfold in its own surprising way can also nurture your soul. (par. 13)

Vocabulary in Context

Locate the following italicized vocabulary items in the reading and see if you can determine their meaning from the context. Then think of an example or situation to illustrate each item, using your personal experience if possible. Do not just define the italicized words and expressions. When you are done, share your answers with a partner.

1 an example of a *grueling* daily schedule (par. 2)

2 the reason some people think it's important to have *idle* moments in one's daily life (par. 2)

3 an example of *serendipity* (par. 2)

4 a task or obligation that you would find *onerous,* and why (par. 3)

5 one of the *culprits,* in your opinion, that cause the increasingly hectic, stressful lifestyle many people lead today (par. 4)

6 an example of someone who is *out of the loop* (par. 5)

7 the amount of time you *allot,* in your weekly schedule, for leisure activities (par. 7)

8 the last time you were able to *savor* something, such as a meal or an experience. (par. 7)

9 a social policy whose *time,* you think, *has come* (par. 11)

10 a way to give people more *clout* in the workplace (par. 11)

Discussion

Choose one of the following activities to do with a partner or in a small group.

1 Make a chart similar to the one on the right. Under each column, fill in Walljasper's ideas about people's lifestyles and schedules. You may also include ideas of your own. When you are done, share your chart with the rest of the class.

Reasons for Stress	Results of a Hectic Lifestyle	Ways to Free People from their Schedules

2 Design a brief survey based on issues raised in this reading. What, for example, do people find stressful in their lives? Do they feel they have too many obligations and activities in their daily schedule? Ask several people to respond to the questions in the survey in written or oral form. Analyze their responses and share your findings with the rest of the class.

3 Access the National Public Radio Web site <www.npr.org>. Click on *Archives* and search for one of the following broadcast titles (remember to include the quotation marks when you search): "Vacationless by Choice," "Do Americans Get Enough Vacation Time?" or "French Vacations." While you are listening to the broadcast, write a list of various people's attitudes toward vacation time. Then discuss these attitudes and your responses to them with your partner or group.

Writing Follow-up

Follow up the discussion activity you chose (item 1, 2, or 3) with the matching writing assignment below.

1 An important aspect of good writing is the ability to create different *tones*, or moods. Practice this skill now with a partner by choosing one of the items in your chart and writing three paragraphs about it. In each paragraph, describe the item in a distinct tone. In the first paragraph, use language that creates a *positive* impression; in the second paragraph, a *negative* impression; and in the third paragraph, a *neutral* impression. You can change the details of the paragraph, the style, or both. (Style includes word choice, sentence structure, and figures of speech.)

2 Write a brief report discussing the results of your survey. Consider peoples' responses and what they have in common. What conclusions can you draw?

3 Write a paragraph summarizing the reactions you heard, in the radio broadcast, to the issue of vacation time. Then write a second paragraph, discussing your response to one or more of these viewpoints.

MAKING CONNECTIONS

Answer two or three of the following questions relating to the three core readings in this chapter.

1 Compare the views of the young women interviewed in the first article, by Sidel, with those of Ventura, the author of the second article. How realistic do you think Ventura would consider the young women's dreams of personal and professional success?

2 The authors of the second and third articles both refer to people as "slaves." What do they mean by this term? In which ways do the authors think people lack freedom in their lives?

3 What kind of advice do you think Walljasper, the author of the third article, might give the young women mentioned in the first article as they pursue their personal and professional dreams?

4 Ventura and Walljasper offer some similar suggestions to help employees feel more in control of their lives. What changes in the workplace do they agree would be helpful? Think of at least two examples.

5 Compare the predominant *tone* of each of the three readings. In which ways are the attitudes of the authors similar or different? Consider especially the level of optimism expressed in the selections.

ADDITIONAL READING 1
The Rage to Know

With several classmates or in your journal, discuss an experience with science that you once enjoyed at school or elsewhere: a class you took, an experiment you did, or a discovery you made. In what ways did you find the experience rewarding, and what did you learn?

Taking Notes While You Read

As you read the selection, note in the margin the various reasons given for scientists wishing to be involved in their profession. Consider especially the satisfactions and challenges they discuss.

The Rage to Know
Horace Freeland Judson

The following reading, "The Rage to Know," is an excerpt from a chapter in Horace Freeland Judson's award-winning book The Search for Solutions (1980), *based on the author's interviews with many scientists about their professional lives. Born in New York in 1931, Judson has made a career of writing books about the history of science and its prominent figures.*

Certain moments of the mind have a special quality of well-being. A mathematician friend of mine remarked the other day that his daughter, age eight, had just stumbled without his teaching onto the fact that some numbers are prime numbers – those, like 11 or 19 or 83 or 397, that cannot be divided by any other integer (except, trivially, by 1). "She called them 'unfair' numbers," he said. "And when I asked her why they were unfair, she told me, 'Because there's no way to share them out evenly.'" What delighted him most was not her charming turn of phrase nor her equitable turn of mind (17 peppermints to give to her friends?) but – as a mathematician – the knowledge that the child had experienced a moment of pure scientific perception. She had discovered for herself something of the way things are.

The satisfaction of such a moment at its most intense – and this is what ought to be meant, after all, by the tarnished phrase "the moment of truth" – is not easy to describe. It partakes at once of exhilaration and tranquility. It is luminously clear. It is beautiful. The clarity of the moment of discovery, the beauty of what in that moment is seen to be true about the world, is the most fundamental attraction that draws scientists on.

Science is enormously disparate – easily the most varied and diverse of human pursuits. The scientific endeavor ranges from the study of animal behavior all the

1

2

3

way to particle physics,[1] and from the purest of mathematics back again to the most practical problems of shelter and hunger, sickness and war. Nobody has succeeded in catching all this in one net. And yet the conviction persists – scientists themselves believe, at heart – that behind the diversity lies a unity. In those luminous moments of discovery, in the various approaches and the painful tension required to arrive at them, and then in the community of science, organized worldwide to doubt and criticize, test and exploit discoveries – somewhere in that constellation there are surely constants, to begin with. Deeper is the lure that in the bewildering variety of the world as it is there may be found some astonishing simplicities. . . .

Scientists do science for a variety of reasons, of course, and most of them are 4
familiar to the sculptor, say, or to the surgeon or the athlete or the builder of bridges: the professional's pride in skill; the swelling gratification that comes with recognition accorded by colleagues and peers; perhaps the competitor's fierce appetite; perhaps ambition for a kind of fame more durable than most. At the beginning is curiosity, and with curiosity the delight in mastery – the joy of figuring it out that is the birthright of every child. I once asked Murray Gell-Mann, a theoretical physicist, how he got started in science. His answer was to point to the summer sky: "When I was a boy, I used to ask all sorts of simple questions – like, 'What holds the clouds up?'" Rosalind Franklin, the crystallographer whose early death deprived her of a share in the Nobel Prize that was given for the discovery of the structure of DNA (the stuff that genes are made of), one day was helping a young collaborator draft an application for research money, when she looked up at him and said, "What we can't tell them is that it's so much *fun!*" He still remembers her glint of mischief. The play of the mind, in an almost childlike innocence, is a pleasure that appears again and again in scientists' reflections on their work. The geneticist Barbara McClintock, as a woman in American science in the 1930's, had no chance at the academic posts open to her male colleagues, but that hardly mattered to her. "I did it because it was *fun!*" she said forty years later. "I couldn't wait to get up in the morning! I never thought of it as 'science.'". . .

Two hundred and fifty years before, . . . Isaac Newton,[2] shortly before his death, 5
said:

> I do not know what I may appear to the world, but to myself I seem to have been only like a boy playing on the sea shore, and diverting myself in now and then finding a smoother pebble or a prettier shell than ordinary, whilst the great ocean of truth lay all undiscovered before me.

For some, curiosity and the delight of putting the world together deepen into a 6
life's passion. Sheldon Glashow, a fundamental-particle physicist at Harvard, also got started in science by asking simple questions. "In eighth grade, we were learning about how the earth goes around the sun, and the moon around the earth, and so on," he said. "And I thought about that, and realized that the Man in the Moon is always looking at us" – that the moon as it circles always turns the same face to the

---

[1] *particle physics:* Branch of physics dealing with the properties and interactions of elementary particles, or units of matter (also called high-energy physics)

[2] *Isaac Newton* (1642–1727): Revolutionary English mathematician and physicist who discovered the law of universal gravitation and used it to explain the motion of planets.

earth. "And I asked the teacher, 'Why is the Man in the Moon always looking at us?' She was pleased with the question – but said it was hard. And it turns out that it's not until you're in college-level physics courses that one really learns the answers," Glashow said. "But the *difference* is that most people would look at the moon and wonder for a moment and say, 'That's interesting' – and forget it. But some people can't let go."

Curiosity is not enough. The word is too mild by far, a word for infants. Passion is indispensable for creation, no less in the sciences than in the arts. Medawar[3] once described it in a talk addressed to young scientists. "You must feel in yourself an exploratory impulse – an *acute discomfort* at incomprehension." This is the rage to know. The other side of the fun of science, as of art, is pain. A problem worth solving will surely require weeks and months of lack of progress, whipsawn between hope and the blackest sense of despair. The marathon runner or the young swimmer who would be a champion knows at least that the pain may be a symptom of progress. But here the artist and the scientist part company with the athlete – to join the mystic for a while. The pain of creation, though not of the body, is in one way worse. It must not only be endured but reflected back on itself to increase the agility, variety, inventiveness of the play of the mind. Some problems in science have demanded such devotion, such willingness to bear repeated rebuffs, not just for years but for decades. There are times in the practice of the arts, we're told, of abysmal self-doubt. These are like passages in the doing of science. Albert Einstein took eleven years of unremitting concentration to produce the general theory of

---
[3] *Medawar, Sir Peter* (1915–1987): English scientist who won the Nobel Prize for his explanation of why the body rejects foreign tissue such as a transplanted kidney or heart.

relativity; long afterward, he wrote, "In the light of knowledge attained, the happy achievement seems almost a matter of course, and any intelligent student can grasp it without too much trouble. But the years of anxious searching in the dark, with their intense longing, their alternations of confidence and exhaustion, and the final emergence into the light – only those who have experienced it can understand it.". . .

One path to enlightenment has been reported so widely, by writers and artists, by scientists, and especially by mathematicians, that it has become established as a discipline for courting inspiration. The first stage, the reports agree, is prolonged contemplation of the problem, days of saturation in the data, weeks of incessant struggle – the torment of the unknown. The aim is to set in motion the unconscious processes of the mind, to prepare the intuitive leap. . . . 8

Identification with the problem grows so intimate that the scientist has the experience of the detective who begins to think like the terrorist, of the hunter who feels, as though directly, the silken ripple of the tiger's instincts. One great physical chemist was credited by his peers, who watched him awestruck, with the ability to think about chemical structures directly in quantum[4] terms – so that if a proposed molecular model was too tightly packed, he felt uncomfortable, as though his shoes pinched. Joshua Lederberg, president of the Rockefeller University, who won his Nobel for discoveries that established the genetics of microorganisms, said recently, "One needs the ability to strip to the essential attributes of some actor in a process, the ability to imagine oneself *inside* a biological situation; I literally had to be able to think, for example, 'What would it be like if I were one of the chemical pieces in a bacterial chromosome?' – and to try to understand what my environment was, try to know *where* I was, try to know when I was supposed to function in a certain way, and so forth.". . . 9

. . . in the classic strategy for achieving enlightenment, the weeks of saturation must be followed by a second stage that begins when the problem is deliberately set aside – put out of the active mind, the ceaseless pondering switched off. After several days of silence, the solution wells up. The mathematician Henri Poincaré was unusually introspective about the process of discovery. (He also came nearer than anyone else to beating Einstein to the theory of relativity, except that in that case, though he had the pieces of the problem, inspiration did not strike.) In 1908, Poincaré gave a lecture, before the Psychological Society of Paris, about the psychology of mathematical invention, and there he described how he made some of his youthful discoveries. He reassured his audience, few of them mathematical: "I will tell you that I found the proof of a certain theorem in certain circumstances. The theorem will have a barbarous name, which many of you will never have heard of. But that's of no importance, for what is interesting to the psychologist is not the theorem – it's the circumstances." The youthful discovery was about a class of mathematical functions which he named in honor of another mathematician, Lazarus Fuchs – but as he said, the mathematical content is not important here. The young Poincaré believed, and for fifteen days he strove to prove, that no functions of the type he was pondering could exist in mathematics. He struggled with the 10

---

[4] *quantum:* Relating to forms of energy and interaction of fundamental units of matter.

disproof for hours every day. One evening, he happened to drink some black coffee, and couldn't sleep. . . . Like Kekulé with his carbon atoms, Poincaré found mathematical expressions arising before him in crowds, combining and recombining. By the next morning, he had established a class of the functions that he had begun by denying. Then, a short time later, he left town to go on a geological excursion for several days. "The changes of travel made me forget my mathematical work." One day during the excursion, though, he was carrying on a conversation as he was about to board a bus. "At the moment when I put my foot on the step, the idea came to me, without anything in my former thoughts seeming to have paved the way for it, that the transformations I had used to define the Fuchsian functions were identical with those of non-Euclidean geometry."[5] He did not try to prove the idea, but went right on with his conversation. "But I felt a perfect certainty," he wrote. When he got home, "for conscience's sake I verified the result at my leisure.". . .

Science is our century's art. Nearly four hundred years ago, when modern science was just beginning, Francis Bacon[6] wrote that *knowledge is power*. Yet Bacon was not a scientist. His slogan was the first clear statement of the promise by which, ever since, bureaucrats justify to each other and to king or taxpayer the spending of money on science. Knowledge is power; today we would say, less grandly, that science is essential to technology. Bacon's promise has been fulfilled abundantly, magnificently. The rage to know has been matched by the rage to make. Therefore – with the proviso, abundantly demonstrated, that it's rarely possible to predict which program of fundamental research will produce just what technology and when – the promise has brought scientists in the Western world unprecedented freedom of inquiry. Nonetheless, Bacon's promise hardly penetrates to the thing that moves most scientists. Science has several rewards, but the greatest is that it is the most interesting, difficult, pitiless, exciting and beautiful pursuit that we have yet found. Science is our century's art.

After You Read

In your journal, write about one of the following topics.

1 Identify the major motivations, according to the author, for scientists who wish to be involved in their field.

2 Discuss a moment of discovery or creation you once had that is similar in some way to an experience described in the reading.

3 Choose a topic of your own related to the reading.

---

[5] *non-Euclidian geometry:* Geometry not based on straight and parallel lines and angles of plane triangles.
[6] *Francis Bacon* (1561–1626): Prominent English philosopher, writer, and statesman.

ADDITIONAL READING 2
Los Pobres

With several classmates or in your journal, discuss one of the following topics.

1 Describe a job you once had that involved physical labor, and your reactions to the work.

2 Which people in your culture do most of the physical labor and menial work?

> As you read the selection, note in the margin what the author learns, as a young man, from his summer job.

 # Los Pobres[1]
Richard Rodriguez

"Los Pobres" comes from Richard Rodriguez's autobiography Hunger of Memory: The Education of Richard Rodriguez *(1982) – a work describing the author's struggles as a Mexican American assimilating to life in the United States. Born in 1944 in San Francisco, Rodriguez received his Ph.D. in English literature from Columbia University and has been a freelance writer and radio commentator. In "Los Pobres," he describes a summer job that led to a revelation about personal and social identity.*

It was at Stanford, one day near the end of my senior year, that a friend told me about a summer construction job he knew was available. I was quickly alert. Desire uncoiled within me. My friend said that he knew I had been looking for summer employment. He knew I needed some money. Almost apologetically he explained: It was something I probably wouldn't be interested in, but a friend of his, a contractor, needed someone for the summer to do menial jobs. There would be lots of shoveling and raking and sweeping. Nothing too hard. But nothing more interesting either. Still, the pay would be good. Did I want it? Or did I know someone who did?   1

I did. Yes, I said, surprised to hear myself say it.   2

In the weeks following, friends cautioned that I had no idea how hard physical labor really is. ("You only *think* you know what it is like to shovel for eight hours straight.") Their objections seemed to me challenges. They resolved the issue. I became happy with my plan. I decided, however, not to tell my parents. I wouldn't tell my mother because I could guess her worried reaction. I would tell my father only after the summer was over, when I could announce that, after all, I did know what "real work" is like.   3

---
[1] *Los Pobres:* Poor and powerless people.

The day I met the contractor (a Princeton graduate, it turned out), he asked me whether I had done any physical labor before. "In high school, during the summer," I lied. And although he seemed to regard me with skepticism, he decided to give me a try. Several days later, expectant, I arrived at my first construction site. I would take off my shirt to the sun and at last grasp desired sensation. No longer afraid, I at last became like a *bracero.*[2] "We need those tree stumps out of her by tomorrow," the contractor said. I started to work. **4**

I labored with excitement that first morning – and all the days after. The work was harder than I could have expected. But it was never as tedious as my friends had warned me it would be. There was too much physical pleasure in the labor. Especially early in the day, I would be most alert to the sensations of movement and straining. Beginning around seven each morning (when the air was still damp but the scent of weeds and dry earth anticipated the heat of the sun), I would feel my body resist the first thrusts of the shovel. My arms, tightened by sleep, would gradually loosen; after only several minutes, sweat would gather in beads on my forehead and then – a short breeze later – I would feel my chest silky with sweat in the breeze. I would return to my work. A nervous spark of pain would fly up my arm and settle to burn like an ember in the thick of my shoulder. An hour, two passed. Three. My whole body would assume regular movements; my shoveling would be described by identical, even movements. Even later in the day, my enthusiasm for primitive sensation would survive the heat and the dust and the insects pricking my back. I would strain wildly for sensation as the day came to a close. At three-thirty, quitting time, I would stand upright and slowly let my head fall back, luxuriating in the feeling of tightness relived. **5**

Some of the men working nearby would watch me and laugh. Two or three of the older men took the trouble to teach me the right way to use a pick, the correct way to shovel. "You're doing it wrong, . . ." one man scolded. Then he proceeded to show me – what persons who work with their bodies all their lives quickly learn – the most economical way to use one's body in labor. **6**

"Don't make your back do so much work," he instructed. I stood impatiently listening, half listening, vaguely watching, then noticed his work-thickened fingers clutching the shovel. I was annoyed. I wanted to tell him that I enjoyed shoveling the wrong way. And I didn't want to learn the right way. I wasn't afraid of back pain. I liked the way my body felt sore at the end of the day. **7**

I was about to, but, as it turned out, I didn't say a thing. Rather it was at that moment I realized that I was fooling myself if I expected a few weeks of labor to gain the admission to the world of the laborer. I would not learn in three months what my father had meant by "real work." I was not bound to this job; I could imagine its rapid conclusion. For me the sensations of exertion and fatigue could be savored. For my father or uncle, working at comparable jobs when they were my age, such sensations were to be feared. Fatigue took a different toll on their bodies – and minds. **8**

It was, I know, a simple insight. But it was with this realization that I took my first step that summer toward realizing something even more important about the **9**

---

[2] *bracero:* Migrant Mexican farmworkers who do hard manual labor for little money (people working with their *brazos* – the Spanish word for "arms").

"worker." In the company of carpenters, electricians, plumbers, and painters at lunch, I would often sit quietly, observant. I was not shy in such company. I felt easy, pleased by the knowledge that I was casually accepted, my presence taken for granted by men (exotics) who worked with their hands. Some days the younger men would talk and talk about sex, and they would howl at women who drove by in cars. Other days the talk at lunchtime was subdued; men gathered in separate groups. It depended on who was around. There were rough, good-natured workers. Others were quiet. The more I remember that summer, the more I realize that there was no single *type* of worker. I am embarrassed to say I had not expected such diversity. I certainly had not expected to meet, for example, a plumber who was an abstract painter[3] in his off hours and admired the work of Mark Rothko.[4] Nor did I expect to meet so many workers with college diplomas. (They were the ones who were not surprised that I intended to enter graduate school in the fall.) I suppose what I really want to say here is painfully obvious, but I must say it nevertheless: The men of that summer were middle-class Americans. They certainly didn't constitute an oppressed society. Carefully completing their work sheets; talking about the fortunes of local football teams; planning Las Vegas vacations; comparing the gas mileage of various makes of campers – they were not *los pobres* my mother had spoken about.

On two occasions, the contractor hired a group of Mexican aliens. They were 10 employed to cut down some trees and haul off debris. In all, there were six men of varying age. The youngest in his late twenties; the oldest (his father?) perhaps sixty years old. They came and they left in a single old truck. Anonymous men. They were never introduced to the other men at the site. Immediately upon their arrival, they would follow the contractor's directions, start working – rarely resting – seemingly driven by a fatalistic sense that work which had to be done was best done as quickly as possible.

I watched them sometimes. Perhaps they watched me. The only time I saw them 11 pay me much notice was one day at lunchtime when I was laughing with the older men. The Mexicans sat apart when they ate, just as they worked by themselves. Quiet. I rarely heard them say much to each other. All I could hear were their voices calling out sharply to one another, giving directions. Otherwise, when they stood briefly resting, they talked among themselves in voices too hard to overhear.

The contractor knew enough Spanish, and the Mexicans – or at least the oldest 12 of them, their spokesman – seemed to know enough English to communicate. But because I was around, the contractor decided one day to make me his translator. (He assumed I could speak Spanish.) I did what I was told. Shyly I went over to tell the Mexicans that the *patron*[5] wanted them to do something else before they left for the day. As I started to speak, I was afraid with my old fear that I would be unable to pronounce the Spanish words. But it was a simple instruction I had to convey. I could say it in phrases.

The dark sweating faces turned toward me as I spoke. They stopped their work 13 to hear me. Each nodded in response. I stood there. I wanted to say something more.

---

[3] *abstract painter:* Artist emphasizing emotional expression rather than realistic representation. (Abstract expressionism was a school of nontraditional painting in the mid-twentieth century.)

[4] *Mark Rothko* (1903–1970): Influential American abstract painter, born in Russia.

[5] *patron:* Boss.

But what could I say in Spanish, even if I could have pronounced the words right? Perhaps I just wanted to engage them in small talk, to be assured of their confidence, our familiarity. I thought for a moment to ask them where in Mexico they were from. Something like that. And maybe I wanted to tell them (a lie, if need be) that my parents were from the same part of Mexico.

I stood there. 14

Their faces watched me. The eyes of the man directly in front of me moved 15 slowly over my shoulder, and I turned to follow his glance toward *el patron* some distance away. For a moment I felt swept up by that glance into the Mexicans' company. But then I heard one of them returning to work. And then the others went back to work. I left them without saying anything more.

When they had finished, the contractor went over to pay them in cash. (He later 16 told me that he paid them collectively – "for the job," though he wouldn't tell me their wages. He said something quickly about the good rate of exchange "in their own country.") I can still hear the loudly confident voice he used with the Mexicans. It was the sound of the *gringo*[6] I had heard as a very young boy. And I can still hear the quiet, indistinct sounds of the Mexican, the oldest, who replied. At hearing that voice, I was sad for the Mexicans. Depressed by their vulnerability. Angry at myself. The adventure of the summer seemed suddenly ludicrous. I would not shorten the distance I felt from *los pobres* with a few weeks of physical labor. I would not become like them. They were different from me. . . .

In the end, my father was right – though perhaps he did not know how right or 17 why – to say that I would never know what real work is. I will never know what he felt at his last factory job. If tomorrow I worked at some kind of factory, it would go differently for me. My long education would favor me. I could act as a public person – able to defend my interests, to unionize, to petition, to speak up – to challenge and demand. (I will never know what real work is.) I will never know what the Mexicans knew, gathering their shovels and ladders and saws.

Their silence stays with me now. The wages those Mexicans received for their 18 labor were only a measure of their disadvantaged condition. Their silence is more telling. They lack a public identity. They remain profoundly alien. Persons apart. People lacking a union obviously, people without grounds. They depend upon the relative good will or fairness of their employers each day. For such people, lacking a better alternative, it is not such an unreasonable task.

Their silence stays with me. I have taken these many words to describe its 19 impact. Only: the quiet. Something uncanny about it. Its compliance. Vulnerability. Pathos. As I heard their truck rumbling away, I shuddered, my face mirrored with sweat. I had finally come face to face with *los pobres*.

---

[6] *gringo:* Term, often used negatively in Spain or Latin America for a foreigner, especially someone of English or American origin.

After You Read

In your journal, discuss one of the following topics.

1 Discuss something important that Rodriguez learned, as a young man, from his summer job.

2 Describe a group of people in your culture that are socially disadvantaged in a way similar to the Mexican workers in "Los Pobres."

3 Choose a topic of your own related to the reading.

ADDITIONAL READING 3
Action Will Be Taken: An Action-packed Story

Before You Read

With several classmates or in your journal, discuss whether the values of action, achievement, and efficiency are stressed in your culture.

While You Read

> As discussed earlier in this chapter, the *tone* of a piece of writing is the author's attitude toward his or her subject, as expressed in the choice of words and details (see page 246). A tone that authors often use to criticize the moral faults or foolishness of people is *irony* – a type of humor in which the words convey the opposite of their literal meaning or in which something that is expected to happen differs from what actually happens.
>
> As you read the story, note in the margin the passages that are *ironic* – that say one thing but actually mean the opposite. Also indicate anything you think the author is making fun of through the use of irony, such as social institutions, values, and attitudes.

Action Will Be Taken: An Action-packed Story
Heinrich Böll

The following short story about a factory employee was written in 1958 by Heinrich Böll (1917–1985), an internationally known German writer of novels and short fiction. An outspoken critic of social hypocrisy and false cultural values, Böll often used humor and satire to portray his moral and political vision. In 1972 he was awarded the Nobel Prize in literature.

Probably one of the strangest interludes in my life was the time I spent as an 1
employee in Alfred Wunsiedel's factory. By nature I am inclined more to pensiveness

and inactivity than to work, but now and again prolonged financial difficulties compel me – for pensiveness is no more profitable than inactivity – to take on a so-called job. Finding myself once again at a low ebb of this kind, I put myself in the hands of the employment office and was sent with seven other fellow-sufferers to Wunsiedel's factory, where we were to undergo an aptitude test.

The exterior of the factory was enough to arouse my suspicions: the factory was 2
built entirely of glass brick, and my aversion to well-lit buildings and well-lit rooms is as strong as my aversion to work. I became even more suspicious when we were immediately served breakfast in the well-lit, cheerful coffee shop: pretty waitresses brought us eggs, coffee, and toast; orange juice was served in tastefully designed jugs; goldfish pressed their bored faces against the sides of pale-green aquariums. The waitresses were so cheerful that they appeared to be bursting with good cheer. Only a strong effort of will – so it seemed to me – restrained them from singing away all day long. They were as crammed with unsung songs as chickens with unlaid eggs.

Right away I realized something that my fellow-sufferers evidently failed to 3
realize: that this breakfast was already part of the test; so I chewed away reverently, with the full appreciation of a person who knows he is supplying his body with valuable elements. I did something which normally no power on earth can make me do: I drank orange juice on an empty stomach, left the coffee and egg untouched, as well as most of the toast, got up, and paced up and down in the coffee shop, pregnant with action.

As a result I was the first to be ushered into the room where the questionnaires 4
were spread out on attractive tables. The walls were done in a shade of green that would have summoned the word "delightful" to the lips of interior decoration enthusiasts. The room appeared to be empty, and yet I was so sure of being observed that I behaved as someone pregnant with action behaves when he believes himself unobserved: I ripped my pen impatiently from my pocket, unscrewed the top, sat down at the nearest table and pulled the questionnaire toward me, the way irritable customers snatch at the bill in a restaurant.

Question No. 1: Do you consider it right for a human being to possess only two 5
arms, two legs, eyes, and ears?

Here for the first time I reaped the harvest of my pensive nature and wrote 6
without hesitation: "Even four arms, legs and ears would not be adequate for my driving energy. Human beings are very poorly equipped."

Question No. 2: How many telephones can you handle at one time? 7

Here again the answer was as easy as simple arithmetic: "When there are only 8
seven telephones," I wrote, "I get impatient; there have to be nine before I feel I am working to capacity."

Question No. 3: How do you spend your free time? 9

My answer: "I no longer acknowledge the term free time – on my fifteenth 10
birthday I eliminated it from my vocabulary, for in the beginning was the act."[1]

I got the job. Even with nine telephones I really didn't feel I was working to 11
capacity. I shouted into the mouthpieces: "Take immediate action!" Or: "Do

---

[1] *in the beginning was the act:* Allusion to the opening line of the Gospel According to John (one of the books of the New Testament – the second part of the Christian Bible): "In the beginning was the Word, and the Word was with God, and the Word was God."

something! – We must have some action – Action will be taken – Action has been taken – Action should be taken." But as a rule – for I felt this was in keeping with the tone of the place – I used the imperative.[2]

Of considerable interest were the noon-hour breaks, when we consumed 12 nutritious foods in an atmosphere of silent good cheer. Wunsiedel's factory was swarming with people who were obsessed with telling you the story of their lives, as indeed vigorous personalities are fond of doing. The story of their lives is more important than their lives; you have only to press a button, and immediately it is covered with spewed-out exploits.

Wunsiedel had a right-hand man called Broschek, who had in turn made a name 13 for himself by supporting seven children and a paralyzed wife by working night-shifts in his student days, and successfully carrying on four business agencies, besides which he had passed two examinations with honors in two years. When asked by reporters: "When do you sleep, Mr. Broschek?" He had replied: "It's a crime to sleep!"

Wunsiedel's secretary had supported a paralyzed husband and four children by 14 knitting, at the same time graduating in psychology and German history as well as breeding shepherd dogs, and she had become famous as a night-club singer where she was known as Vamp[3] Number Seven.

Wunsiedel himself was one of those people who every morning, as they open their 15 eyes, make up their minds to act. "I must act," they think as they briskly tie their bathrobe belts around them. "I must act," they think as they shave, triumphantly watching their beard hairs being washed away with the lather: these hirsute vestiges[4] are the first daily sacrifices to their driving energy. The more intimate functions[5] also give these people a sense of satisfaction: water swishes, paper is used. Action has been taken. Bread gets eaten; eggs are decapitated.

With Wunsiedel, the most trivial activity looked like action: the way he put on 16 his hat, the way – quivering with energy – he buttoned up his overcoat, the kiss he gave his wife; everything was action.

When he arrived at his office, he greeted his secretary with a cry of "Let's have 17 some action!" And in ringing tones she would call back: "Action will be taken!" Wunsiedel then went from department to department, calling out his cheerful: "Let's have some action!" Everyone would answer: "Action will be taken!" And I would call back to him too, with a radiant smile, when he looked into my office: "Action will be taken!"

Within a week I had increased the number of telephones on my desk to eleven, 18 within two weeks to thirteen, and every morning on the streetcar I enjoyed thinking up new imperatives, or chasing the words *take action* through various tenses and modulations: for two whole days I kept saying the same sentence over and over again because I thought it sounded so marvelous: "Action ought to have been taken"; for another two days it was: "Such action ought not to have been taken."

---

[2] *imperative:* Verb form expressing a command, request, or instruction.

[3] *Vamp:* Woman who uses charm and deceit to seduce and exploit men.

[4] *hirsute vestiges:* Hairy traces of an early human being.

[5] *intimate functions:* Bathroom needs (urination and defecation).

So I was really beginning to feel I was working to capacity when there actually 19
was some action. One Tuesday morning – I had hardly settled down at my desk
– Wunsiedel rushed into my office crying his "Let's have some action!" But an
inexplicable something in his face made me hesitate to reply, in a cheerful gay
voice as the rules dictated: "Action will be taken!" I must have paused too long, for
Wunsiedel, who seldom raised his voice, shouted at me: "Answer! Answer, you know
the rules!" And I answered, under my breath, reluctantly, like a child who is forced
to say: I am a naughty child. It was only by a great effort that I managed to bring out
the sentence: "Action will be taken," and hardly had I uttered it when there really
was some action: Wunsiedel dropped to the floor. As he fell, he rolled over onto his
side and lay right across the open doorway. I knew at once, and I confirmed it when
I went slowly around my desk and approached the body on the floor: he was dead.

Shaking my head I stepped over Wunsiedel, walked slowly along the corridor to 20
Broschek's office, and entered without knocking. Broschek was sitting at his desk,
a telephone receiver in each hand, between his teeth a ballpoint pen with which
he was making notes on a writing pad, while with his bare feet he was operating a
knitting machine under the desk. In this way he helps to clothe his family. "We've
had some action," I said in a low voice.

Broschek spat out the ballpoint pen, put down the two receivers, reluctantly 21
detached his toes from the knitting machine.

"What action?" he asked. 22

"Wunsiedel is dead," I said. 23

"No," said Broschek, "that's impossible," but he put on his slippers and followed 24
me along the corridor.

"No," he said, when we stood beside Wunsiedel's corpse, "no, no!" I did not 25
contradict him. I carefully turned Wunsiedel over onto his back, closed his eyes,
and looked at him pensively.

I felt something like tenderness for him, and realized for the first time that I had 26
never hated him. On his face was that expression which one sees on children who
obstinately refuse to give up their faith in Santa Claus, even though the arguments
of their playmates sound so convincing.

"No," said Broschek, "no." 27

"We must take action," I said quietly to Broschek. 28

"Yes," said Broschek, "we must take action." 29

Action was taken: Wunsiedel was buried, and I was delegated to carry a wreath 30
of artificial roses behind his coffin, for I am equipped with not only a penchant for
pensiveness and inactivity but also a face and figure that go extremely well with
dark suits. Apparently as I walked along behind Wunsiedel's coffin carrying the
wreath of artificial roses, I looked superb. I received an offer from a fashionable
firm of funeral directors to join their staff as a professional mourner. "You are a born
mourner," said the manager, "your outfit would be provided by the firm. Your face
– simply superb!"

I handed in my notice[6] to Broschek, explaining that I had never really felt I 31
was working to capacity there; that, in spite of the thirteen telephones, some of

---

[6] *handed in my notice*: Submitted a letter announcing my intent to quit.

my talents were going to waste. As soon as my first professional appearance as a mourner was over, I knew: This is where I belonged; this is what I was cut out for.

Pensively I stand behind the coffin in the funeral chapel, holding a simple bouquet, while the organ plays Handel's *Largo*,[7] a piece that does not receive nearly the respect it deserves. The cemetery café is my regular haunt; there I spend the intervals between my professional engagements, although sometimes I walk behind coffins which I have not been engaged to follow, I pay for flowers out of my own pocket and join the welfare worker[8] who walks behind the coffin of some homeless person. From time to time I also visit Wunsiedel's grave, for after all I owe it to him that I discovered my true vocation, a vocation in which pensiveness is essential and inactivity my duty. 32

It was not till much later that I realized I had never bothered to find out what was being produced in Wunsiedel's factory. I expect it was soap. 33

After You Read

In your journal, write about one of the following topics.

1 Identify the main idea Böll is conveying in the story.
2 Give an example of *irony* in the story and the point you think the author is making.
3 Choose a topic of your own related to the story.

---

[7] *Handel's Largo:* Famous slow and sad piece of music by the German-born English composer George Frideric Handel (1685–1759), often played on solemn occasions.
[8] *Welfare worker:* Unemployed worker receiving financial aid and other types of assistance from the government.

ADDITIONAL READING 4
To Be of Use

Before You Read

With several classmates or in your journal, discuss whether you agree with the following statement: "Some types of work are more valuable than others."

Taking Notes While You Read

As you read "To Be of Use," note in the margin the things that the speaker of the poem values most in work and people's attitude toward it.

To Be of Use

Marge Piercy

The following poem, written by the U.S. poet, novelist, and essayist Marge Piercy, appears in a collection of her poetry titled Circles on the Water *(1982).*

The people I love the best
jump into work head first
without dallying in the shadows
and swim off with sure strokes almost out of sight.
They seem to become natives of that element,   5
the black sleek heads of seals
bouncing like half-submerged balls.

I love people who harness themselves, an ox to a heavy cart,
who pull like water buffalo, with massive patience,
who strain in the mud and the muck to move things forward,   10
who do what has to be done, again and again.

I want to be with people who submerge
in the task, who go into the fields by harvest
and work in a row and pass the bags along,
who are not parlor generals[1] and field deserters   15
but move in a common rhythm
when the food must come in or the fire be put out.

The work of the world is common as mud.
Botched, it smears the hands, crumbles to dust.
But the thing worth doing well done   20
has a shape that satisfies, clean and evident.
Greek amphoras[2] for wine or oil,
Hopi[3] vases that held corn, are put in museums
but you know they were made to be used.
The pitcher cries for water to carry   25
and a person for work that is real.

After You Read

In your journal, write about one of the following topics.

1 Identify the things Piercy values most in work and people's attitudes toward it.

2 Indicate the major tone, or tones, expressed in the poem.

3 Choose a topic of your own related to the poem.

---

[1] *parlor generals:* High-level military commanders who stay indoors (in parlors, or conference rooms) instead of fighting in battle.

[2] *Amphoras:* Ancient Greek jars or vases.

[3] *Hopi:* Native American people living primarily in northeastern Arizona.

ADDITIONAL READING 5
Humor: The Purpose Of Work

With a partner, read the following joke and cartoon and discuss the issues relating to work.

 ## The Purpose of Work

An American businessman was at the pier of a small South Pacific Island village 1 when a small boat with just one fisherman docked. Inside the boat was a dorrado and several large groupers.[1] The American complimented the Islander on the quality of his fish and asked how long it took to catch them.

The Islander replied, "Only a little while." 2

The American then asked why he didn't stay out longer and catch more fish. 3

The Islander said he had enough to support his family's immediate needs. 4

The American then asked, "But what do you do with the rest of your time?" 5

The fisherman said, "I sleep late, fish a little, play with my children, take a late 6 afternoon nap with my wife, Helia, and stroll into the village each evening, where I sip rum and play my guitar with my friends. I have a full and busy life."

The American scoffed, "I am a Harvard MBA[2] and could help you. You should 7 spend more time fishing and, with the proceeds, buy a bigger boat. With the proceeds from the bigger boat, you could buy several boats and eventually you would have a fleet of fishing boats. Instead of selling your catch to a middleman, you would sell directly to the processor, eventually opening your own cannery. You would control the product, processing, and distribution. You would need to leave this small fishing village and move to Australia, then Los Angeles, and eventually New York City, where you could run your expanding enterprise."

The South Seas fisherman asked, "But how long will this all take?" 8

To which the American replied, "Fifteen to twenty years." 9

"But what then?" 10

The American laughed and said, "That's the best part. When the time is right, 11 you would announce an IPO[3] and sell your company stock to the public and become very rich. You would make millions."

"Millions? Really? Then what?" 12

The American said, "Then you would retire and move to a small fishing village, 13 where you would sleep late, fish a little, play with your kids, take a late afternoon nap with your wife, and stroll to the village in the evenings, where you could sip rum and play your guitar with your friends."

---

[1] *dorroda . . . groupers:* Large fish found in warm oceans.

[2] *Harvard MBA:* Graduate of Harvard University with a master's degree in business administration.

[3] *IPO:* Initial public offering – a company's first sale of stock to the public.

DILBERT. Reprinted with permission of United Feature Syndicate, Inc.

ESSAY TOPICS

Write an essay on one of the following topics. Support your points with an appropriate combination of references to the readings in this chapter, library and Internet sources, and personal experiences and observations.

Refer to the section "The Essentials of Writing" on pages 102–132 to help you plan, draft, and revise your essay. Use this special section, too, to assist you in locating, integrating, and documenting your sources.

1 Analyze the qualities of your ideal job. Consider the type of work you wish to pursue, the work environment, and anything else that would make your job enjoyable and rewarding.

2 Explain your career goals and how you hope to achieve them. Consider such issues as education, job training, and the challenges and difficulties you anticipate in fulfilling your aspirations.

3 Examine the reasons some people find their jobs rewarding and fulfilling and others find their work unrewarding and unfulfilling.

4 Discuss your personal definition of success, material or otherwise, in your professional and/or private life. What does success mean to you? How do you hope to achieve it?

5 Explore employment opportunities and limitations in your culture. Are certain groups of people restricted in their job opportunities because of such factors as race, ethnicity, religion, gender, social class, sexual orientation, or educational background? Consider the social factors that limit the employment opportunities of a certain group of people.

CREDITS

The author and publisher would like to thank the following for permission to reproduce copyright material.

Text Credits

Page 5, Gary Althen, "American Values and Assumptions." From *American Ways: A Guide for Foreigners in the United States,* Second Edition. Copyright © 2003 by Gary Althen. Reprinted by permission of Intercultural Press, Inc.

Page 19, Lisa Davis, "Where Do We Stand?" From *In Health* (September/October 1990). Copyright © 1990 by Hippocrates Partners. Reprinted by permission of the publishers.

Page 27, Robert Levine, "Time Talks, With an Accent." From *A Geography of Time: The Temporal Misadventures of a Social Psychologist, or How Every Culture Keeps Time Just a Little Bit Differently.* Copyright © 1997 by Robert Levine. Reprinted by permission of BasicBooks, a division of HarperCollins Publishers.

Page 36, Yaping Tang, "Polite but Thirsty." From *MATSOL Currents* (Fall/Winter 1995–1996, Vol. 2, No. 1). Copyright © 1996 Yaping Tang. Reprinted by permission of the author.

Page 40, Margaret K. (Omar) Nydell, "Friends and Strangers." From *Understanding Arabs: A Guide for Westerners,* Revised Edition. Copyright © 1996 by Margaret K. (Omar) Nydell. Reprinted by permission of Intercultural Press, Inc.

Page 44, Premchand, "A Coward." From *Deliverance and Other Stories,* translated by David Rubin (Penguin Books India Pvt. Ltd., 1988). Reprinted by permission of the publishers and translator.

Page 52, John Godfrey Saxe, "The Blind Men and the Elephant: A Hindu Fable." From the Preface to *Cultural Awareness Training Techniques* by Jan Gaston (Brattleboro, VT: Pro Lingua Associates, 1984). Reprinted by permission of the publishers.

Page 59, John Holt, "School Is Bad for Children." From *The Saturday Evening Post* (February, 8, 1969). Copyright © 1969 by The Saturday Evening Post Company. Reprinted by permission of The Saturday Evening Post Society.

Page 68, David Rothenberg, "How the Web Destroys the Quality of Students' Research Papers." From *The Chronicle of Higher Education* (August 15, 1997). Copyright © 1997 by David Rothenberg. Reprinted by permission of the author.

Page 71, Richard Cummins. Letter to the Editor of *The Chronicle of Higher Education* (October 1997). Copyright © 1997 by Richard Cummins. Reprinted by permission of the author.

Page 77, David Miller Sadker and Myra Pollack Sadker, "Multiple Intelligences and Emotional Intelligence." From *Teachers, Schools, and Society,* Sixth Edition. Copyright © 2003 by McGraw-Hill Companies, Inc. Reprinted by permission of the publishers.

Page 88, Nicholas Gage, "The Teacher Who Changed My Life." From *Parade* (December 17, 1989). Adapted from the book *A Place for Us.* Copyright © 1989 by Nicholas Gage. Reprinted by permission of the author.

Page 93, Ji-Yeon Mary Yuhfill, "Let's Tell the Story of All America's Cultures." From *The Philadelphia Inquirer.* Copyright © 1991 by Ji-Yeon Mary Yuhfill. Reprinted by permission of *The Philadelphia Inquirer.*

Page 220, reprinted by permission of American Indian College Fund, Denver, Colorado

Page 224, "How Joe's Body Brought Him Fame Instead of Shame©" and "Charles Atlas®" 2003 under license from Charles Atlas, NY, NY 10159 (www.CharlesAtlas.com).

Photo Credits

Page 25, from *Japanese and Caucasian Facial Expressions of Emotion* photo set (David Matsumoto and Paul Ekman, 1988). Copyright © 1988 by Paul Ekman. Reprinted by permission of Paul Ekman.

Stock Photo Credits

Cover: Getty Images; page 2: Getty Images; page 19: Tim MacPherson/Getty Images; page 56: Punchstock; page 92: Gabe Palmer/Corbis; page 102: Stewart Cohen/Getty Images; page 134: Getty Images; page 186: Punchstock; page 238: AP/Wideworld Photos; page 271: Ernst Haas/ Getty Images

Every effort has been made to track down rightsholders of third-party material to clear permissions. If any rightsholder has concerns about any such material, Cambridge University Press would be pleased to hear from them.

INDEX

The following items are key terms relating to reading and writing that are discussed in the text.